THE

POWER OF SOUL

THE
POWER OF SOUL

LIVING THE TWELVE VIRTUES

ROBERT SARDELLO

HAMPTON ROADS
PUBLISHING COMPANY, INC.

Cover design by Marjoram Productions
Cover art by Loyd Chapplow

Hampton Roads Publishing Company, Inc.
1125 Stoney Ridge Road
Charlottesville, VA 22902

434-296-2772
fax: 434-296-5096
e-mail: hrpc@hrpub.com
www.hrpub.com

If you are unable to order this book from your local
bookseller, you may order directly from the publisher.
Call 1-800-766-8009, toll-free.

Library of Congress Cataloging-in-Publication Data

Sardello, Robert J., 1942-
  The power of soul / Robert Sardello.
     p. cm.
ISBN 1-57174-319-7 (5 1/2 x 8 1/2 paper w/flaps : alk. paper)
1. Conduct of life. 2. Spiritual life. 3. Soul. I. Title.
BJ1581.2 .S242 2003
179'.9--dc21

                    2002013095

ISBN 1-57174-319-7
10 9 8 7 6 5 4 3 2 1
Printed on acid-free paper in Canada

Acknowledgments

Richard Leviton is a remarkable editor. I thank him and the wonderful people at Hampton Roads for taking on this book and helping it come to clarity. My work with the virtues began with a consultation contract with the John E. Fetzer Institute and the forward-looking administrators, Carol Hegedus and Rob Lehman, who saw that the power of virtue can transform institutional settings. Cheryl Sanders, codirector with me of the School of Spiritual Psychology, inspired this work. Therese Schroeder-Sheker, director of the Chalice of Repose Project in Missoula, Montana, has welcomed this exploration of virtue into the curriculum in music thanatology. The small band of spiritual warriors in Greensboro, North Carolina—Janet Hampton, John Hampton, Kate Wagner, Sally Anderson, and Judy Boyd—are forever encouraging. The students of Spiritual Psychology in Greensboro eagerly took up the work with virtue, showing the practicality of this effort. My dear friends in Dallas—Gail Thomas, Joanne Stroud, and Larry Allums—exemplify courage with their work at the Dallas Institute of Humanities and Culture, where I was privileged to present workshops on the virtues. I also thank the spiritual psychology group in Seattle—Randy Morris, Sue Maro, Rob Staveland, and the many others there who provided ongoing discussion that led to many of the insights in this writing. None of the writing would have happened without the many students of the School of Spiritual Psychology in Greensboro, Dallas, Missoula, Seattle, Portland, Baltimore, Stamford, Toronto, Sydney, Vancouver, New York, and Manila.

Contents

Introduction

The word "virtue" is highly charged. It is a word with a great history, maybe as old as humankind. It exists in Eastern as well as Western cultures. We do not hear much of this word today, partly because we are interested more in the shadowy side of life than in the doing of the good. I think our culture is ready for a turn-around. The new door to concern for virtue was shown to us on September 11, 2001, in New York City, Washington, D.C., and the skies over Pennsylvania, where all of the virtues described in this book were displayed, initiating us into a new era of doing the good (see the Epilogue). Given this situation of our culture, telling you how I use the word "virtue" might be helpful as a beginning.

I do not approach virtue from a religious perspective. This book is not about being a virtuous person, if you hear that word as referring to being pious. This book is about locating the essence of our soul, and coming to have an inner sense of how soul wants to function in the world to bring about the good. We are now accustomed to hearing about soul in its sufferings, its need for beauty, its love of story, myth, creativity, and more recently, the soul of the world. Soul also wants to act. And when we enter deeply into soul life, we become receptive to what comes to us from the spiritual worlds.

The virtues are the glimmerings within the soul of the spiritual urgings to bring our life into harmony with the rhythms of the cosmos. Virtue concerns closing the gap between the earthly world and the spiritual worlds. There are not two worlds unless we go away from acting in accordance with the Great World and create an artificial separation where there is none. Such a separation produces cultural egotism of the crudest and cruelest kind. We can certainly forget that we are citizens of the cosmos, that Earth and her beings are part of the functioning of the whole. This writing seeks to remind us that we not only belong to the whole but also bear responsibilities to act in accordance with the grandeur and beauty of the universe.

These days, spiritual development, popularly understood, often means learning to concentrate on the chakras, do various forms of meditation, search for one's higher self, engage in shamanic work, image work, dream work, and a myriad of other possible practices. Very little attention is given to inner moral development, in spite of the fact that absolutely every spiritual tradition places priority on the importance of character and very little on the kinds of experiences many present-day spiritual practices seek. It is certainly the case that working to develop and deepen in the virtues has as one of its effects the gradual opening to kinds of experiences not available to ordinary consciousness. It is not at all the case, however, that working to develop psychic or even spiritual capacities alone results in becoming a person who seeks and does the good.

Spiritual development can and often is sought for questionable reasons. Having out-of-body experiences, journeying to other worlds, becoming clairvoyant, developing healing capacities, finding a connection to the higher self—all such matters are considered to be of little importance to spiritual development in the great religious and spiritual traditions. In fact, developing such capacities is seen in these traditions to present great challenges. We must learn to look beyond them and never become enamored. In other words, we must actually learn to overlook the capacities that develop in order to continue deepening in soul. This caution toward seeking spiritual experiences indicates that spiritual work, as understood for thousands of years, is never done for the sake of ourselves alone, but always for the whole of the world. The virtue of virtues is that through them our spiritual efforts are always kept in touch with the earthly world and the soul and spiritual needs of others.

The context in which every person can develop in the qualities of the virtues is our daily life, in the midst of our connections, trials, difficulties, and joys with others. Another way of seeing the virtues would be that they are the soul medium of our spiritual relationships with others. The virtues constitute the way of sacred service in the world, for they are the means through which we serve the soul and spirit of other human beings. Only when we serve in this manner can a whole community flourish. However, serving the soul and spirit of others has to be distinguished from serving another person or serving the outer needs of another. Further, such serving must be freely chosen and not based upon power or authority or position.

In daily life we are often in situations in which a kind of serving of others is demanded. These demands occur in family life, in work, in intimate partnerships, in social situations. We typically respond to overt or covert demands out of love for the other person, duty, obligation, or fear. None of these ways of responding, in themselves, can be considered a practice of virtue. These situations, however, can be the place of labor, the laboratory for the practice of the virtues.

What is being asked for in all of these contexts, seen from a soul/spiritual point of view, is that a demand be transformed by us into an act of virtue toward the person making the demand. This transformation requires that the demand not be attended to directly, but rather seen through. By seeing through, I mean an act of imagination in which the suffering soul and spirit of the individual making the demand—whether the demand be overt or concealed—can be perceived and responded to. For example, I have been told by quite a number of people that I am very patient in my work as a teacher. Quite often in classes, individuals ask what seem to be rather frivolous questions. I try not to turn away from such questions, or on the other hand, to answer them directly, as they most often come from the personality of the individual. I attempt to see through the question, comment, or observation to the soul and spirit being that is that person and speak directly to the soul substance of the person. In order for me to do so, my immediate emotional reaction to the person must be tempered. It is not a matter of thinking these things through, but of having taken on the discipline of seeking soul perception of others.

Virtue does not concern solely oneself, either in the dimension of going inward toward soul development or going upward toward spiritual development. Virtue concerns the soul/spirit gifts we give to others. Further, these gifts are not something that we already have at hand, ready to give. The other person gives us the gift of having to develop them to give. All of the virtues thus have a polarity about them. We have to, for example, develop in the virtue of patience, and patience is also our spiritual gift to others. Or we have to develop in the virtue of balance, and balance is also a spiritual gift to others.

Then, a further aspect centers on the fact that virtue as a way of acting toward others is to be oriented toward the soul/spirit levels of the other person and not to their immediate needs. Thus, the transaction of virtue may well remain a quite invisible process. The effects of such transactions do show up in the visible world in the form of the gradual shifting of relationships to more refined levels, but the effects are almost always subtle.

The term "more refined levels" requires clarification. Virtue does not operate simplistically; it is not a matter of my treating someone nicely resulting in the other person transforming his view of me and quite suddenly treating me nicely in return. The difficulty with this way of thinking about the matter, and of operating in relation to others in terms of this kind of imagination of virtue, is that it quickly turns into a power strategy, oriented toward achieving the results one wishes to achieve.

Virtue does not work in this manner, which would turn soul/spirit relationships into materialistic cause-effect relationships. We cannot simply insert virtues into our lives, remaining at the same level of consciousness as before. Once we enter into the task of developing in virtue, we enter into an alchemical process of transforming our soul life into capacities for helping others gracefully, and with subtlety and nuance.

The alchemy of virtue, becoming engaged in a process of soul refinement, does not shift difficult situations piecemeal, but rather shifts, or refines, the functioning of the whole. Suppose, for example, in a particular relationship with another person at work, it becomes apparent that the situation asks that I develop in the capacity of faithfulness. Development of the virtue here would mean that I cease moving around my views and opinions and ways of operating according to what serves me best at the moment, and that I develop the ability to stand firm in soul and spirit toward the other person. This would mean that I have to deepen in mindfulness of this other person and be able to have a sense of reverence for the soul of this other person. As that ability develops, the character of the whole community of work slightly shifts toward becoming more soulful; we find that people begin to care for one another rather than compete against each other.

As we develop an imagination and an inner feeling of each virtue as well as work at the practice of them, the nature of virtue itself becomes clearer. Virtue becomes a way of acting in the world wholly. This domain, long dormant, is also opening in the wider culture, at least indirectly. Is it not the case that wherever we find a holistic approach to science, or healing, or medicine, or ecology, or any other endeavor, we find an inherent ethical dimension playing a central part in the formulation of those endeavors? Perhaps the healing qualities so characteristic of holistic knowing have to do with the qualities of virtue inherent in these practices. Something is added in holistic work that goes beyond the exploration of new paradigms of healing—and that something is that the soul of the healer is understood as central and essential to the work.

These new ways of knowing recognize that the act of knowing is not a neutral act, that we can know wholly only through virtue. Such recognition does not make our knowing subjective, and in fact it is quite the opposite. To be aware that virtue enters into how and what we know makes us more objective, while to remain ignorant of these factors keeps an unknown subjective element at the center of knowing. That is, the notion that knowledge remains ethically neutral keeps the ethical dimension of knowing private, or it is shuttled off to experts, the ethicists, to debate.

We can imagine virtue as a vast and differentiated cosmic medium through which it becomes possible to enter into relationships of soul and spirit, not only with other people, but with the human body, and the world of nature, including the plant world, the animal world, and even the mineral world. Would we not have quite a different science—a different biology, chemistry, medicine, botany, agriculture, technology—if these matters were approached through the twelve virtues of equanimity, patience, selflessness, love, compassion, devotion, balance, faithfulness, courtesy, truth, courage, and discernment? If an education into virtue constituted an important part of becoming a scientist, or a researcher, an educator, or a lawyer, the realms of research and practice would appear quite different than they do to the eyes of one trained only in the professions as they now exist.

The recovery of virtue involves much more than prescribing a list of things to do, that if done in the right way, would make us into honorable persons. This work on virtue is concerned with re-visioning consciousness in such a manner that virtue encompasses cognitive, emotional, spiritual, soul, and behavioral acts.

Virtues seem to be inner qualities that, once we become aware of them and seek to strengthen them through practice, can be brought into behaviors that have effects on others. I want to be quite cautious in speaking of virtue in this way, and be aware of a possible misunderstanding. This would consist of imagining the virtues, once developed, as factors that can cause direct changes in the outer world. Such a misunderstanding is almost inevitable, given the fact that we still live within a scientific and technological worldview. One of the aspects of such a worldview is that everything is viewed in terms of cause and effect. Whatever belongs to the realm of the soul, and whatever belongs to the realm of the spirit, does not, however, belong to the sphere of cause and effect as these terms are usually understood. We cannot, for example, say that the practice of patience will produce the result that other people will treat you more kindly. Nor can we say that practicing patience will have an observable effect on those who experience being in proximity to one who practices patience.

The matter is even more complex. The virtue of patience, for example, relies upon the presence of those who try our patience. Such obstacles have to be considered as part of the phenomenon; that is, we have to begin to imagine a kind of circular causality.

We need stubborn people in order to develop the virtue of patience. The same can be said of all the other virtues.

The virtues are among the elemental qualities of human existence, the very power of the soul. They are among the foundational aspects defining what it is to be embodied beings of soul and spirit, conscious of that existence, standing forth in the world, always in relation with others. We can speak of the virtues as among the existential categories of being human. This way of approaching the matter constitutes the attitude and outlook of the meditations on virtue in this book.

When I speak of practicing the virtues, I do not mean learning a skill, but rather recognizing that we have to work at awakening and being present to our full humanity, awake to our existence as beings of body, soul, and spirit. Only the potential of being human, it seems, is given to us. We have to enact that potential, put it into operation. The descriptions of virtue that constitute the core of this book are not prescriptive; they are not intended as instructions concerning what to do to be human, but as portraits of the dimensions of our inherently moral existence.

Is the term "virtue" any longer viable? This may seem a strange question, in view of the fact that I have attempted to recover the very notion of virtue, as well as develop the phenomenology of a number of specific virtues. I have also attempted to provide some specific suggestions concerning the practice of the virtues in our time. Nonetheless, it remains an ongoing work to retrieve the notion of virtue from any kind of outmoded "churchiness," piety, or dogma, and restore it to a vitality and vigor that can have application in the present world. In the past, people made a concerted effort to live a virtuous life. To speak in this way now sounds antiquated; and it is.

We know too much about the darker sides of human nature, and of the necessity of recognizing the shadow aspects of the soul, to believe in being virtuous in the older ways in which this was understood. Whereas in the past, practices centered around trying to restrain oneself from certain actions, keeping certain kinds of thoughts and feelings from intruding into consciousness, guilt, and penance as the way to virtue, today, self-observation is all-important. We need to develop the capacities to observe the most subtle of our inner states and outer acts, the connection or lack of connection between them, and the subtle results of our acts. These practices form the new field within which reinvigorating virtue can take place.

I have not in this book referred to or promoted an idea or an ideal of being virtuous. The intention of practicing the various virtues is not to turn oneself into a virtuous person. Engaging in developing qualities of soul can perhaps be better described as a way toward transmutation of our ways of action. Even our seemingly most altruistic acts are typically filled with self-interests. No judgment is placed on this observation. Rather, because egotism, left to itself, follows a strict law of increase, separation from others, and self-absorption, a need and an impulse exist in everyone to reorient the ego toward genuine interest in others, care for the world, and love of the divine. I take the stance that egotism comes about primarily because our standard ego mode of consciousness, having nothing sacred to do, becomes preoccupied with its own pleasure, preservation, and extension. A reorientation is required.

Practice of the virtues does not ask, demand, or require that we renounce that psychic factor that gives us each an immediate and concrete sense of ourselves, our ego. In earlier times, it was perhaps so that the practice of virtue did demand such renunciation. It was as if there existed a fear of the newly discovered sense of self-centeredness that the ego brings, and a hope that one could continue to live in innocent submission to the divine by trying to root out this psychic factor before it took permanent hold. That hope became less and less possible to actualize.

Now, after having assiduously developed the ego dimension of soul life, human beings have a different task. We cannot any longer hope to renounce this factor in order to be in connection with the grace of holiness. Rather, we have the new task of transforming the ego rather than ignoring it, trying to get rid of it, or letting it live in the illusion of being the whole of our conscious being. This transformation consists in letting our ego consciousness receive the soul substance created by acts of virtue.

I approach the virtues as the work of metamorphosing ego consciousness. The process of metamorphosis does not work in opposition to the ego, but constitutes the manner in which our ordinary consciousness comes to encompass more than itself and to be filled with more than itself. As the larva metamorphoses into the butterfly, so ego consciousness can metamorphose into soul consciousness that is open and receptive to the spiritual worlds. In the case of the larva, the imprint of the earlier stage is retained with the body of the butterfly, though the transformed body now has wings. Similarly, the process of virtue does not diminish the ego but rather changes its form, makes it in its own way have wings, be that which it has been prepared for and longs for. The ego becomes a spiritual ego, but does not seek to abandon the world for the allures of the heights. It seeks to experience all that is here in a soulful manner.

1 The Twelve Spiritual Virtues

The virtues are inherently practical because they are concerned with the good, and it is never sufficient to simply think about the good or to feel it; it must be engaged. For Plato, the True, the Beautiful, and the Good exist as three archetypal realms and are grand imaginations toward which we aspire as human beings. We orient our thinking to the True, our feeling toward the Beautiful, and our actions, our willing, toward the Good. In such striving, we seek to unite our merely human ways with the ways of the spiritual worlds. The Good is the object of willing, that which our actions attempt to achieve when we act out of a harmony of body, soul, and spirit.

Aristotle has a more empirical approach to virtue, but echoes Plato in many respects. In the *Nichomachean Ethics* he seeks to discover the good, and comes to define the good as what it is we are aiming at in life, what we are here to do. As there are many ways of doing the good, there must be one chief good, with which all the rest we can imagine are connected. This chief good Aristotle calls *Eudaimonia,* which is best translated with a quite beautiful word: "flourishing." The chief good is the flourishing of the harmonious life of body, soul, and spirit.

What sort of human life is most flourishing? Aristotle holds that a virtuous life is most flourishing; the best human life is one of excellent human activity. In book three of the *Ethics,* he turns to the question of what constitutes virtuous activity. Virtues, first, are aspects of "soul," those aspects primarily concerned with mediating our emotional life. For example, anger is lived in a virtuous manner when we feel it neither too violently nor too weakly. Virtue concerns expression and action in the realm of emotion that finds the mean between extremes. The doing of virtue does not so much concern what is done as how it is done. He does not say that we are not virtuous if we become angry; on the contrary, we may not be virtuous if we do not express anger. Virtue is not a matter of making a list of what counts as good and what counts as bad and focusing only on the one, trying to exclude the other. We see that there exists a dynamism of soul that is not subject to simple rules and regulations.

Living the virtues can be imagined as developing the art of the soul. You have to get the knack of it by doing it. Aristotle's view is that the virtues are acquired by doing; we are not born with them, and we do not acquire them in any other way than by exercising them. An artistic skill is required in exercising virtue. Still, there must be an inner quality of soul that recognizes a virtue when it sees one, and if seen clearly enough, becomes inclined toward that virtue. Otherwise we become involved in a rather impossible regress.

If virtues come wholly from the outside, then who determines what counts as virtue and what does not? That is to say, if virtue comes completely from the outside, then this realm would be simply a matter of what is socially or culturally conditioned. Here we have to tread a careful path. The way we take up and live virtue must indeed be sensitive to context. The acts themselves, no matter what the content might be, are not virtuous. A genuinely fair action, for example, is not one that can be determined in an abstract way. It must be an action that a person knows to be fair in a given situation, chooses to do for its own sake, and does in such a way that it expresses the soul character of the person.

We need to make a clearing for the consideration of virtue by differentiating virtue from ethics on the one hand and from values on the other. The primary difference centers in the concern with the soul, which we shall be following in an explicit way. When doing the good issues from the inner life of the soul, there is active enjoyment in what one does. We take pleasure in our virtuous activity; it is not a matter of duty or obligation, following a moral code, or doing what one is told to do. Ethics is a code of conduct based upon moral duties and obligations that indicate how one should behave. Values are core beliefs or desires that guide or motivate attitudes and actions. Values are not necessarily ethical.

Look, for example, at the act of treating other people fairly. Fairness can be a value, a characteristic of social life that is held in affective regard. One then acts in fairness toward others because that is what is valued by the group or society; there may or may not be pleasure involved in such action. Fairness can also be an ethic, a matter of moral duty and obligation, connected with the perception of what is right. For fairness to be a virtue, it must express the inner soul life of the person acting in a fair way, and therefore carry a particular quality characteristic of that individual; the individual must also choose to act in this way, and in so doing experiences pleasure, not from what may come from acting in this way, but in the act itself.

If virtuous action brings pleasure to the soul, then it is necessary to know how soul pleasure is experienced. It is not the same as sensory pleasure, emotional pleasure, or the kind of satisfaction we might experience by doing something that brings the approval of others, or even that which accompanies doing something well. Try to remember a time when you did a courageous act simply because that was what the situation called for. You did not do this act in order to be praised, or because it was expected that you do it; in fact, you did not even consider whether you would benefit. The quality of pleasure involved in this action can be described as feeling free, as if an existing inner barrier had been removed and you were acting in perfect accord with who you are.

In such a moment, in fact, you discover more of who you are as a spiritual being than you had known before. While the pleasure connected with each of the virtues has its own particular quality—and we shall try to describe these qualities in detail—the inner quality of freedom characterizes them all.

How are we to approach the question of what specific virtues to consider? There are the three theological virtues of faith, hope, and charity, and there are the four cardinal virtues of prudence, justice, fortitude, and temperance; these will not be the ones we shall focus on. The cardinal virtues are needed for noble actions in the world. The theological virtues are the way the spiritual worlds grace us. We do not acquire faith, hope, or love, but rather find the way to be open and receptive to these virtues. It is more accurate to say that we are visited by faith, hope, and charity than it is to say that we develop them. For example, in Dante's *Divine Comedy*, Dante the pilgrim does not encounter anything of these three virtues until he reaches paradise. He is there tested for his knowledge of these virtues and declares that they are gifts from the heavens.

The cardinal virtues characterized the pagan world; they were the mark of the highest nobility a human could attain—arete, or excellence. The theological virtues characterized the medieval world. They characterized the receptivity of human beings to the spiritual worlds. The new realm of virtue that is the concern of this book are the actions needed in the world to elevate our doing, making what we do an offering to the spiritual worlds. The spiritual virtues are ways of spiritualizing our actions in the world, of making action holy. Any action.

The number of virtues varies, from perhaps the single virtue of love to as many as 545 in one religion of India. My method of determining what to focus on is based upon three considerations. The first consideration comes from the meaning of the word itself. The word "virtue" means: "the power or operative influence inherent in a supernatural or divine being"; or "an embodiment of such power, especially one of the orders of the celestial hierarchy"; or "the act of a divine being."

These initial *Oxford English Dictionary* definitions precede the more common definitions of virtue as acts of conduct carried out by human beings. Re-visioning virtue first requires going to this source meaning, recognizing that the more common meanings have become deadened by being immersed in the dogma of one or another religion. I am interested in developing the spiritual rather than the religious way of attending to the life of virtue because this way invites separate individuals to find their particular way of expressing their soul and spirit life rather than doing so according to arranged practices.

A second consideration follows: we most likely cannot directly perceive the acts of spiritual beings, but we do have evidence of their action in the archetypal patterns of the universe. We can take an archetypal approach to virtue, seeking the imaginal and spiritual background to our practice of particular virtues as ways of reaching toward the divine arrangements of the cosmos. A specific relation, for example, exists between the twelve constellations of the zodiac and twelve virtues. This relation has been pointed to by various individuals, but not yet developed.

H. P. Blavatsky spoke of such a relation in *The Secret Doctrine*. Rudolf Steiner was asked if he agreed with the list of twelve virtues suggested by Blavatsky, and he said yes. He also said that these twelve virtues can be traced back to the great initiate Mani. Herbert Witzenmann more recently wrote a brief book of meditations of the virtues, *The Virtues–The Seasons of the Soul*, based on the indications of Blavatsky and also of Rudolf Steiner. Recently an astrologer, Paul Platt, has attempted to phenomenologically verify the relation of twelve different virtues to the twelve constellations in his work, *The Qualities of Time*. My work extends these efforts and utilizes only the naming of the twelve virtues; the rest of what follows is original research rather than a reporting of these previous efforts.

For our purposes, it is not a literal connection of virtue with the zodiac that is of importance; rather, what is important is to have a cosmological imagination in relation to virtue. Such an imagination will help us feel we are in harmony with the larger universe when we act out of virtue and prevent virtue from becoming a code of ethics to follow or a moralistic system attempting to impose modes of behavior.

A further consideration in approaching the virtues through an archetypal imagination of the zodiac concerns the mobility of such an imagination. The year is an archetype of becoming; we move from one month to the next, from one season to the next; and then return to the start again. The virtues, then, are not fixed ways of acting but a path of inner development that we go over again and again, deepening and expanding our experience of these attributes of the soul throughout our lives. The zodiac, for us, is an imagination within

which we can place this work and not a system that in any way pre-
dicts, for example, that someone born under a certain sign will be
characterized by a predominance of a certain virtue. Nor does this
imagination provide a new system for astrological reading.

We can think of the virtues as twelve stages of development,
but these twelve stages repeat because we are not engaged in learning something conceptual; if we were, then once we got the concept we would have clarity. Virtue educates emotions and feelings,
and that takes not only practice but repetition.

Our emotions have a quality that is much like the realm of
dreams. You may have a most vivid and moving dream, only to forget it within a few hours. We experience emotional life in a similar
way. While we are in the midst of a particular emotion, it domi-
nates our consciousness totally. Yet, after the emotion passes, we
usually have trouble describing exactly what we experienced. Thus,
emotional life does not develop in the way that, say, intellectual life
develops. The virtues are not intellectual concepts but rather purifi-
cations of emotion; for this reason, it is perhaps not to the theolo-
gian or to the philosopher of ethics that we should look for
guidance in the practice of virtue, but rather to a depth psychology
bearing a spiritual orientation, that is, to spiritual psychology.

The correlation between the zodiac constellations and the
virtues we will be considering are the following:

Region	Virtue	Time Period
Aries	Devotion	March 21–April 21
Taurus	Balance	April 21–May 21
Gemini	Faithfulness	May 21–June 21
Cancer	Selflessness	June 21–July 21
Leo	Compassion	July 21–Aug. 21
Virgo	Courtesy	Aug. 21–Sept. 21
Libra	Equanimity	Sept. 21–Oct. 21
Scorpio	Patience	Oct. 21–Nov. 21
Sagittarius	Truth	Nov. 21–Dec. 21
Capricorn	Courage	Dec. 21–Jan. 21
Aquarius	Discernment	Jan. 21–Feb. 21
Pisces	Love	Feb. 21–March 21

My naming of these twelve virtues differs in four instances from the naming given by the individuals mentioned above. In place of the virtue under the sign of Aquarius, which is named by Blavatsky as "Silence," I use the term "Discernment." I do this because it seemed to me that the primary activity that goes on in meditative silence is discernment. In addition, Steiner links up the two. Silence is not itself a virtue; what goes on within it can be. Besides, discernment is one of the main characteristics of the sign of Aquarius. This activity is the act of discerning among various spiritual operations.

A second change is that I use the term "Faithfulness" rather than the term "Perseverance," as originally given. The two are obviously related, but "faithfulness" conveys a more spiritual connotation than does "perseverance." The third change is that I use the term "Equanimity" as a virtue rather than "Contentment." "Contentment" also does not convey an active quality very well. The fourth change is that I use the term "Truth" rather than "Control of Speech." This latter term is unwieldy and seems to be trying to convey something of the way that truth needs to be expressed. Truth also is attributed to Sagittarius by astrologers.

I want to emphasize that the previous writing on the twelve virtues all stems from the report that a list was given to Rudolf Steiner, a list that supposedly came from the work of Blavatsky. The person giving Steiner this list asked him if it was correct. He reportedly said yes, and that practicing the virtues would result in significant changes in soul life. Thus, since Steiner, to my knowledge, never lectured or wrote about the twelve virtues, there is considerable leeway in how they are presented. It is a matter of ongoing research. I have also relied in my naming on extensive reading of astrological texts and the qualities and attributes of each of the signs of the zodiac.

One further comment needs to be made concerning what Steiner said about the twelve virtues. He said that the practice of the virtues would lead to very specific changes in soul life, and he named the changes associated with each virtue:

Devotion becomes the Force of Sacrifice
Balance becomes Progress

Perseverance becomes Faithfulness
Selflessness becomes Catharsis
Compassion becomes Freedom
Courtesy becomes Tact of Heart
Contentment becomes Equanimity
Patience becomes Insight
Control of Speech becomes Feeling for Truth
Courage becomes Redemptive Power
Silence becomes Meditative Power
Magnanimity becomes Love

What practice of the virtues leads to in the soul relies, however, on clear understanding and a feeling for the virtues themselves. The effort needs to be placed here, and not on what spiritual advances might result. I know a number of anthroposophists, followers of Rudolf Steiner, who carry around a card listing all the virtues and their development into new qualities. I once asked a medical doctor who practices anthroposophical medicine, who once pulled out such a card to show me, to describe just one of the virtues; he was not able to do this. I dared not ask him to describe what is meant by the soul development that results from the virtues. We need a careful phenomenology of these new virtues with suggestions on how to work with them and how they can enter into our daily actions.

The procedure I follow in this book consists of giving an initial, brief description of each of the twelve virtues listed above. Then, the twelve subsequent chapters develop the phenomenology of each virtue in depth. Then, some specific suggestions on methods of working with the virtues will be given along with a reflection on the nature of virtue. The challenge of these descriptions will be to find the most adequate way of finding language that is a language of the soul, since virtue concerns soul education. The language varies considerably in these twelve chapters because it also attempts to be a language of each of the constellations. Aquarian language, for example, is necessarily more abstract than Taurean language.

When we imagine the circle of the zodiac as a whole, while at the same time we try to imagine one region separate yet belonging to that whole, then it is possible to feel that one virtue is not separated from the rest. A further feeling arises: that these virtues, taken as a whole, can be named, just as the virtues of faith, hope, and charity are named the theological virtues because they are those soul qualities needed to approach God. Similarly, the virtues of prudence, justice, temperance, and fortitude are named the cardinal virtues because they are the principal ways to develop our moral relationships with others.

The twelve virtues listed above, seen through the imagination of the zodiac, that great embrace of the cosmos, could be named the spiritual virtues. These twelve virtues to be considered have primarily to do with how to engage in the practice of finding our ongoing connections with spiritual reality in the practical activities of daily life. The attempt is to gradually form a community of earthly beings and helpful spiritual beings. We perhaps do not get very far by trying to form intentional communities, or trying deliberately to live as a community of one sort or another. The suggestion here is that by engaging the virtues, those that hold together the whole of spiritual and human worlds, we might find ourselves a living community. Thus, as we proceed to describe the twelve qualities of the whole, we will do so bearing in mind a concern for what constitutes a flourishing community.

Devotion

We have to move into the image of each virtue gradually, being careful not to drown out the feeling-voice of the virtue itself by trying to know it rather than feel it first. An image is not a static picture but rather the activity of the soul in the act of creating a picture. Devotion itself cannot be pictured because it stands there as a static word, a word that perhaps can be defined but not easily imaged.

To aid in developing an image, begin by noticing that in the zodiac circle, devotion stands between love and balance. Love precedes devotion, and balance follows from devotion. Devotion builds on a basis of love, and anticipates balance. Devotion concerns a steadiness of the depth of love. To practice devotion concerns developing the ability to deeply love in a steady, ongoing, balanced manner rather than, say, sporadically. In devotion, we approach whatever we are doing, or attend to who is with us, as if the task, the event, the person were sacred and holy. The practice of this virtue requires a certain specific kind of attention, of focus, of concentration—the concentration of love.

Every virtue can also be looked at in terms of its excess and its lack. These two qualities are the shadow of every virtue, and we must look at these excesses and lacks in ourselves quite closely (see chapter 14). Such qualities are not to be denied, turned away from as if they were not there, for then they return as obsessions. On the other hand, we have to be able to look at these adverse qualities in ourselves without identifying ourselves with these qualities. For example, the shadow of devotion on the side of excess is malice. The shadow of this virtue on the side of lack would be the incapacity to sustain a concentration of love toward a single goal. If we do not recognize our own malice, then devotion can have no real, embodied strength. If we do not recognize our own shallowness, then our devotion will have no breadth.

Balance

In order to experience the virtue of balance we have to be moving toward a future in a soulful and spiritual way. Even in the realm of physical life, it is when we go to take the "next step" that balance comes into play. In the spiritual realm, a good image for the point of balance is the crossing point of a lemniscate. This is the point of concentration between two spiritual factors—the effort that comes from us in our attempts at spiritual development, and the presence of spiritual reality, which opens itself to us according to its own laws, not according to how hard we work to attain authentic spiritual experience. The virtue of balance concerns the capacity to concentrate, without effort, at the crossing point. Our own personal efforts toward spiritual development must be in perfect balance with the grace offered or not offered by the spiritual realms.

The virtue of balance is also reflected in everyday practical life and concerns the relation of the efforts we bring to a situation in order to influence it, and what the situation itself requires in order to be true to its own internal, and often mysterious, order. The disorders of balance often show up here either as an attempt to impose our understanding and/or desires onto the situation or as an inability to act at all, a kind of apathy or inertia. Such unbalance in the horizontal direction of our work in the world, I suspect, reflects an unbalance in the vertical direction; that is, lack of balance in spiritual work precedes lack of balance in everyday life.

Developing the virtue of balance entails moving from the constant oscillations of the mental life into the rhythmic movement of the feeling life, centered in the realm of the heart. This development also entails discovering the exact relationship between matters of the mind and matters of the heart. While balance can only be found in the rhythm of the heart, moving into this rhythmic domain does not mean abandoning thought, but rather, switching what takes precedence. The location of balance in the zodiac circle between devotion and faithfulness gives an image of the work entailed here. Balance relies on the devotion of the heart and requires the development of faithfulness, that is, adherence to the ways of the heart.

Faithfulness

The virtue of faithfulness concerns, before all else, faithfulness to our soul and spiritual life. Quite often, we may lose the actual experience of the soul and of the spirit. Faithfulness truly exists only when it defies absence. When, for example, I speak of an individual as a faithful friend, I mean this person is someone who does not fail me, someone who stands up to whatever the circumstances may bring, someone I find there when I confront difficulty. Such a friend is truly faithful, though, when his or her presence is not forced, is not a matter of duty or felt obligation.

Now, with respect to our soul and spirit, the virtue of faithfulness means that we stand in and for these realms, regardless of the times in which we do not actually experience them. Further, to be faithful means that we are present to and for the realms of soul and spirit, that it is something we do for them, not for our own sake. It may seem somewhat strange to suggest that the worlds of soul and spirit rely upon our active attention; it is the nature of these realms of reality that, while they certainly have an independent, autonomous existence, each individual is a part of the objective existence of these realms. Our individual soul is a drop in the soul of the *anima mundi,* and our spirit is a drop in the spirit of the *spiritus mundi.* So, giving attention to soul and to spirit is something that is really oriented toward these larger realms in which we participate, and in part, sustain.

I am suggesting that it is really not possible to exercise the virtue of faithfulness in our lives—faithfulness to another person, an organization, a work—unless we are first of all faithful in the realm of soul and spirit. It is possible to be constant, to force ourselves not to change, to be present in a constant way as a matter of duty, to be conscientious. But faithfulness goes beyond constancy because it contains an essential element of spontaneity. I am not faithful out of obligation; hence, faithfulness must be something essentially creative and founded in freedom.

Suppose I enter into a relationship, either of a personal and intimate sort, or even of the sort involved in day-to-day work. How would the virtue of faithfulness be practiced? It cannot be simply a matter of commitment, of saying that no matter what happens I will not change in my commitment. No relationship can flourish under such circumstances. Faithfulness is created in the act of doing it, and thus it must be every moment created for it to exist. We do not have to be conscious of this act every moment, but only a certain awareness of this creativeness, what the philosopher Gabriel Marcel has called "creative fidelity," shifts the burden of commitment to the joy of faithfulness.

Selflessness

The virtue of selflessness lies between the excess of self-abandonment and the lack of self-centeredness. A total loss of boundaries occurs with self-abandonment, which leads to the possibility of being taken over by the needs and desires of others, while the one taken over feels he or she is actually being of service. After a time, one who has served others in this manner becomes completely confused and feels an inner emptiness. On the other hand, placing oneself at the center of whatever one does, making sure that personal benefit of one sort or another results, leaves the person or institution being "served" in this manner empty.

The virtue of selflessness is not easy to come to. Much of what we do for others tends to be either self-serving or done out of the need to be approved of by others; both are forms of egotism. The way through these two difficulties that lie in the way on the path to selflessness does not involve trying to become egoless. Rather, the ego needs to be given a sacred task. Our ego so voraciously grabs at whatever it can get for itself because, typically, it does not have what it needs, which is connection with something holy. Not having this connection, our ego tries to get hold of anything—power, position, status, material things—and since none of these is satisfying, our ego becomes involved in repeatedly trying more of the same.

Development of the virtue of selflessness begins with orienting our ego toward our self, ourselves in our spirit aspect. For example, when someone takes up a practice of meditation, this is an instance of the ego becoming oriented toward the self. Once given this sacred task, which takes repetition and discipline, the self is able to do its work in the world, to fulfill its desire, which is to serve.

The position of selflessness in the zodiac circle as occurring after faithfulness and before compassion shows us more about this virtue. Selflessness must be based upon the capacity to creatively be oriented toward others and must also partake of the capacity of entering into the experience of others as if it were one's own.

Compassion

As a virtue, compassion has a more restricted meaning than it does as a central aspect of the practice of Buddhism. I have already alluded to this more restricted meaning by giving the ego an important place in the development of virtue. Thus, compassion here does not rely upon taking the ego as illusion, as it does in this great religious tradition. Compassion does require that one live and work in relation with others and with the world more out of the center of the heart than out of the mind. The mind, or thinking, is certainly not excluded, but rather becomes a feeling-thinking. We can see that the virtue of selflessness is a kind of prerequisite to compassion; the ego, occupied with the sacred task of keeping connection with our spirit, leaves thinking free to enter into intimate relation with the heart.

Compassion concerns feeling the thoughts, feelings, joys, and sufferings of others, and of the things of the world as if they were our own. I want to extend compassion beyond a relationship with other human beings and also include the animal world, the plant world, and even the physical world; in doing so, I stand in the tradition of the *anima mundi,* the tradition going back as early as Plato and certainly before that, of seeing everything in the world as having soul. Further, when this virtue is developed in a further reflection, I will show that it is really not possible to have compassion for another human being without this larger, more inclusive sense of compassion.

A further aspect of compassion to be developed concerns how this virtue is active, that it is not simply something that one has for others, but something one does for others, an activity of radical receptivity that has real effects in the world. And while we can readily understand how feeling the suffering of others may indeed be a virtuous act, we will have to show how this act must be extended to those who do not appear to be suffering at all. Can we have compassion for the tyrant, or for the person at work who seems completely occupied with his own advancement, or for those around us who seem to have no feelings whatsoever toward us, or perhaps even hostile feelings?

Courtesy

The virtue of courtesy concerns holding back one's own emotions—not repressing or denying them—but holding them in order to give a place for the soul life of the other person to be expressed. Certainly, the word "courtesy" is related to the term "to court," which is to honor the presence of another, to outwardly acknowl-edge the person as a being of soul and spirit substance. In some ways this virtue may seem to be minor, but that mistake is due to courtesy falling into outward manners with little inner feeling. The virtue must be related to the tradition of courtly love, the troubadour poets, the right restraint in the expression of love.

Courtesy recognizes beauty as being at the very center of human life. Further, this virtue shows that beauty is not simply something to be looked at, to be admired, but that it can be a prac-tice, a discipline. Interestingly, the word "courtesy" is also related to the word "courtesan," which on the one hand means the guardian of the court, guardian of the royalty of soul and spirit, and on the other hand means a prostitute. If we restrain judg-ment, then a prostitute serves the bodily needs of a person. This helps us see that courtesy is a very bodily act, one honoring the soul and spirit in body. Of course, this kind of honoring of the body can become a perversion when the sense of soul and spirit is excluded; prostitution has all sorts of different forms.

We cannot bypass the fact that courtesy honors the feminine face of the world. Thus, we can ponder how this virtue can become more extensive, where we can see manners as having to do with the manner of relating. Because courtesy is a matter of the heart, how we do something is as important as what we do; in fact, per-haps even more so. Courtesy makes our act sensuous, full of body, erotic—every act an act of making love. Without courtesy our com-passion becomes sentimentalized, and without courtesy we cannot find the way to equanimity. Instead, we fall into carelessness—we couldn't care less—which is a lack of courtesy.

Equanimity

Equanimity may be the primary virtue needed for the devel-opment of communal relationships. In the zodiac circle, this virtue lies opposite to devotion. Oppositions in the zodiac do not signify conflict but rather show a particular sort of helping relation that goes on between polarities. For example, if the planet Pluto hap-pens to be in the seventh house, the house of relationships, and is in opposition to the Sun in the first house, then a person can expect that a transformation (Pluto) will occur in the individual (Sun) through relationships.

In terms of the virtue of equanimity, we could say that equanimity is brought about by devotion, and devotion is brought about by the practice of equanimity. For example, a saying that beautifully expresses the relation of devotion and equanimity can be found in the Bhagavad Gita (12:20): "He who holds equal blame and praise, who is restrained in speech, content with anything that comes, who has no fixed abode and is firm in mind—that man is devoted and dear to me." I introduce here the notion of looking at the opposite of each virtue as another help in understanding the nature of the virtues, a practice that can be applied to all the virtues, not just to equanimity.

Equanimity concerns the capacity to be even in emotional life, neither swinging into highs nor dipping into lows. It does not mean detachment from emotion, but does indicate the ability to see, to observe one's emotions while they are happening and thus avoid being completely taken over by the emotion occurring at the moment. All emotions are held with equal honor. Through equanimity a refinement of our emotional life occurs, and without this virtue emotions remain crude. On the other hand, overrefinement leads to superficiality.

Equanimity is of extreme importance because through this virtue we are able to develop a realistic imagination of our faults together with our virtues, and thus the practice of virtue does not fly off into an impossible and even destructive direction. For example, if I experience strong anger, the virtue of equanimity makes it possible to be fully present to this anger without however being wholly taken over by it. In this manner, the anger itself can be taken over into the practice of virtue.

Patience

Patience is the virtue that shows us that the time of the soul and the time of the spirit are different than everyday time. Patience is required to be in healthy connection with soul and spirit. Patience concerns a particular form or way of waiting; it is one filled with expectation. One waits patiently, expecting something to happen. The virtue requires living in such expectation without hastily seeking the completion of the expectation. When we do break the tension of patience and try to make something happen, then the soul and spirit involved in the expectation are left behind. Patience is the virtue that holds together the outer events of our lives with the inner workings of soul and spirit so that both occur together with the right timing.

While patience involves waiting with expectation, it is necessary that the expectation not be filled with any content; it is rather a kind of plentiful void. If that plentiful void becomes filled with our imaginations of what should or might happen, or with what we wish to happen, then we are living in illusion. The difficulty with such illusion is that it obscures the possibility of seeing what lies right in front of us now.

The lesson of patience is patience; that is to say, this virtue is unending. We are not just patient until something happens. Rather, patience is an enduring state of the soul that, if it has a purpose at all, is to deepen our receptive capacities. Patience is strained by the fact that things do happen, and that makes us impatient and anxious for something to be always happening. The events of our lives, however, are always—always—less than the life of possibilities experienced by the soul. Patience shows us in fact, in a very gradual way, that soul life consists of the imagination, which is the activity of living in the possible and not any particular content.

There is always a kind of surplus to any event that we experience, something that goes beyond the content of what has happened. It is this surplus that is the effective agent in bringing about transformation in ourselves, in others, and in the world. The impatience of efficiency tries with technical means of every sort to get rid of this surplus, and thus, the world completely lacks patience.

Truth

As a virtue, truth does not concern having knowledge of what is right and correct and knowledge of what is false. The virtue of truth is more connected with emotion; it concerns the ongoing development of the capacity of a feeling for truth. It is more like taste than, say, sight. One has to acquire a subtlety for differences and nuances rather than have something presented before one clearly and completely. We tend to confuse truth with judgment, taking our judgment of what we say to be true as truth. Such judgments reveal more about the individual than they do about the reality being judged.

The need for the virtue of truth shows in its deviations of gossip, slander, moralizing, and subjectivity of opinion. All of these deviations reveal the rather universal attempt to possess the truth. We do not ever have the truth because truth has its own autonomy; it exists independently of what we may think or judge. Nonetheless, its power can reveal itself only insofar as we practice the virtue of striving for truth. We reach for the truth, try to feel it, come close to it, get acquainted with it, befriend it.

When we attempt to have the truth, to know it completely, we are actually trying to seize not truth but the power that lies within truth. At that moment, when we think we have it, the truth we think we have turns into subjective judgment, gossip, slander, or moralizing. Metaphorically, the seeker of truth has to be a person without a place, always on the road, peripatetic, and if the seeker wants instead to take up residence, to feel secure, then the truth turns into lies.

The development of a feeling for the truth intensifies, strengthens, and brings into form our powers of attention, focus, and concentration. These capacities involve not just the mind, but the feelings and the will as well. We seek truth with our whole being, not just with our mind. We may find that the greater the concentration the more we find ourselves also practicing silence, and that those great deviations from truth all involved the violation of silence.

Courage

We can begin to sense courage as a virtue to be exercised daily rather than imagining it as expressed only in acts of heroism by picturing the other sides of courage—ambition and timidity. Ambition looks much like courage except that it moves too quickly and too self-consciously. Ambition has too much self-will attached to it, so that strong, decisive action, which may indeed look courageous, serves only the one doing the action and not those whom it may seem to serve. Timidity also relates to courage; it is courage that gets blocked by coming to rest in consciousness rather than flowing over into action. The timid person often sees events and situations quite clearly, but is content with being conscious, abdicating giving inner shape to what is seen and taking responsibility for acting according to what one sees needs to be done.

Genuine acts of courage really do not happen on the spur of the moment and spontaneously; they may look that way, but that is because we do not have access to or knowledge of the development and inner life of the person who acts courageously. Such a person has had to develop and now lives more from the center of the heart, but not in a sentimental way. Perception, however, cannot be at a distance, as it is for many people; it is, for the courageous person, an engaged perception, fully conscious, but not overbalanced in the direction of self-consciousness. The heart can be conscious in this way, whereas the mind cannot because it is forever self-reflective of itself. With courage we have a perfect harmony of bodily experience, centered in the heart, with the experience of soul and spirit. For this reason the courageous person has the greatest range of imagination, and is able to move comfortably from the depths to the heights.

Courage, as a way of being, reveals itself in thought and feeling as well as physical action. One's whole life can be an act of courage. It is not at all necessary to face some seemingly insurmountable obstacle to engage this virtue. The person who moves along in life with clear aims and clear values, moving toward these step by step, can certainly be called courageous, provided the way is accompanied by the embodied experience of soul and spirit. Ambition seeks the top but cannot see that the high summit really belongs to the spirit, and instead courage is thwarted into having authority over others rather than recognizing the authority of the spiritual worlds.

Discernment

We typically think of discernment as the ability to make choices based on trying to be clear concerning the difference between choices, particularly when we find ourselves attracted to more than one thing at the same time. As a virtue, discernment is not quite so easy as this sounds because of two factors. The first factor concerns the nature of desire, and the second concerns the fact that the objects of choice do not involve things easily apprehended. Thus, the process of discernment must take place in two ways at the same time; we have to be able to feel the often subtle differences in desire, and we have to be able to tell the difference between objects that often have the substance of something like air, such as ideas, destiny path, a future outcome, or the effects of what we do on the lives of others.

Where do we find the inner resource capable of the virtue of discernment? First, a different way of thinking has to be practiced than what we are accustomed to. We have to learn to be present to the activity of ideas, their coming into being, their process. When we "have" an idea, it is already thinking crystallized, no longer fluid and part of the creative process. Such solidified ideas, which constitute the material of typical thought, occur too late in the thinking process for discernment of a soul and spirit nature to take place.

A similar kind of presence, presence to the activity rather than to the momentary result of inner activity, is required in the realm of feeling in order to be able to practice discernment. We have to develop the discipline of being present to the inception of feelings more so than feeling those we already have.

The virtue of discernment can be imagined as the way we ride the current of our soul and spirit destiny, and thus concerns the way that we move from where we are in our lives into what is coming to meet us from the future. Without discernment we are in fact always living in the past—in past ideas, in past emotions and feelings, in habits from the past.

Discernment does not enter as something we even recognize as important unless we actually experience the reality of the freedom of our spirit. While freedom of spirit sounds like something wonderful, it involves living in the regions of not-knowing and having to learn to navigate these regions. We can do so only by seeking to harmonize the various elements of our inner life—our thinking with our feeling, with our perception, with our desires, with our intent. If one of these elements becomes too strong, then discerning where we are in the process becomes confused. The primary discipline in the development of the virtue of discernment is thus inner stillness and listening.

Love

Love constitutes a huge topic unto itself, so we must try to be clear that here we are interested only in the virtue of love, something slightly different than the whole realm of the reality of love. The practical question, the question of virtue, is how love is actually practiced. How do we do it? We could begin by saying that as long as we are feeling love, we are not doing it as fully as it could be done. Love feelings, of course are most important, but they also indicate we are trying to hold on to something whose nature is wholly that of being given away; that is to say, the nature of the virtue of love is to give it away.

Since love is not an object, a thing, what does it mean to give love? To experience this virtue, it is necessary to become intimately acquainted with our need to receive love, because this need is perhaps the source of holding on to the love that wants to be free to circulate in the world. Thus, self-love confuses the virtue of love, yet self-love is certainly necessary, and is in fact a prerequisite for the virtue of love. Self-love consists of the endeavor to be ourselves rather than who someone else might want us to be. Love cannot be given unless it is given freely of our own individuality; otherwise, the acts of love that we engage in are really for ourselves and not for others and for the world. Self-love makes it possible to choose to give rather than to hold on to love.

I do not want to try to define love, but we must try to characterize it so that it is not confused with certain kinds of feeling states or, alternately, too quickly spiritualized. Perhaps we could say that love consists of universal friendliness fraught with beneficence to all creatures. Given such a broad characterization, we can see the wisdom of love standing in the zodiac circle between discernment and devotion. Discernment is needed for the practice of love in order that love may be universally specific. And because love does take us into the whole of creation, as well as the whole of the soul and spirit realms, it must look forward to being practiced in very specific ways, an anticipation of devotion.

The virtue of love is experienced as an encompassing field existing within ourselves and the beloved but also pervading the soul space around both. The central aspect of the virtue of love consists of learning to perceive the reality of these currents of love as an autonomous reality to which we are called to participate in and follow. These currents open new levels of perception so that everything becomes more intensely vibrating, showing its soul and spirit being.

With these brief characterizations of the virtues as a starting place, we can now go on and develop a more extensive and deep description of each virtue, how they function and what they do in the soul and as forces of power in the world.

2 **The Virtue of Devotion**

Devotion may be the most difficult virtue, not only to actually put into practice in our lives, but also to adequately and accurately describe. The word seems easy enough to understand. We know what it means to be devoted to someone or to some work, or to God. It is when we try to say what we mean by devotion that things become more difficult.

We might say, for example, that devotion is extremely dedicated love that is selflessly oriented toward the good of another. The soul capacities needed to actually bring such a notion into actuality are manifold. We do not simply decide to try this virtue out. Certain soul capacities have to be developed and made conscious. There are some very strong dangers connected with trying to live this virtue without clear understanding. A primary danger concerns losing ourselves, which actually turns devotion into something more pathological, for love at this level has to be given freely and consciously; if it is not, what looks like devotion is sentimental piety that is detrimental to one's own soul life and to that of others.

Devotion is the ability to be completely and wholly engaged with someone in a manner in which wholehearted attention is given to that person at all levels of their being. We can also imagine devotion to an ideal as well as an individual, or even to an organization; and certainly, religious devotion comes to mind. Devotion, though, has real force to it. It is fiery, hot, impulsive, and can even seem militant or rash. One thing for sure, we shall have to change our minds about devotion and release any kind of

sentimental and pious notions that picture someone quietly pray-
ing, or exuding a peaceful, caring presence. We may look this way
when we attend someone with devotion, but the interior soul life
is filled with fire. We are on fire with devotion. Perhaps we see so
little devotion in the world because there is fear that it could con-
sume us. We have to learn how to hold the fire, how to develop an
adequate vessel of soul that can both contain and express the
intensity of devotion at the same time.

Devotion seems to be such a quiet virtue. Perhaps because it is
just the opposite of quiet, because it is so active and so restless and
so full of force that we have covered it over with a sentimentality
as a way of avoiding dealing with the depth of its forceful reality.
We have to work at entering into the sense of devotion as a force
of immense strength, as a living activity, as an act, a virtue that is
essentially penetrating, reaching out, searching, looking, yearning,
seeking rather than inward, whole and calm.

Let's look for a moment at the archetypal qualities of the element of fire as a first orientation to the virtue of devotion. Fire is
always imagined as an active force, the archetypal force of
willpower and energy. Fire destroys and renews, chars or purifies,
is a creative force, and at the same time, a destructive force. In
alchemy, the first of seven alchemical operations leading to the
treasured philosopher's stone is the operation of fire, called calci-
nation, which is a heating and pulverizing of a solid to drive off
water and other volatile compounds. Considered psychologically,
the "solid matter" that is being burned away is our ego. The act
of devotion puts us in the fire that separates the essential from the
dross. When our ego is under the fire, we become expansive,
explosive, disruptive, and impulsive.

Perhaps these characteristics can be seen, though, as the first
step into an initiation into devotion. Acting in an expansive manner looks like anything but devotion, but that is only because, at
first, such a force as devotion is most difficult to contain, and
sparks go shooting all over the place. In its very first phases, devotion actually looks like an expansion of ego into the world; and in
fact, the possibility of devotion can easily get sidetracked into
being nothing more than ego expansion. Let me give an example.

The possibility of the development of devotion often begins with some life-changing experience that sets us on a totally new course, a new beginning. Imagine a person who has been convicted of a crime and sent to prison, although the person did not commit the crime. While in prison, the person studies law and eventually becomes a lawyer, having the intent of helping others who may be unjustly charged and treated. Such a person might well become devoted to this work. Perhaps, however, such a person, when released from prison, becomes quite good as a lawyer and begins to make a lot of money and receives much notoriety. What began as an ideal, and then moved into a devoted work, can at this point turn into ego expansion, an ego trip characterized by an obsession to work that only looks like devotion.

An intention toward devotion needs the help of the virtue of equanimity as its complement. Without the stabilization of equanimity, it is quite likely that devotion never gets beyond its initial fiery stage. Equanimity concerns the point of balance between efforts we bring to a task and the realization that no matter what we do or how hard we work, what we accomplish is a matter of grace. The capacity to feel the presence of grace, of being graced by help from the spiritual realms, can cool the intense fire of devotion. The forcefulness of the application of so much energy toward something that characterizes devotion can lead to burnout; or what initially inspired the devotion can get lost or forgotten unless this balance can also be felt.

For example, the act of devotion begins with an ideal, something toward which we apply all of our energy. It is easy to see here the seeds of devotion. The danger, however, lies in the fact that an ideal almost always begins as an intense vision carried almost wholly as head or mental force without the necessary will and feeling to turn the vision into an actuality. For the initial impulse to turn into steady devotion, something must come in to hold the exuberant force and transmute the impulsiveness.

If equanimity can be found, the ideal has a chance of maturing. Even when this balance comes about, devotion does not necessarily follow. The balance only makes possible extending the ideal into taking some of the initial steps toward actualizing it.

When we become attracted to some ideal and initiate devoted work toward that ideal, incineration begins, and the possibility of devotion getting sidetracked into egotism occurs. A great deal of heat is generated when one feels devotion, which means a lot of will-force, love, concentration, and energy. This initial heat, however, centers in the region of the head, and has a lot of ego involvement. It is this strong ego involvement that must be incinerated if the ideal is to serve others and not just oneself. If the ideal involves only our own self-aggrandizement, then a behavior that may look like devotion, but is not, may develop. The possibility of devotion turns toward mere ambition. We see this devolution occurring all the time in the various professions. People go to medical school, law school, or graduate school with high ideals, which could be transformed into devoted service to others and to the world. Most often, the idealism gets mixed with a great deal of egotism, with the result that "professionalism" sets in and people become concerned with making money, reputation, professional status, and career advancement.

Noticing how the degradation of devotion happens gives us a clue for the further exploration of the virtue and why it can so easily get diverted. The "professionalism" of the professions shows how order and outer structure can come in and provide the riotous vigor of sparking enthusiasm with form. The soul purpose that initiates devotion can be subverted and harnessed into tight structures that utilize the energy of devotion but cut it off from its true intent.

When we feel an urge toward devoting our lives to our work—perhaps medicine, or teaching, or service—we feel this urging so strongly that we often change our lives completely in order to follow such an impulse. We want to be of help to others. Then, when we begin to find our way into the actual work, we often encounter strong institutionalized structures. These structures are intended to legitimize our acts of devotion, but they often divert them. How to follow our devotion, never losing sight of it, goes together with the virtue itself. That is, devotion is not only the initial dedication but also the finding of inner resources to sustain that initial dedication no matter what. We have to be devoted to devotion itself or it will get lost.

Rather than just following our idealism or letting it burn out, it is perhaps important to work at holding in abeyance the object of the ideal and trying to get closer to the fire itself. If I feel a very strong desire to change my profession from being a stockbroker to being an addiction counselor, what is the quality of the urging? Rather than too quickly looking into available training, and how I might get an internship and set up a practice, and make my decision to go in this new direction, I will look at the urging itself for a long time.

We quickly find that this fire that characterizes the urging is indeed the fire of love. Whatever we love, we idealize; and whatever we idealize, we feel devoted to. But it is the particular form of love that is a pure fire that begins in the head, as an idea, that we must try to understand in order to get a better feeling for the virtue of devotion.

We do not typically know why a particular ideal we hold develops. We may have been exposed to this ideal in our family, or in the church, or in education, but this exposure does not account for why so few who are exposed to an idealistic stance actually take it up. An ideal has an instinctive base, or else it does not have force and power and instead is simply living out someone else's ideal. By instinctive base, I mean that we don't know why something grabs our attention so strongly and will not let go. The ideal seems just to appear, but it has, in addition to its idea side, a strong bodily aspect; the idea is also an impulse. We feel compelled, drawn, pushed, almost forced toward this ideal. The instinctive basis of idealism, and thus of devotion, easily takes the turn toward the base side, however, and devotion goes awry. This kind of deviation tends to happen if an inner, reflective side to the impulsiveness that leads us on toward something is not awakened at the same time as the ideal.

If we are able to temporarily forgo focusing only on the object of our idealism and look at the urging itself, we can discover a factor belonging to devotion that provides the possibility of contributing reflection to the impulsiveness of idealism. In addition to the aggressiveness, strength, and heart characteristic of devotion, there is another, more hidden soul quality that it is necessary to get in touch with. A mercurial, reflective quality also accompanies the urge toward devotion, though at a more subtle and hidden level. It is this mercurial quality that we can look to as helping to move our initial idealism into sustained acts of devotion.

We may think we know what our idealism is about, and usually think that it concerns only some external goal that we are trying to reach. We set out to attain that goal and then become permeated with whatever the goal requires of us. For example, a person may feel a strong impulse to be of service to others. This idealism, due to the abilities, history, and circumstances of the person, may focus on, say, becoming a doctor and helping others. Once the ideal is known, in this case to be doctor, years and years of education, a level of intellectual ability, the desire to put aside all rewards for a very long time, and so on are required.

For a long time, the idealism feeds into the particular goal and sustains the sacrifices needed. However, all that is required in becoming a doctor does not necessarily produce a doctor whose idealism matures into the virtue of devotion in this chosen path. The possibility of devotion developing can only occur if, at some point, the person is able to reflect back to see that becoming a doctor was not really the ideal, but was rather merely the vehicle for being of service to others. If this reflection does not occur, the person will either drop away from the study of medicine or will be taken into the structures of the profession that do not require that one be devoted to that profession.

For idealism to mature into devotion, the element of reflective thinking must be brought into the fiery urge to do something significant, which projects an ideal to go after. It is as if we feel our idealism and an impulse toward devotion before we really know what we intend to be devoted to. What seems to be the goal of our devotion is always simply the medium through which the devotion finds expression. However, reflective thinking alone is not sufficient to bring about the transformation of idealism into devotion. Certain qualities of feeling are also needed, and, as well, certain qualities of will.

The feeling quality of devotion is that of being oriented toward something wholeheartedly, something that, in essence, lies in the domain of the unknown. We can even specify the particular quality of feeling more clearly; devotion consists of an intense feeling of unwavering love, but why we feel devotion is something mysterious and remains, for the most part, unknown. Thus, while the initiation of devotion begins as idealism, this beginning has to be brought into reflection, and reflection deepens into feeling. If devotion does not unfold in a manner something like this, it is momentary infatuation, or an obsession, or romanticism, each of which cannot last.

This circuitous route into the heart of devotion is necessary, for following the pathway carefully is the only way of avoiding the simplistic notions that we might have about this virtue. These preconceived notions are bound to be either sentimental, thinking of devotion as sweet peacefulness, or completely cynical, thinking that anyone who lives out of devotion must have foolishly relinquished their own existence for someone or for some ideal for which there is no profit.

While the route to devotion begins with a primacy of an impulsive idealism, the route changes drastically, and a strong heart feeling of love oriented toward something true but unknown must come to take precedence. This quality of love is different than other kinds of love. All love is not oriented toward what is not known. With devotion, however, love comes to be present and strong before we are able to conceive of what it is that we are loving; this quality is essential to devotion.

Actually orienting our lives out of a strong feeling of love that is not completely understood, taking this feeling and doing something with it, is the will component of the virtue of devotion. We are led into the unknown, and here, thinking shows up again, now in a new way. We begin to think deeply into what we are so devotedly engaged with. We begin to be self-aware of the depth and the mystery of what we are doing. We may discover that the most central dimension of the devotion we are now living is that we are being drawn to the eternal, and our soul longs to unite with the eternal. We discover that longing for the eternal, though, has to go through the thickness, the density of the world, and this involves being dedicated, in love, to someone or something, some actuality. We discover that longings for the eternal that bypass the density of the world are flighty, ephemeral, not lasting, or completely lack a foundation in soul life.

Reviewing the complex action of entering into the virtue of devotion, we note that two simultaneous movements are involved. The inner life has to be strengthened at the same time as we move out into the world and do something of service. The inner life has to be strengthened in such a manner that it remains extremely open and flexible and does not fall into the hardness of egotism. And as we move out into the world, we have to do it in such a way that soul does not lose itself there. The will, living in and oriented toward love, has to be strengthened, or else we lose ourselves in an unhealthy way in the service with which we are engaged. For example, we may devote ourselves to our work for many years and come to a point that we no longer know who we are and really have no identifiable inner sense of self outside that work. This would be unhealthy devotion.

Healthy devotion is always accompanied by thought. There must be a resolve to think about, to consider deeply, the object of the soul's devotion. This thinking is of no use, however, if it is problem oriented. It cannot be the kind of thinking that says over and over, why am I devoted to this work, or this person, or this service. It has to be a creative thinking, a constant work of putting the element of reflection into the act of devotion. This kind of thinking is a kind of witnessing. We develop the capacity to witness the act of devotion itself, and that witnessing becomes part of the devotion.

If creative thinking does not form an essential core of devotion, then love turns into sentimental enthusiasm. We cannot do the work devotion requires in the world through the element of sentimental enthusiasm. The result would be that whatever we are so strongly engaged in becomes a kind of drudgery, loosely connected with a dreamy sense that this must be of service to others and to the world. Living in this state of sentimental enthusiasm is most dangerous for the soul because, in this condition, we are most subject to being utilized by the enthusiasms of others, which come to stand in for our own weak capacity of devotion.

We come, then, to the rather surprising point of understanding that the capacity of creative thinking is most essential in the practice of the virtue of devotion. Devotion, at first, does not at all seem to be something mental. I do not want, however, to suggest that creative thinking is the same thing as ordinary thinking, or even that it is something mental. The way thinking has been developed in describing this virtue, it is a thinking that permeates body, soul, and spirit. We are so accustomed to imagining thinking as "thinking about" something, that the nature of mercurial thinking, of hermetic thinking that is characteristic of devotion, needs to be emphasized. In devotion, our thinking is a loving permeation by the spirit of what we are devoted to.

A picture of the virtue of devotion as developed thus far can be found in the act of religious devotion. Our interest though, is in the gesture of devotion, seeing what happens in religious devotion as a prototype that can be expressed in many different ways in the world and not confined to the forms we find in religion. Devotion is an act of "looking up." In devotion we bend our knees, fold our hands, look up to the revered. Anyone who has gone into church and participated in such gestures discovers something right away.

The holy is not immediately present when we humble ourselves. These gestures have the effect of raising to the surface images and feelings, impulses and thoughts that do not seem at all to belong with these gestures of reverence. We have made a movement of the body that, in effect, subordinates the ordinary ego; the gestures, in effect, say, "There is someone much more exalted than myself, to whom I give the highest honor." It is most interesting that with these gestures, what first comes to consciousness are not images of this holy other, but our own complexes, fantasies, shadow, and pictures bubbling up from the sub- and unconscious regions of the soul.

The subordination of our ordinary ego is in fact immediately responded to by whom we give devotion to. It is not that the subconscious and unconscious regions rebel and come forth as an attack. Rather, who we give devotion to lights up and illuminates our being so that we are at least somewhat present to the fullness

31

of who we are. A strictly religious understanding of the pouring forth of the regions that we are not ordinarily conscious of would most likely see as temptation the upsurging of impulses, passions, fantasies, and such—temptation oriented toward keeping us away from the holy. A soul understanding would not see matters in this way. Including the fullness of who we are is central to the act of devotion; it changes the imagination of devotion from religious piety, in which sweetness is pitted against forceful ugliness, to devotion with the force of imagination.

Imagining the gesture of devotion, and how it brings forth the deeper realms, indicates that devotion concerns not only orienting ourselves to what is, so to speak, "above us," but also to what lies below. The act of devotion, as brought out in this description of what happens when we enact the gestures of devotion, also brings the startling discovery—something at first very difficult to absorb—that what is above is the same as what is below. When we set out to engage the virtue of devotion, in a way, all hell breaks loose. Ordinary thought would say, "Stay away from those lower regions, orient yourself wholly toward the higher realms." Creative thought says, "The true power and force of what is above is pictured for you by what comes so strongly from below; hold these two together until they become one."

Only creative consciousness can, through its fluidity, through its being an imaginal form of consciousness that does not categorize and cut one thing off from another, hold these tensions together, seeing that the one realm is a reflection of the other. By imaginal I mean that the images and impulses that well up when devotion is engaged are symbolic rather than literal. If I am devoted to my partner, I may find, for example, that strong images of being attracted to someone else begin to appear. Such images are not literal—they do not mean I really love the person fantasized. The images simply reveal the strength of the devotion.

It is the gesture itself, the gesture of genuflection (which need not be literal; it can be an internal gesture) that brings our creative thinking into being. We cannot self-initiate truly creative thinking. We can only do something that opens the possibility of it appearing. We bend ourselves down and look up, which simultaneously invites in the holy from above and leans toward, in an act of honor, the unknown depths within.

There is a further aspect to creative thinking that tells us something of the nature of devotion. Creative thinking is the same as image-thinking. When we engage in the gesture of subordinating ego consciousness, we are at the same time opening up image-consciousness. The forces from above stream in and the images from below arise. The task concerns making these two streams into one. Here, it is necessary to understand the nature of image-thinking. A proper understanding—one that takes into account the nature of what was just stated, that this consciousness has to hold together the "above" and the "below"—indicates, first, that image-thinking is something more than being present to the image-pictures that come into consciousness from below.

We must also characterize what streams in from "above" in the gesture of devotion, and then we must be able to imagine the synthesis of the two. What streams in from above is much more difficult to speak of because it has no form. We cannot quite say it is a feeling for God or some spiritual reality, for that is too conceptual. The feeling itself is one of pure awe. It is the presence of the ineffable, the unknown, the holy, perhaps of light, warmth, and really, the essence of love.

The act of devotion, we could say, consists of subordinating ego consciousness and the kind of thinking that goes with this consciousness—detached, a "thinking about" things, categorized, functional, practical, manipulative—to meditative thinking, in which what we think about becomes bathed in the warm light of love and the soul depth of being. In devotion, we think *with* rather than *about* the theme of our thinking.

This type of thinking can also be called intuition, but it is sustained intuition, not just the kind of momentary flashes usually denoted by this term.

We have come far from the sense of devotion as religious piety to a kind of stance we can take up in our daily lives. When we are devoted to another person or devoted to our work, this means that, in the midst of the practical aspects of what we are doing, we work at the same time to develop another level of consciousness toward what we are doing. If, for example, I am devoted to the practice of medicine, this would mean that, while I need to be skilled in the knowledge and techniques of the science, I also subordinate what I know to something larger, more comprehensive, more mysterious; and I subordinate what I do to something deeper, stronger, and also more mysterious; and I do so consciously. I gradually begin to be aware that I am devoted not to medicine per se, but rather, through the vehicle of medicine, to the whole vastness of the outer and the inner world; then the conjunction of the visible and the invisible begins to open. Then, even the most simple of procedures is carried out, not out of the solitary ability of ego consciousness, but in conjunction with a sense of the presence of the holy.

Would someone practicing medicine in this devout way be the kind of doctor you would want to care for you? Would you perhaps prefer someone who relied solely on technical knowledge and skill? Doesn't this notion of devotion seem just a little bit off-the-wall?

First, a physician who lives in this manner, placing the virtue of devotion at the center of practice, would most likely not speak about devotion at all. This kind of consciousness, while thoughtful and reflective, shows up as a style, a manner of behavior, rather than as an ideology. It would be wise indeed to avoid the physician who had to speak about a concern for devotion. Further, the person living the virtue of devotion would actually be just as skilled in a technical sense as one who relied on the usual ways of knowing. Devotion, as it has been developed here, does not separate itself from the particularities of everyday existence.

A number of years ago I had to have extensive dental work done. I was referred to a nearby dentist. He did excellent work, technically speaking. And while he made use of an anesthetic and all of the most modern of equipment, while he was working on my teeth, it was much as if an auto mechanic had stepped inside my mouth. Afterward, for a very long time, my mouth was extremely sore, and I was ill for quite a long time, apparently due to the high level of anesthesia administered.

About four years later, I again had to have some dental work done in the midst of travel. I was referred to a dentist I did not know and had never heard of. He was a most interesting person. Quite off the cuff, because he knew I was a psychologist interested in spiritual matters, he began speaking of the inner work that he did. This dentist not only had continued his education into his profession, but also continued his self-education. Further, he did not engage in soul work for his own benefit alone. He was vividly aware of how this alters his professional practice. The dental assistant, and even the person taking care of the records, all seemed to exude a kind of radiance; nothing "new age" about it, just a quiet radiance. This dentist was also very skilled.

I noticed, however, that as he was working, pulling one tooth and doing a root canal on another, I did not have anything like the impression I had with the previous dentist. It did not feel like someone was prying around with a wrench, a hammer, and a screwdriver. Even more interesting, afterward, not only was there no soreness, I actually had more energy. This dentist, I would say, was devoted to his work. From the viewpoint of an observer, the difference between the two dentists probably would not be visible. They both used the same procedures, the same tools, the same medication. Yet there was an absolutely tangible and real difference between them.

I find it fascinating to think that a dentist who thinks about his place in the cosmos, who explores his dreams, who thinks about how this kind of attention can be brought into his professional practice, brings something into the world that the strictly technical dentist does not. Devotion is not just a private matter; it has actual effects in the world.

The effects of devotion in the world, in the story of the dentist, did not just have to do with my feeling less pain and undergoing a minimum of aftereffects. It is better, in fact, to consider these effects as side effects, for the purpose of working in this devoted way is not to produce a certain result. The purpose of devotion is to develop a conscious soul orientation that moves fluidly between the above and the below, taking the realm between, the world of our everyday endeavors, as the place of their confluence. While I said above that, from the viewpoint of an observer, how the two dentists functioned would appear the same, that statement cannot be completely accurate. There must be visible differences, even if they are very subtle. Let me see if I can describe the actions of the devoted dentist in a way that shows the gesture of devotion.

First, everything the dentist and the assistants did was completely professional. One certainly could not tell any difference between this office and any other dental clinic. We could not call the practice performed there "alternative dentistry." But even at the moment of stepping into the waiting room, I felt honored. And honored not merely as a customer. The receptionist spoke in a way that touched the level of soul. No particular content can be pointed to as making what she said any different than any other receptionist. I would say, though, that my soul felt welcomed.

As I waited, the level of anxiety characteristic of such waiting was almost imperceptible. Then the dental assistant called me to the chair. This space was also not different than that of any other dentist. There was, for example, no sweet music being played, nothing external set up to put me into a dreamy state. Once again, though, I did not feel like a car that had just been put into the shop, but like a person, and this was due to the manner of the assistant. I would describe this manner as disinterested interest. By this rather strange term I mean that there was clearly an interest in me but it was not a feigned interest. It was warm interest, focused primarily on why I was there, but it was more than just an interest in my mouth.

When the dentist came in, this same quality, though a bit more intense was also present. He went about his work in a straightforward manner. What most amazed me was that he could be engaged in a series of complex actions while at the same time never losing a presence to the whole of the situation, which included me as a person. I never for a moment felt myself slipping away and becoming a mouth. He was working with me. A part of me did not become objectified, yet for him to do his work as dentist, he had to be objective.

To describe what went on and how it differed from other dental experiences is not easy. The wholeness I felt had to do with a kind of choreography of his actions. "Choreography" is a good word because it approaches describing the manner of his movements that were whole and complete and brought me into the whole action without leaving out any aspect of my being.

The devotion of this dentist consisted of a style of behavior that lived, thoughtfully, in and through his body. By saying that he was fully present, I mean that the fullness of his being was brought to the situation. I could see, for example, that he was concerned with whether I was feeling pain. This concern was more than technical, and consisted more of his gestures coming into resonance with mine so that he could actually tell if I was feeling pain before I felt it. Thus, his actions, while remaining completely skilled, were actions acting not *on* something, but *with* someone. For him to be able to do this required that he move and act out of a presence to the soul level. His skill and ability also had a kind of "light" about it. What I mean is that being surrounded by drills, tools, strong lights, grinding sounds, metal on tooth, did not have the intensity of being invaded by something "foreign" as it typically would. That element was present, but it had a much lighter feel to it than I had experienced before. I would say that the technical skills of this dentist were pervaded with the sense that he was engaged in a sacred rather than a technical act.

If you reflect on this story, all of the elements of the act of devotion can be seen to be present. I hope that the story makes clear how devotion now can go on in daily life in the world, how the virtue can be practiced everywhere and is not to be confined to special times of religious practice. In particular, this virtue—or rather, the absence of this virtue in the world—reveals a need for inner development work as a central aspect to the training in the professions. People enter education in the professions yearning and longing to devote their lives to a work. They are invariably surprised that the course of education is strongly oriented toward killing this idealism.

3 The Virtue of Balance

The word "balance" conveys a sense of finding a midpoint, a pivotal place between two polarities. We work, for example, to find balance between work and recreation, or between thinking and feeling, or between the many competing factors in our lives. Many times, such polarities have the quality of being opposites, each of which we find to be of value in life.

The notion of a midpoint of balance, however, covers over the spiritual nature of the midpoint itself; it sounds as if it were merely a matter of coming to value opposites equally and being able to attend to each side of the polarity, giving something to each. I am balanced if I care for my work but do not let it take over my home life. I am in balance if I give time to charitable work to even out the time I give to making money.

However, such a notion raises as many questions as it seems to answer. What within us can know where and what constitutes a midpoint between two qualities, each of which may be so vast and complex that the boundaries of either of them cannot be known with any precision?

The usual way in which we understand the term "balance" is in fact a quantitative notion, like the point of equilibrium between two weights at opposite ends of a long board, or the two weights on either side of a scale. The virtue of balance is not such a point of equality between two or more life demands. It is good to have the capacity to distribute our concerns in life so that we are not focused on one or two to the detriment of the rest. The virtue, though, is something else because the dimension of soul is involved.

Soul is always understood as being between—between spirit and matter, between ideas and action, between two very different levels of qualities. Thus, the virtue of balance concerns soul qualities of this "between-place" and how to be conscious of them and maintain them. It concerns the right relation between the efforts we bring to any situation and the receptivity necessary for that situation to unfold according to its own inherent design and what is needed for our soul life.

Suppose, for example, I have to make a presentation at a business meeting in which I propose bringing a new product into the market. I do a great deal of background work, including surveys, demographics, costs, profits, and so on. I also develop a strategy of presentation, figure out who will be at the meeting and how to meet their objections. I also know the politics of the company and have factored in how to appeal to everyone. The virtue of balance enters only if, with all this effort, I am also able to be receptive to what seems to want to happen, what seems to be beyond what I can control. Balance is the perfect relation between the efforts we bring to a situation and what comes to us that keeps this effort in connection with the life of the soul. The virtue is not easy. We want something to happen, and that desire can easily obscure the subtle dimension of making sure that our soul is not neglected.

We might better begin with an inner picture of the point of equilibrium as a magical point rather than as a physical point on a scale. Quite different laws are involved than those involved with the physics of the middle. Shifting into an imagination of a magical place where there is the perfect coming together of physical factors with soul and spirit factors helps in gaining a better orientation toward the notion of balance and how it might be a virtue. While the physical realm follows the laws of cause and effect, the magical realm follows the laws of resonance.

In the example above, the usual way of thinking holds that if I am out of balance, then there is too much of one thing and not enough of another; maybe I have overplanned and don't allow for spontaneity. However, implicitly, with this kind of imagining, I am thinking quantitatively. If there is too much control, then add an amount of spontaneity. I am also thinking that if I don't have balance, then that will cause something to go wrong. If I don't balance office work with exercise, then this lack of balance might cause a health difficulty. If I don't bring balance between the responsibilities of being a parent and the joys of marriage, then my irresponsibility may bring disaster to my marriage.

The quantitative imagination of balance carries another notion that obscures the virtue. The notion is that we are normal if we have balance and tend toward abnormality when we are out of balance. This notion, if adhered to, works against the virtue of balance. In seeking balance we are not seeking normalcy. In many ways, normalcy is the bane of virtue. We think that being normal means being just like everyone else—adjusted, productive, middle-of-the-road, liked, not one-sided, not too visible, accepting the collective values. Rather than a virtue, however, this notion is deadly to the soul. It leaves out all the soul wishes to express—imagination, fantasy, dream, feeling, innerness, darkness, fecundity, genuine warmth, a sense of destiny, and true individuality.

To get to a true imagining of this virtue, we have to leave behind quantitative and causal thinking. We have to leave behind thinking that we can get what our soul needs solely by our own efforts. We cannot achieve balance wholly on our own. We cannot cause it to happen. We can, however, develop the capacity to know when it is present and how to extend this presence in time.

Balance resonates within us. A good example of resonance is what happens with a musical string instrument. If you play a chord and sustain it, something in the room will begin resonating to that sound. The virtue works like this. We are in balance when a level of our ordinary activity resonates with our soul-being. Then there is a feeling of harmony between what I am doing in the world and the innerness of life.

To experience this happening, however, the instrument, in this case our bodily life in union with our soul life, must be allowed full amplitude. That is, it is necessary to tune the body to be receptive to the vibrations of the soul in its connections with events in the world. For example, imagine walking down the street and coming upon a beggar. If we walk on by, oblivious to the beggar's needs, we are not in balance. If we stop and give the person some money because we think we ought to, we are not in balance. If we feel something from the person as we walk by—feel, not necessarily know—something of the person's real needs, and help out of that presence of feeling, that would be an example of the virtue of balance.

Coming to balance is thought of better as a tuning process than as something that can be done by the will. We tune the soul to the body and we tune the soul to the world. You can do this tuning as a daily practice of just paying attention to how your body feels in relation to your individual perceptions of things around you. It is a matter of paying attention to the body. Not the reactions of the body to what goes on, but to the different qualities of bodily experience in relation to what is happening. When someone laughs loudly and nervously, perhaps the body feels a jaggedness. When we see an atrocity on the news, the body feels constricted. When someone lies to us, the body feels ugly. It is important, though, not to label the experience of the body's resonance. If we enter into the tuning process, over time we find a right language for it.

Not only is our usual way of understanding the term "balance" too filled with a quantitative imagination, it is also too external. We imagine looking at two sides of something we are involved with, and seeing both, come to a point of equality. Even when such an imagination is taken in a more interior way, it carries the strong connotation that balance is something that we find. We think that we come to it—we find our balance. The virtue, however, does not come into action by our looking around at the various factors in our lives and finding a point of equality among them all. When we look at balance in this way, we are left with the very big question of what it is within us that has the capacity to look around in this way and evaluate what constitutes having just the right measure of each thing in our lives.

Let's try to pose the question of balance differently. Where is the inner place in which an interflow occurs between activity that is, at least in part, under our control, and receptivity, where something comes to us over which we have no control? What is that place of the soul like? What are its qualities? What is the importance of that place? What are the practices associated with it? What are the conditions under which the qualities of this soul place can be experienced? If we can enter into and describe this landscape, then we are describing the virtue of balance.

One further aspect of clearing away our usual imagination of balance must be mentioned. We are accustomed to understanding balance as existing on the horizontal plane. We have to add to that imagination a picture of balance in the vertical direction. Here we have to consider the relation in our lives of the above to the below, adding that to the relation between the interior aspects of our lives with the exterior aspects. Does what I am doing resonate with an inner listening to the spiritual worlds as well as to the depths of soul? This dimension is essential to the virtue of balance.

The complex relations involved in the virtue of balance cannot be achieved on the basis of our usual capacities of consciousness. Balance cannot be achieved through thinking through how important and necessary it is to have this quality in life. The virtue of balance also cannot be achieved by willfully setting out to bring balance into our lives. Nor can balance come about through trying to find it in the realm of feelings, though here, we can have moments in which we do feel the qualities of this virtue. These moments, though, do not constitute the virtue; to be a virtue they would have to be sustained over time. We all have moments in which there seems to be inner harmony with outer events, where we feel an inner connection between our soul and spirit life with our physical and practical life. These are moments of the complex interflow spoken of above. It is possible, however, to orient ourselves so that balance is more than a matter of chance, or of having a good day.

The virtue of balance is founded in the region of the heart rather than the head, so it is necessary to find our way into an actual experience of the heart. Balance has to do with how it is possible to live in the region of the heart and be open to the soul and spirit, to the realms of the invisible, and at the very same time live a very grounded, practical, mundane earthly life. When we find our way into the heart, our outer life rings with certain soul qualities. A description of these qualities will help in coming to recognize when we have located the virtue. It is more helpful to think of virtue in this way—as a subtle region of experience that we work to find—rather than as certain kinds of behavior we seek to achieve. A careful description of the experience of the region, then, can be of assistance in knowing the virtue.

Balance concerns the way in which we experience the world around us as intimately interwoven with the deepest aspects of our being. "World" here is taken in its broadest possible context and meaning, and includes not only the physical world of things, but also events, experiences that happen to us, encounters with others, as well as the natural world. In the region of balance, the world resonates with amazement. We look at something and experience it as both known and unknown at the same time, experiencing it as if for the first time in spite of the fact that we may have had this experience many times. Our ordinary perceptions and thoughts and feelings are, in a state of wonder, filled with the experience that something deeper is at work than is at the surface. We experience the vastness and deepness of things, but at the same time, we are not taken away from the most mundane level of those very same things.

Amazement is not primarily an intellectual quality. It can and should lead to thinking, creative thinking, which does not kill the sense of amazement but extends it into knowledge and even practicality. Amazement is the basis of philosophy, which simply means that the philosopher looks at the same things that everyone else looks at, but sees them differently. The philosopher sees the unknown in the known and then goes on to explore the element of the unknown. Thus we can have a philosophy of anything—from paper to the origin of the universe.

Wonder does not have to be taken in the direction of intellectual knowing; it is, however, cognitive. We are present to the wisdom of the world, to all the processes we are involved in, usually without even being aware of them. We experience, for example, how our body belongs to the body of the world, to the Earth, the minerals, the plants, the animals. We experience something of how we belong to the cosmos, that each thing that happens to us in the daily world is leading us either closer to our destiny or away from it. And it is all amazing! These moments of amazement are the opportunity, the opening to the region of this virtue. Rather than just experience the wonder and then move on, if we are more attentive to such moments, they will enlarge because a tuning process is going on. We begin to be able to consciously live the virtue.

What is it that happens with balance that goes beyond our more ordinary experience of the world? When we experience balance, we are remembering something. I am not referring to ordinary memory. What is the difference, for example, between waking in the morning and hearing the singing of the birds outside and going on with the things we have to do, and waking up and hearing the long, lamenting call of the hawk, the crackling of the crow, and the chirp of the sparrow? When we hear only with our ears, we hear the songs of birds. When we hear with our heart, we hear something of the soul quality of the song and even have an immediate experience of some other world, a world that is even beyond the strangeness and the beauty of these creatures as they exist in nature. In the moment of wonder we experience an immediate presence of the spiritual world from which these extraordinary feathered beings originate. This kind of experience is a memory, a memory of something beyond the sensible world. At the same time, this kind of experience is a self-recollection. In balance, we come home to ourselves.

At the moment we experience balance, we do not know in a reflective way that we are participating in the soul and spirit worlds. Yet balance is a way of knowing. It is knowing that is a "being with" what we know, rather than a "thinking about" something. This kind of knowing is an experience of balance, of the interflow of worlds, and occurs through the center of the heart. It is a feeling-knowing.

For balance to be a virtue, of course, means that we consciously take up the task of coming to the world in an attitude of wonder. In more philosophical terms we might call this attitude one of "ideal realism," which synthesizes the attitude of wonder toward the soul and spirit regions characteristic of the Platonic stream of philosophy and the attitude of wonder toward the physical world characteristic of the Aristotelian stream of philosophy. Only the middle region of the heart can accomplish such a synthesis. Philosophy in the modern world has all but lost its origins in wonder and the capacity to sustain its work out of a sense of balance. Thus, in pointing to philosophy as a kind of prototype for the experience of wonder, I am not suggesting that balance is to be found by studying philosophy. I do mean to indicate that while balance is located in the space of the heart, this experience is as much cognitive as it is emotional; and it is also as much imaginative as it is emotional. However, these relationships must be understood in the proper way.

It is not a matter of balance in the usual sense of that term: balance between the cognitive and the emotional and between the emotional and the imaginative. To think of balance in this way puts us back into the imagination of weighing qualities on either side of a scale. A more adequate image of balance here would be that of picturing our imaginative life nesting within our cognitive life and our emotional life nesting within the imaginative, and all these nested within the region of the heart.

A great challenge in giving attention to the virtue of balance is how to do so in the situation of having to live in such a decidedly chaotic culture. We can experience moments of balance in the natural world, where we can be spontaneously put into the region of the heart by the overwhelming beauty surrounding us. It is much more difficult to practice balance as an attitude of wonder in the everyday world. The natural world calls us to balance. The everyday world pulls us out of balance. Unless we can find our way into the interior of the heart, it is not possible to sustain this virtue because the chaos is now overwhelming the natural balance of the world.

I mentioned above that balance, while occurring through the region of the heart, is nevertheless cognitive. What does such a statement mean? It may not be at all apparent what is meant by a heart cognition, a heart-knowing. I do not mean feelings, though feeling is involved. A first difference between head-thinking and heart-thinking concerns a quality of rhythm. When we engage in head-thinking, our thoughts take the form of motions with gaps. We have a thought, followed by another and another. The gaps are filled in by logic, which moves us from one thought to the next.

With logical thinking we attempt to bridge the gap between one thought and the next thought so that one follows rightly after the other. Logic itself, however, follows upon feeling. Feeling is first, logic and thinking are secondary in the operations of the soul. We have to have a deep feeling of the truth of the reality that has our attention, and then go on to think about it in the form of logic to know this reality further. Logic itself does not and cannot prove anything. The proof is already present in the feeling, and then we try to put that comprehensive, yet deep, feeling into thought-form using logic.

The premise of any logical statement cannot itself be logically proved. For example, the syllogism: All men are mortal; Henry is a man; therefore Henry is mortal. The first of these statements cannot be arrived at through logic. Nor can it be arrived at empirically, for that would require examining every person on Earth. The first statement of a logical syllogism is something known intuitively. We know it through the feeling of wonder. Wonder, then, is not logical, but intuitive.

Heart-thinking, which is the basis of amazement and amazement as opening into balance, occurs at a level right below consciousness. We can be present to it, but cannot quite articulate it. When we are able to be true to the feeling level of our existence, then we know more from the heart than through the head. This kind of cognitive-feeling does not proceed from one concept to another. When we know something in an attitude of wonder, we know it, not exactly all at once, but rhythmically. The immediate presence of something—a sense experience of the natural world, or something someone says, or an idea—exists for us in a perfect rhythm with the deeper resonance of that event, opening the event to the invisible realms, to the depths of soul and to the heights of spirit.

Whereas in the natural world this kind of rhythmic experience is aided by the existing rhythms found in places of beauty, in the everyday world we have to supply that quality of rhythm much more ourselves; it has to be generated from the heart. When we think with our heads, logically, we think about something. In contrast, we do not think with our heart but from our heart. Thinking from the heart, when it does not involve an immediate experience in the natural world, lacks the outer support to sustain it; it has to sustain itself from within. At the present time we mostly cannot do this for very long and have only momentary experiences of balance.

In many respects, the virtue of balance is like being able to live in the world as a work of art. Rather than *looking at* something, as we do when viewing art, however, we participate every moment in this work of art and are part of it at the same time that we are able to experience it. Even more, we are not just participant-observers; each of us is the brush making the art. Experiencing the world in this way requires the virtue of balance.

In times of balance, the everyday obviousness of things around us takes on a quality of transparency. Something shines through them. We see beauty shining through the mundane. The experience of such beauty has another characteristic. In balance, the beautiful object and our most intimate self are grasped together. The subject-object dichotomy is transcended. The beauty we experience in balance is not a subjective experiencing of an object, event, or another person. Nor, however, is beauty understood here as the beholding of a purely objective value. The experience of beauty in balance does not come from "within," nor does it come from "without." We are now in a world where these ways of thinking do not apply. We are in the logic of "what presents itself."

Balance, then, is being present to what is present, doing so fully conscious, with thinking, feeling, and willing awake, in which the usual and the unusual are thrown together. The act of balance as a virtue is not an act of any particular human faculty; all the dimensions of our existence are involved.

Moments of balance can be moments of joy. We can work toward achieving balance, a practice of the virtue, but we have no control whatsoever of the production of joy. Joy is a fundamental happiness and comes always as a gift. This kind of happiness has nothing to do with sheer pleasure or comfortable relaxation, but is something more in the way of grace. Joseph Pieper, in his book *Happiness and Contemplation* (New York: St. Augustine Press, 1998, p. 25) says, "We are, whenever happiness comes our way, the recipients of something unforeseen, something unforeseeable, and therefore not subject to planning and intention. Happiness is essentially a gift; we are not the forgers of our own felicity." The purpose of working toward the virtue of balance is not to achieve joy or happiness. Balance is not a utilitarian virtue, which, if practiced, leads to the state of bliss. All it is possible to say is that sometimes, when balance occurs, there is also the experience of joy. We can also say that in the absence of balance, joy is not possible. Further, it must be pointed out that joy as described here is not bliss. In fact, what accompanies joy, as a kind of backdrop, is anxiety.

This anxiety is not due to any psychological difficulty, but is the necessary "other side" that always accompanies joy. It is a fundamental existential anxiety, which is always with us but is usually veiled behind our daily functioning. Surprisingly, then, working toward balance also places the possibility of experiencing deep anxiety before us. This tells us that it takes courage to work on the virtue of balance. In facing the possibility of the fullness of being, we also encounter the facelessness of nonbeing.

In balance, the qualities of the space we live and work within changes. The space of balance certainly differs from the abstract conception of the three-dimensional space of classical physics. In space as understood mathematically, there is no surrounding world; there is only a multiplicity of "points," an absolute homogeneity, within which objects are located. The space we live in, by virtue of being embodied and being in a world, is not this characterless emptiness. Space, as lived, is dynamic and constantly changing, depending on our moods and circumstances.

For example, if I am occupied by an interest in trying to find a book, the bookstore across the street is closer to me than the barbershop that stands right next to where I am at the moment. When people are in love, they feel their beloved near, no matter what objective distance holds them apart. This "lived-space" is not something merely subjective, in contrast to what is real and objective. "Lived-space" is the space of our everyday existence. The space that physics knows is an abstract construction of the mind, a space without environment, distance, perspective, depth, and world. As the "objective" abstraction of space enters more into everyday life, which comes about by living what science says is real, we lose the qualities of lived-space and take up residence in a homogenous world.

The virtue of balance returns us to the natural capacity of experiencing the spatial world in its dynamic qualities. This is because this virtue, like all of the virtues, is not an abstract idea but a fundamental operation of our embodied soul and spirit. Balance takes us out of the abstractions in which we live, which we have completely forgotten are abstractions. Our experiences of the world and others begin to change. Balance does more even than help us to become aware of the immediacy of our body and our soul/spirit relation with our surroundings. The qualities of nearness and distance become something more than what can be known through measurement. Nearness and distance alter according to our particular concerns and interests. To begin to be aware of these changes in existential space indicates that we have entered the dynamic realm of balance.

Our soul life has now become engaged with our daily interests in others and in the world. In our body we feel the attracting and repulsing qualities of things, and on that basis can find the proper point of balance. It is not a matter of going toward the attractions and away from the repulsions, though. It is much more a matter of coming into the region of dynamic forces that can be felt, for balance is real. Without balance we get physically dizzy, or tired, or depressed. Then, when we can feel the push and pull of the world-forces, another dimension opens up with balance. This is the quality of depth.

What does it mean to experience the depth of the world? It is not the horizontal depth of our everyday existence. A vertical depth opens in balance. The things we encounter take on the quality of being infinitely remote and infinitely close at the same time. Depth carries this quality of the dynamic play of the infinite coming close to us and receding, a play that keeps us engaged with spiritual reality. We feel pervaded by the inner mystery and glow of things, while at the same time these very things remain at a distance from us and retain their own autonomous character. One small part of the world is perceived as if it were, for the moment, all the world.

There are three qualities to the depth of balance. First, this depth is intimate. Our perception of the things of the world alters in balance from one in which we perceive surfaces and have the impression that there are only things in the world standing side by side, to the perception of something of the utter particularity of each and every thing. There are no "its" from the viewpoint of this virtue, only the particularity of the "thou." Perceiving becomes meeting.

The intimacy characterizing this virtue relativizes our ego. We are, in our ego-being, outside observers only. The intimacy focuses on the more impersonal aspects of our being and the being of the things of the world. Our body, externally and internally experienced, feels in intimate relation with the unseen.

A second quality of the depth of balance can be described as a particular sense of entering into the world as a liturgical drama. Balance is not static. From within this virtue, the world is experienced as sacred drama. We have dramatic form whenever there is the experience of polarities, opposites, contradictions held in irresolvable tension. Opposites such as perception of the utterly particular in tension with perception of the deepest meaning of the things around us. And, the tension that balance is something I do and do not do at all—it comes to me. Then, there is the dramatic quality of being within a reality while being able to observe it as an objective reality. It is like being within soul and being able to observe it at the same time. And, being able to engage in this kind of observation without splitting off part of oneself to become the observer.

In the place of balance there is anticipation. This is the third quality of the depth of silence. The anticipation is not ours. What does it involve? An anticipation of what? By whom? It is as if balance poises and just about speaks. That is the anticipation felt;

something about to be said. You know what it is like when you have something to say, something that comes quite spontaneously and yet has an urgency to be expressed. That moment before it is said, that is the quality of anticipation that characterizes the depth of balance. A preparedness, an about-to, a coming, or as they used to say in the 1960s, a happening.

I want to emphasize that these descriptions of the world in balance are to be understood not as what *results* from engaging the virtue. Rather, they are descriptions of balance itself. Balance does not *cause* us to experience the world in new ways. If we understand the descriptions in this reductive manner, we are doing no more than conceiving of balance as if it were a drug. These descriptions, on the contrary, attempt to demonstrate that balance, rather than being some kind of static point that we search around and try to find within ourselves, is actually a creative, dynamic relation between ourselves, our body, soul and spirit, the world and the cosmos.

We can also describe the time of balance. Just as the space of balance is different from the abstract conception of space and even different than "lived-space," the time of balance differs considerably from ordinary time. The abstract notion of time is that it is an infinite sequence of instantaneous "nows" that successively come along and pass away. The time of balance also differs from the way that we usually live time, which is different than clock time. "Lived time" is experienced as the spacious or not spacious qualities of change we live within every day, the various activities and involvements of our lives. For example, "work time" is different than "love time," is different from "meditative time." The time of illness differs from the time of health, for in illness time expands into duration. The time of nature is different than the time of the city. Lived time expands and contracts according to what we are doing and how we are engaged.

In balance, there is a wondrous coming together of lived space and lived time. The "here" and the "there," the "now" and the "then," merge. This experience is difficult to describe because we hardly have adequate language for it. It is as if time gets spread out into a feeling of spaciousness. This quality of time also stands out, as if past, present, and future were gathered together and go on simultaneously. But then, we find ourselves within time, as if time were space. The time of balance is not "no-time" or timeless, but a reposeful time; it is not motionless, but motion-at-rest.

In relation to ordinary time, the time of balance seems to be a useless waste of time. Balance is certainly nonutilitarian, and for that reason it is life-giving and life-renewing. Many things can happen through balance. Inspirations come during such time. Inspiration cannot happen when we are engaged in ordinary, utilitarian functioning. We do not do something with balance. Rather, balance does something with us.

It can cure us of the illness of activity that is not desired for its own sake, but that we are always doing for the sake of something else. If I hurry and wash the dishes in order to sit down and watch television, that activity is done out of balance and I cannot feel the spaciousness within that time. If I wash the dishes with an attitude that doing so is an activity that within itself is worthy, time opens up into the spaciousness of wonder. Without the virtue of balance, time has no space, and in this time-condition, we feel empty and in despair.

Little has been said in this reflection on the virtue of balance about how to actually practice the virtue. We have to work at becoming aware of the dimension of nondoing in whatever we do. We also have to work toward stepping out of the usual, habitual ways of doing things, where we have control and thus do not typically let anything new come in. We also have to have a strong sense of initiating the direction of our lives and not just living them passively. It is possible to be too receptive, which takes us out of the activity of doing something in the world. People who engage in spiritual practices, such as meditation or inner image work, can find themselves taken into this kind of passivity. It is also possible to find that we keep the active side of our lives quite separate from the receptive side. The practice of the virtue consists in holding these two aspects in close relation to each other.

When we do work to keep a relation between activity and receptivity, we find that a new kind of wholeness enters. What we do, and what we receive, what comes to us simply by being open, turns out to be not only related, but of a whole piece. When these two dimensions are held apart, we cannot usually even see a connection between what we actively do and what comes to us, except as two events that seem to exist side by side. For example, if I work hard and a promotion comes, then it appears that the promotion comes as a result of my activity I have engaged in. There is no virtue in thinking of achievement in this cause-effect way. When we can see such an occurrence, however as revealing a wholeness— that my years of activity prepared me for the right receptivity, and when these two soul qualities match each other in resonance, something new happens—then we are doing the virtue.

Making a practice of attending not only to the content of our activity but to the inner, motivating aspect of it, and as well, the qualities of energy entailed in the activity and how these qualities affect others, opens the way for the other half of this activity, which is receptivity. Here, we move away from a cause-effect mentality. Instead, we move into a wholeness of consciousness in which activity and receptivity belong together and go on simultaneously.

This union comes about when we attend, not only to the content of what comes to us in an attitude of receptivity, but to the quality of the energy that comes toward us from others and from the world. These qualities will always, without exception, be intimately related with the qualities of our own action. The universe and the earthly world are whole. When we work toward the virtue of balance this wholeness becomes a real experience.

4 The Virtue of Faithfulness

We associate faithfulness with certain kinds of close or intimate relationships. Friends are faithful to each other, so are lovers, and married couples are supposed to be faithful. We also have the cliché picture of a "faithful" pet, such as a dog or a cat. We can perhaps also include in this picture being faithful to a task or a work, or in carrying out any kind of long-term effort. In all of these instances, and in any we might think of, faithfulness is taken to mean simply that the behavior of the faithful one evidences a quality of commitment. The relationship is one of endurance without question, and typically includes refraining from deviating in any way from being present for and with another, the one to whom we made a commitment—spoken or unspoken.

Such an ordinary assumption concerning faithfulness certainly expresses a dimension of truth. However, this kind of picturing of the virtue is also extremely limited—so limited, in fact, that almost no force can be felt in imagining faithfulness in this way.

Understanding this virtue as unwavering commitment carries little significant emotional tone or inner force. In fact, to be truthful, imagining the virtue in such a manner deadens it rather than vivifying and reawakening the soul quality that constitutes the virtue. The characterization is too external; it comes dangerously close to being a formulation that can be imposed on others in an attempt to control behavior. If we are someone's friend, lover, husband or wife, then we are supposed to be faithful—that is the expectation, the voiced or unvoiced rule. If the rule can be trusted, then we can relinquish any anxiety we might hold concerning the steadiness of our relationship with another person and fears we might have that the person might be forming additional bonds behind our backs. Faithfulness comes close here to being a vow, one made to assure the parties involved that no deviation from a commitment will ensue once this "vow" is taken.

This standard way of understanding faithfulness, seen more from within the soul element involved, moves toward dogmatism. Virtue can slide into one-sidedness, particularly when it is taken literally and imagination is not engaged. Then virtue becomes a rule to follow rather than an imaginative way of living in relation with the wholeness of the cosmos. The absolutist character of the standard way of picturing faithfulness almost assuredly brings the opposite polarity up in the soul life. If we try to live faithfulness according to the way our ordinary understanding, and indeed, the understanding of the term occurs in society at large, the soul will be so unsatisfied, so suffocated, so trapped, that the other extreme will be sought.

An unrelenting notion of constancy without deviation invites frequent and constant violations of that way of going about being true to a relationship. These violations are not likely to be seen as the soul's attempt to find breathing room in the impossible state to which it has been subjected. Rather, we will feel the deviations to be of no true consequence, or alternately, will come to a point of relinquishing altogether any semblance of faithfulness. In either instance, the intention to be true to someone becomes a sham.

When people marry, a vow of faithfulness is involved. It is always understood very literally—neither person will become romantically interested in another person. All love and all devotion will be directed toward the marriage partner. Any deviation from this is considered a breaking of vows. Consider how making such a vow affects the people involved. Perhaps you can remember taking that vow. I do. I remember standing at the altar, resolutely convincing myself that this way of life could be done, and in fact was just exactly what I wanted. I remember squeezing out of imagination any doubts, and any thoughts of others. It was a moment that felt like a new birth.

Later, over the years, I was very surprised that attractions toward others did not disappear altogether. I thought that taking the vow would mean that from then on the love between my wife and me would be so strong that any other attractions simply would not exist. Naturally, these forbidden attractions became all the more enticing because they were not supposed to be there. The vow of faithfulness was supposed to bestow a magical veil, and marriage partners were supposed to find all their needs, desires, wants, and hopes satisfied in each other.

This kind of literalizing of faithfulness almost always leads the soul to find a way to express the opposite. There is no imagination in dogmatic steadiness, so the soul is not satisfied. Soul always finds its expression between polarities. We know we are not in soul when paradox, irony, tension, drama, are absent. The soul will not cancel a one-sided understanding of faithfulness, but will find ways to relativize it in order to get room to expand. The soul lives a rhythm of expansion and contraction, and if confined to one side only, it must find ways of expressing the other. The only alternative is to cut off soul life altogether. Then a committed relationship turns from being something holy in itself to becoming a means to other ends. Marriage, for example, is adhered to for the children, or for the relatives, or for appearance's sake. Or marriage becomes a matter of convenience or comfort, an economic commodity. More and more, relationships involving faithfulness are done for the sake of other things, not to enter a particular path of initiation experience.

If the virtue is not done with soul consciousness—with the inner conviction and experience that something valuable develops in the soul—then we feel we are being deprived of something we need. A relationship of steadiness feels incomplete, but it is usually hard to determine why there is such a feeling.

In order to try to fill the void of incompleteness, we unwittingly begin to try to derive other, outer things, from our relationship, as if that would take care of the emptiness. Without knowing we have done so, by exercising the virtue only as an outer form of behavior, we become psychopathic, using another person in order to get other things we value, such as security, comfort, steadiness, reliability, while feeling we are deprived of depth in our relating. Faithfulness seems to be for the sake of these other values rather than being a value in itself. Except, we don't know that we are using others that way. Faithfulness in itself seems to have no soul value.

I hope my way of using the term "psychopathic" is clear. I am referring to a quality of soul life: that not particularly happy quality of thrashing around, searching for some sense of freedom when bound by a soul-killing condition. The dogmatic manner in which faithfulness has been incorporated into the relationship actually obscures the possibility of the soul partaking in the pleasure of the true virtue of faithfulness. Thus, while there may be an external semblance of commitment, there is not an interior living of the virtue.

The dogmatic and almost wholly external way of considering faithfulness quite often results in seeking out other relationships of an intimate nature. However, understood from the point of view of the soul and of the soul's engagement with this virtue, such deviations from a commitment cannot so easily be judged to be a mere lack of faithfulness. Rather, the other extreme of the virtue is being sought in order that faithfulness can be an act of the soul rather than meeting some external demand. The immobile quality of faithfulness as never questioning a commitment seeks its polarity—that of engagement that does not at the same time deprive the soul of an inner feeling of freedom. Strange as it might seem, flitting from one encounter to another might well express a search for a more healthy form of the practice of faithfulness.

I am not, of course, suggesting that this action alone will be successful in that regard. It produces great guilt on the one hand and an attraction toward the forbidden on the other. A terrible suffering ensues, all based on attempting to live a virtue. We have, unfortunately, the notion that all the virtues involve doing something that is hard and excluding something that is enjoyable. We are expected to give up the joys of life and attempt to follow a prescribed version of being virtuous. Such ingrained notions of virtue have to be erased, and a complete re-visioning must take place.

Nowhere is this need more evident than with the virtue of faithfulness.

Rather than taking the word "faithfulness" to mean adhering unquestioningly to a commitment made, it might be helpful to dwell on a primary component of this word, "faith." Is it not true that faithfulness implies approaching our relationship with someone in such a manner that we have ongoing faith in the strength and continuity of the connection no matter what must be gone through? Faith, however, is not to be equated with belief. It would be a mistake to take faithfulness to mean that I live in the belief that my relationship with someone is not subject to question. Faith is something stronger than belief; it is a particular form of knowing something. If I really have faith or experience an inner sense of faith, a quality of knowledge inheres with this state. True, we speak of "blind faith," as if knowledge were not involved; however, that cliché simply means that the kind of knowing that characterizes faith is decidedly different than intellectual and cognitive forms of knowing. We do not practice faith with our heads but rather with our hearts.

Faith, I want to suggest, is a mode of knowledge characteristic of the heart, one that *feels* truth. Faithfulness, then, would consist of a fullness of feeling for another existing within the space of the heart. What then, can be said concerning this way of knowing?

Faithfulness as knowing something through the heart is here intended to be more than a mere metaphor. Faithfulness occurs within the organ of the heart that beats within our chest; that is where this quality of knowing can be felt. In fact, the very action of the heart reveals a physical basis for this virtue each and every moment. One beat follows another, systole follows diastole, expansion follows contraction. Between expansion and contraction, however, there is a tiny moment within which there is a gap. If we focused only on this gap, we would experience the ongoing presence of death as an integral part of life. This gap, though, is filled by the faithfulness of the heart to its own process, a process that includes an inner knowing that the gap will not remain. This ongoing rhythm of expansion and contraction is also the rhythm of the soul. Without the sense of the rhythm, however, soul life only exists as a pull of polar opposites. Faithfulness has to fill the gap.

Faithfulness is the rhythmic movement between the soul polarities of dogmatic, rigid adherence to a commitment (contraction) on the one side and frivolously being pulled into any and all attractions on the other (expansion). The virtue is the steady rudder in the constant currents of the forces of love existing within the soul. For the virtue to function, however, it is necessary to experience all the tows and undertows of the currents. It is necessary to be in the contradictory motions of the heart, to suffer their vicissitudes. We need to be able to experience the fullness of commitment, the gap where nothing seems to exist, and the attractions that tempt us away from steadiness toward someone—all together.

As a first approximation toward coming to a real and actual experience of what is meant by faithfulness, it is extremely helpful to shift attention from the region of the head to the place of the heart and concentrate for a few moments within the heart rhythm. Do not just pay attention to the rhythm of the heart from the place of the head, which would be to focus *on* the heart rather than from *within* the heart. It is possible to actually develop a kind of inner-heart awareness.

It is as simple as practicing, for a few moments every day, shifting awareness from the region of the head to the region of the heart, moving from the constant ongoing thoughts we have to the inner, active silence of the heart. At first, you may experience strong anxiety as you try to leave the head for the heart. Try to make this shift for a few moments, at a regular time, each day. After a while, the anxiety ceases and it becomes possible to experience the interior sense of the rhythm of the heart.

Finding the language to express what we experience within an inner awareness of the heart is not so easy. We have to translate something quite wordless back into words and realize that in doing so, the head has again become engaged. The heart, experienced from within, is not an experience of an object but more like an experience of a space, a vast interior—all interior. If even for a moment I become aware in a mental way of being within this interior space, a strong anxiety, even a strong sense of fear, comes crowding in that immediately removes my consciousness from this sacred center. It is quite difficult to stay for a while within the space of the heart. If you shift your awareness there and find you become aware of this awareness, that is the intervention of the mind. Anxiety and fear will immediately accompany such an intervention. Recognizing that this interference has occurred, return attention to the space within the heart. It will be possible to remain there for a bit longer this time.

The interior space of the heart is not like the interior space of a room. Qualities exist within this space; this space is not empty space. For example, it is fully accurate to call this interior space "moral space," though the nature of this space needs careful articulation. The term here has nothing to do with morality or moralism. From the interior place of the heart we perceive everything we do as having meaning and consequence. In heart space, it is immediately apparent that how we treat another has an effect on the soul life of the other. The interior currents of our heart forces are in direct connection with the interior forces of the heart currents of others. The virtue of faithfulness recognizes the reality of these currents as the medium within which it must steer a course. The virtue, then, is a particular way of being *with* another person, rather than acting in a certain way *toward* another person. This way of being with a person has real, ongoing effects that change both people, and is better imagined as an active force than a behavior.

This new definition of faithfulness as having to do with the interconnection of heart currents between people means that when the virtue is there, a particular kind of resonance is experienced between two people, or between ourselves and whatever we are faithful to. This resonance is an inner heart-knowing that we are in constant connection with whomever we are faithful to. Our outer behavior becomes secondary. I do not mean that behavior does not matter. Rather, the outer behavior will partake of the inner resonance, but not in prescribed ways. For example, I feel completely free to engage with another person at deep levels without feeling I am being unfaithful—as long as I retain the resonant feeling and remain true to it.

It is also accurate to further this characterization of the interior space of the heart as emotional-space, and as feeling-space, which are two quite different qualities. By emotional-space, I mean that the interior region of the heart is the source of the energetic activity of the soul. This energetic activity is what we feel as emotion. When we are present to the life of the heart, we experience things emotionally. Emotion is a pure form of heart and soul energy. I do not mean here having specific emotions such as anger or desire or joy. I mean the heart-center is the felt sense of soul as dynamic activity rather than soul simply as inner feeling or as having images. Emotion is the felt push and pull of the soul, its liveliness and its ardor. Emotion makes images feel rather than just be there as inner pictures.

The interior of the heart as having a quality feeling-space is different than the emotional quality of the heart. I mean by this quality that the heart is a cognitive capacity, a way of knowing—the very source of all true knowing of others. We know objects through the head. We know others through feeling. It is an alternate knowing that differs from intellectual knowing in that what we know through feeling is the innerness of things, of everything. Intellectual knowing is restricted to knowing things from the outside only, a spectatorial knowing.

Regardless of what we know in a biological way or a medical way about the heart and what goes on within the heart, the immediate experience of the inner space of the heart is that the inner regions are occupied with currents of these qualities. It is within these three currents of the heart—the moral currents, the emotional currents, and the feeling currents—that we locate the central action of faithfulness.

In addition to these qualities, there are additional heart activities that one might expect to become aware of through the shifting of consciousness from head to heart. We might expect to become more aware of the rhythm of the heart, of the heartbeat itself, or even of the flow of the blood into and out of the heart. If you pay very close attention, however, you will notice that when you become aware of these actions of the heart, your consciousness has gone from the interior center of the heart more to a place right outside the heart, where it becomes more like a spectator, albeit a pretty intimate spectator. Or, in a similar way, you will notice that your awareness shifts back and forth from the interior space of the heart to this place exterior to the heart. In actuality, the interior space of the heart is very still, very quiet, but not static.

Indeed, you have the impression that that familiar activity of the heart—the systole and diastole, the flow of blood—is the activating condition that gives rise to the interior, deep-space qualities within the heart, but does not itself partake of the qualities of that space. Rather than thinking that we have moved our intellect to the center of the chest through the practice of shifting our awareness from head to heart, it is more helpful and more accurate to imagine that the experience of the interior of the heart is blood-knowledge. We shift from the nerve-knowing of thought to the blood-knowing of feeling.

What do these qualities of the interior space of the heart (moral space, emotional space, feeling space, sacred space) have to do with the kind of knowing spoken of above as faith? And what do these interior qualities have to do with the virtue of faithfulness?

In order to address these questions, the term "space" that is being used to describe the interior quality of the region of the heart needs qualification. This term does not convey precisely enough the charismatic sense of the interior of the heart—it seems a bit too static. The interior space of the heart is all dynamic motion, a flow of the subtle soul currents of moral feeling, emotion and feeling and the many subcurrents they create—the forces of passion, desire, longing, waiting, loving. This dynamic flow also holds the soul experiences of mourning, sorrow, woundedness, hurt, and absence.

The interior space of the heart feels vast, while at the same time this vastness feels immensely concentrated—a concentrated vastness. Or we could also say—a vastness of concentration. These two seemingly contradictory qualities are here one and the same quality. We can get lost in the interior of the heart, then someone comes along who calls forth the desire of faithfulness from us, and at last, there seems to be a reason for the subtle forces of the heart being arranged in this seemingly chaotic way. We suddenly find someone who focuses the streaming forces of the heart, giving them focus. The entry into the virtue requires not just maintaining focus on someone in an act of commitment. It also means the commitment of entering into the dynamic, inner swirl of the forces of the heart, staying true to those motions and learning how to read them, how to understand what they are doing, where they want us to go.

This way of imagining faithfulness and entering into its demands develops a new capacity. It develops the capacity of staying within impossible, irresolvable opposites without seeking resolution. Faithfulness is a way of imagining the impossible. When we become truly intimately involved with another person—where the deepest emotions are revealed, the deepest longings, desires, hopes—then something very contradictory happens. We find ourselves strongly attracted to others. We do not feel any less connected to the person with whom we have a commitment, but other attractions are actually intensified. It cannot be any other way. The heart, when open, is not selectively open. It is just open.

Faithfulness, first of all, involves stepping into these contradictory currents and staying with them. Faithfulness means that we take this impossible swirl of contradictory feelings as a way of knowing something that we cannot know in any other way. What we know through the faithfulness of the heart is that love only enters through the gateway of contradictory opposites held in irresolvable tension. From the viewpoint of the heart, it is quite foolish to think that loving someone deeply and through the heart thereby excludes others. The more deeply I love someone, the stronger the attraction to others. It sounds heretical, I know. Love is not supposed to work that way. But it does. And the virtue of faithfulness requires that we adhere to the love that is primary, but without denying, turning away, or shutting down the attractions that now become more vivid. Now, under these conditions, the virtue has room to breathe and can operate within its full range of possibility.

A second aspect of this interior space takes us into another contradiction that surfaces when we enter into the soul work of faithfulness. This interior space is at one and the same time exceedingly dark and exceedingly light. We feel attacked by all of the darkest thoughts and emotions imaginable when we practice faithfulness. It is as if we are suddenly thrown out of a boat into treacherous currents. In a completely contradictory way, these currents are, at the very same time, currents of light—under a certain condition. The condition is that we have to give ourselves over to the dark currents of all our desires, needs, wants, and even those of hurt, woundedness, abandonment, and let the divine light carry us through the torment. This is the act of faithfulness—staying with dark torment as being mysteriously the same as the divine light.

I believe that the quality of the interior space described above can be verified by anyone willing to spend time doing the kind of exercises described. One additional quality needs to be mentioned. Actually, it is not so much an additional quality as it is a closer and more differentiated description of the particular quality of feeling that characterizes the interior of the heart. Here again, we come up against a contradiction. The feeling-quality of the interior of the heart can be described as "pain-joy." This feeling-quality does not, for the most part, alternate between these two qualities, nor is it really a combination of these two qualities. The term "pain-joy" is meant to convey a particular kind of feeling.

As far as I know, we do not have a term that expresses this feeling-quality because it is not a quality of feeling life that is experienced in our ordinary feeling states as they occur in daily life. In daily life, this feeling quality seems to bifurcate into its two separate qualities of pain and joy. This feeling-quality of pain-joy united perfectly describes the feeling of faithfulness.

As with all of the virtues we have considered thus far, our interest in the virtue of faithfulness centers on describing the virtue from an inner standpoint. We have reimagined the virtue as an act of the soul rather than as a desirable form of behavior that I wish I could do, but leave to the saints to do. A second focus concerns providing suggestions on the inner development that can strengthen the soul quality of the action of the virtue.

As a beginning point, it is possible to say that there is a secret life to faithfulness. It does not live in the daylight of conscious awareness except in certain reflective moments when we may be thinking about or mulling over or remembering a certain relationship that we have with someone. The other, more intimate way of becoming aware of faithfulness is to consult your heart by shifting consciousness as described above into this interior region. Now, however, hold in awareness the image or a thought of a person with whom you feel a connection of faithfulness. You will be able to feel the presence of this person in the interior region of the heart. What are the felt qualities of the interior presence of this individual like?

The first thing we are able to say concerning faithfulness from the point of view of the interior presence of the heart is that this virtue is not the same as love, even though its point of operation is the interior of the heart. Love may also be present, but it is not the essence of this virtue. On the other hand, if I cannot really locate a sense of the individual within the interior of the heart, then it is likely that faithfulness does not exist in relation to this person. Or if faithfulness does exist, it is of a wholly external nature—a mental ideal held or something that has been imposed.

The difference between the two—interior presence and external form—in relation to the manner in which the other person is regarded is striking. If faithfulness is an external act of behavior toward another based upon an idea that this behavior is important, faithfulness does not include the other person in any intimate way. Here, faithfulness has the quality of an obligation. As such, I live within this sense of obligation that is more or less imposed upon the other person. This kind of faithfulness can actually feel suffocating to the other person.

Wholly external faithfulness means that I have taken on the obligation of being a constant presence in the life of another. I do it with constancy, day in and day out. As the cliché goes, I am there for that person. This kind of faithfulness has the power to kill the interior life of the relationship, even though, from an exterior point of view, it seems to provide a steadiness that is admirable. This kind of faithfulness, we could say, is faithfulness without faith.

A faithfulness of the heart operates quite differently than externalized faithfulness. If, for example, I feel a real faithfulness toward another person, then my inner connection with that person partakes of all of the contradictory qualities characterized as belonging to the interior qualities of heart-awareness. Faithfulness here does not mean "steadiness." In fact, considered from an interior standpoint, the relationship is always in "motion." I "know" this person in an entirely different way than I know someone with whom this virtue does not take part in the relationship. It is a kind of not-knowing, but it is not ignorance.

Faithfulness obliges me to proceed with another person by staying as close as possible to the rhythms of the heart, knowing the person through how I treat that person, how I emotionally respond to that person, and following the knowledge of feeling. Entirely new aspects of this person for whom there is a relationship of faithfulness continually reveal themselves. Similarly, aspects that I am aware of, at times, completely disappear, become concealed.

When faithfulness is a wholly external matter, if the qualities of the person that led me to be faithful in the first place disappear, then the whole relationship is brought into question. I find myself saying, "This is not the person that I decided to be faithful to. This person has changed and there is no longer a basis for holding to that obligation." Little do we see, however, that it is most likely that the way we have taken up the virtue in the first place does not allow for changing qualities of the relationship.

When faithfulness is lived as interior, heart qualities, what I am faithful to is the ever changing nature of the person to whom I am faithful. This kind of orientation is creative. It creates the possibility for the other person to grow and develop and change in life. This virtue frees the person, while externalized faithfulness is binding. The philosopher Gabriel Marcel has a beautiful term for the virtue understood in this way. He calls it "creative fidelity."

Creative faithfulness conveys the truth that this virtue creates something that is otherwise not there—it creates the freedom of the other person. It is not that faithfulness, understood in the manner suggested here, merely lets the person have their freedom;

it is a strong constituting element of that freedom. We may have the inborn capacity of freedom as human beings, but this capacity has to be triggered, set into motion, and that initial impulse toward the actual living of freedom is not something we do on our own, out of our own soul forces.

This deeper understanding of the virtue of faithfulness reveals that the virtue is not confined to our most intimate relationships. It can and needs to extend to others, first in the circles of family, then to friendships, then to the many individuals we know but with whom we do not feel a particular intimacy. The extension of the virtue is necessary because it creates something in the world that cannot be created in any other way—a true experience of freedom, for both giver and receiver.

When a relationship begins to be repetitive, comfortable, working with ease, then there is the strong possibility that we have tumbled into external steadiness and have lost touch with the interior swirl of heart currents, that inner maelstrom which serves as the oceanic life-fluid within which the rudder of faithfulness thrives. It is illusory to think of the virtues as leading to inner peace. They lead to the interior of life, not to peace. They do creative work in the world, and creating is never peaceful.

Experienced polarities such as those that describe the rhythmic center of the heart are agonies, paroxysms of creation. As a primary experience of these agonies taken all together, faithfulness takes on its true dimensions as a quality of soul over which we do not and cannot ever have complete control. We have to suffer our faithfulness, let it show us its ways, which may seem like complex morasses and complications that keep us entwined with the soul of the individual or work or task with which a relationship of faithfulness is being enacted. We cannot meaningfully say, "I am going to be faithful" to someone. It is a lovely intention, to be sure, but we can at best decide, with great trepidation, to jump into the oceanic depths of faithfulness and, looking around for some small twig, hold on for our lives.

Virtues are challenges for the soul, invitations for the soul to take on the task of developing into the spiritual soul. They are not a set of pious rules to follow that will make us more spiritual.

Virtues are for warriors of the soul; they are the weapons with which the soul can enact its battles in reaching for the spiritual realms. Without these weapons, soul is doomed to the depths of the depths, to shadeland rather than spiritland.

What does faithfulness do in the world? As the word suggests, we gradually enter into an inner, full-knowing of the inner soul essence of the other person, in which we are able to undergo a kind of sensing of the full possibilities of that person. In faithfulness, we do not experience the person exactly as he or she is; we experience the person as who he or she is intended to be. Faithfulness consists, then, of a peculiar kind of knowing of the future. The agony of the virtue concerns relating to the individual in terms of this heart-foreseen future. Psychology would see such a notion as dangerous and perhaps even pathological on the part of the person who adheres to the ways of this virtue. All kind of suspicions of projection, denial, not being present to the moment or to who is right here with us, would be leveled at anyone who would espouse relating to the potential of a person rather than to who the person actually is. In addition, it might seem cruel and inhuman to relate to what, from an ordinary point of view, is not really present.

But from the viewpoint of the spiritual soul, we are what we *can* be, not what has shaped us from the past, and not just what we seem to be in the moment. Faithfulness is not prognostication or divining. It is rather a particular stance of the soul taken toward the soul-being of another. I am faithful to the destiny of the other person, to who that person is *becoming*. Being present to the other person in this way, in part, creates the possibilities of who that person can become.

From an outer point of view, it is not very possible to distinguish between a connection of faithfulness and one of fatedness. "Fate" is another term that brings out the nature of vowing to be externally steady in our relationships. A relationship of fate is certainly not necessarily a dire thing; it can be entirely fulfilling, pleasurable, and deep; or it can be agonizing. So too with a relationship which, at heart, has faithfulness at its center. However, the agonies and the pleasures of each of these forms of connection are centered in a different soul-space. The content of what is lived out in each form of relating may well be exactly the same, so the difference lies not in the kind of experiences encountered in each of these ways of enduring relationship. The difference lies in the more subtle aspects of the experience, and turns on whether our experiences with another are felt as enactment or as improvisation.

A relationship with the quality of enactment carries a quality of repetition, of habit, of the same thing lived in the relationship over and over—the same pleasures, the same trials, the same difficulties, revisited time and time again. If we see from an outside point of view, or live outside our own soul life as spectators to our own inner life, then this kind of relationship may look like faithfulness. This pattern is not necessarily static; repetition often deepens the lived qualities of relationship. Faithfulness, on the other hand, does not give us the same kind of assuredness in relating. What may come about in the next moment has much more of an unknown quality. We cannot rely on the repetitive habits of the past to take care of what comes up next. We have to improvise the next moment, and do so from a sensing of the interior regions of the heart. Relating as jazz.

The strong element of fate, or of the life of the soul in its archetypal enactments, has a part to play in a relationship based in the virtue of faithfulness. We do not and cannot avoid this aspect of soul life. However, whereas in a relationship where all that is felt is that it is fated and patterns are relived over and over, in a relationship of faithfulness, these repetitious patterns become the artistic material through which we discover new aspects of the soul of the other person. Patterns of the past now become the material of soul improvisation that allow stepping into a future current of the soul, where a beginning shaping of entirely new soul experiences begins to form for both individuals involved in the virtue of faithfulness. To be faithful means to be committed, from the place of the heart, to this process of soul improvisation.

In our ordinary relationships, even those that are lasting, and where there seems to be commitment and certainly an outer form of faithfulness, the relationship serves not the soul of the other person but rather our own soul. This seemingly self-serving nature of relationship is not necessarily egotistical or self-centered. The relationship does serve soul. However, a relationship of faithfulness serves the soul of the other person, and cannot help but do so; it belongs to the very nature of faithfulness. I am not faithful to another person for myself, not even for myself at the level of soul. I am not served by being faithful, certainly not in a direct way. Faithfulness is lived for someone else, and because it is lived in the interior of the heart, at the level of the soul, it cannot become captured by our own egotistical needs and desires.

5 **The Virtue of Selflessness**

Aristotle spoke of virtue as the mean between the extremes of emotional life. It is a helpful formulation because it clarifies that virtue is a *way* of doing something rather than the content of what we do. Virtue is never just for the sake of virtue, but rather is the soul's intent to make whatever we do essentially spiritual while fully worldly.

I can, for example, approach any task or relationship, or even an idea, selflessly. To do so requires the soul to be aware of the extremes of selflessness. On the one hand, if I just give myself away, that is not selflessness; it is self-abandonment. On the other hand, if I guard myself and always make sure that I get something from whatever I do, that is egotism. Selflessness is the emotional mean of these extremes.

One way of approaching understanding selflessness is to carefully describe the extremes of self-abandonment and egotism, which will keep us close to the dynamic character of the virtue. It is, for example, quite helpful to realize that when we feel tendencies toward self-abandonment or the press of egotism, then we have the opportunity to develop in the direction of selflessness. We need our urgings toward self-abandonment—the wish to be rid of ourselves, not in a literal way, of course, but in that everyday sense of feeling something in ourselves holding us back from being engaged with others without reservation. We also need our incessant egotism, the nagging self-inflation that puts us at the center and the periphery of the universe at each moment.

Without these emotional qualities nagging at us, making us feel anything but spiritual, we cannot discover selflessness. Selflessness is not achieved by getting rid of these pesky distractions from living spiritually. Our virtue consists in how we go about living in intimate *contact* with them—neither sliding into them, rejecting them, feeling bad about finding ourselves taken by them over and over, but always striving toward the mean.

Self-abandonment looks a great deal like selflessness. However, having no sense of self, or in effect giving that sense away, does not constitute living in this virtue; that is to say, selflessness, in spite of the literal meaning of the word, does not at all mean having no self or no ego. While we logically have no difficulty whatsoever agreeing with this assessment, in actual practice, in life, the two—selflessness and self-abandonment—are often confused. Sometimes, in fact, loving another person is taken to mean giving completely over to another with self-abandon, not just in a momentary act of loving, but in an ongoing way.

To begin to get an actual feeling of the virtue, it is necessary to feel this tendency toward complete abandonment. It exists as a tendency within us all. If we do not or cannot feel such an impulse, an urge, a desire, it is because this propensity exists in polarity with its opposite, the polarity of egotism. When this other side of the polarity has strength, its reliance on the self-abandonment side of the polarity goes unrecognized. Egotism can be an inner fight against the fear of self-abandonment. Another way of stating the relation is this: extreme egotism is but a face of self-abandonment. Can you see how this is so? Imagine how much egotism is involved in the thought, "I can and want to give myself fully and completely away"—to someone, to some ideal, to some project. The egotism involved, though, remains silent, in the background, the polar opposite necessary for such one-sidedness.

To begin to develop a true and accurate imagination of self-abandonment and egotism, we have to refrain from any kind of judgment of these qualities. They are not bad, and trying to rid ourselves of such tendencies will only disperse the possibility of finding connection with the virtue of selflessness. These two qualities are the pregiven polarities of soul life, existing as the needed impulse for the development of soul life. Each, in its own way and in tandem with the other, instills a tone of discomfort. The first work is to feel this discomfort, which requires setting in imagination these two poles in tension, trying not to let one exist without an accompanying awareness of the other one. If the opposites are split, then it may indeed be a very long road back to the possibility of developing the virtue of selflessness.

The discomfort felt by recognizing the emotional quality of living in the tension of these opposites is the initial impulse toward selflessness. The particular character of this discomfort can be described as a feeling of emotional self-suffocation; we find ourselves facing ourselves no matter where we turn. We feel that there must be something other, something else, someone else to be interested in. If this condition of suffocation did not exist at some level, and the eventual hopelessness that comes with it, we would not be able to find that other orientation that we call selflessness.

A most typical manner in which the polarity—self-abandonment and egotism—splits into opposites is in our relationships with others. Often, one partner in a relationship carries one of the polarities while the other partner carries the other. One partner, in his or her actions, acts out self-abandonment, while the other partner acts out egotism. But since the polarity cannot under these circumstances be felt within individual soul life, a kind of destructive stasis results. The other person is needed to feel any sense of soul life, but the other person carries that soul sense, and no inner impetus for development can be felt. Only the friction with the other person is felt. "Why are you so self-centered?" says the one holding the position of self-abandonment. "Why aren't you totally subservient to me?" says the one holding the position of egotism.

These are the kinds of feelings that go on between people who live soul life one-sidedly. The feelings take innumerable forms, but always have this underlying dynamic. Under these circumstances, an emotional neediness exists between the individuals, along with great strife and each trying to get away from the other, accompanied by deep fear that the relationship will not continue.

The first movement toward selflessness consists of becoming aware within ourselves of the polar tension between self-abandonment and egotism; not one without the other. Selflessness consists of a metamorphosis of this dynamic polarity. What may be most difficult in considering this polarity is realizing that, even more than any of the other virtues, selflessness concerns, in a very strong way, the life of feeling. The three terms—"self-abandonment," "egotism," and "selflessness"—are not words that particularly carry strong feeling tones. To understand the metamorphosis into selflessness, however, it is necessary to begin with the feeling tone of its two polar extremes.

Self-abandonment, at first, carries an ecstatic feeling, the quality of living on the edge, an initial breath of incredible freedom, of leaving all of the burdens and the heaviness of the past behind, of starting life all over, afresh. Another side to the feeling quality of self-abandonment consists of the remarkable sensitivity that comes through living free from the reserve involved in retaining a sense of self-reflection. Living in an immediacy of feeling and the senses can make us feel intensely alive, but also intensely vulnerable. Desire is thus strong, making us restless and changeable, craving more feeling and more sensation. These feeling qualities all make for deep capacities of receptivity, for nothing is held back. Such receptivity can be overwhelming because there has not really been a giving of self, but rather an abandoning of self. Thus, in the background, silently, a gaping hole lurks, an unfillable emptiness felt.

A fundamental aspect of the possibility of metamorphosis of such vulnerability into selflessness consists of uplifting this sensitivity, along with its deep background painfulness, toward spiritual realms, which can change emotional sensitivity into practical mysticism.

Idealistic understanding of what constitutes spirituality often hinders the actual practice of spirituality because we have imagined it in ways that are far too lofty. The same holds with the virtues. The approach taken here is that we *are* our foibles, not that we have to find the way *out* of our foibles to something more perfect. Spirituality, or the practice of virtue, then consists in finding the right relation with our defects, our faults, and our insufficiencies. The right relation to our imperfections is far more fruitful than striving for perfection.

Egotism, as the polarity of self-abandonment, means holding strongly to oneself, where the strongest feeling becomes self-feeling. Egotism expresses fear of nonbeing, and thus we have to feel ourselves in order to know that we are. We hang on to egotism and do all sorts of things to further it because it gives us a sense of being someone. All of the sensitivities suggesting self-abandonment equally characterize egotism, though in a different manner. Here, these sensitivities are utilized to retain the needed feeling that one really exists. Self-feeling gives us the bodily experience of existing, since we typically identify ourselves with our body, and this is even more so with egotism.

In order to have and continue having this most necessary experience of existing, self-feeling continually perpetuates and enhances itself. Perhaps, in developing an understanding of the virtue of selflessness, it would be better to employ the term "self-centeredness" rather than egotism as the polarity to self-abandonment.

How, out of this polarity of self-centeredness and self-abandonment, can the virtue of selflessness can be born? It is not a matter of finding the mathematical mean between the two extremes—feeling some sense of self-abandon, but not too much, and feeling some sense of self-centeredness, but not too much. Virtue, as the mean between extremes, does not consist of this kind of balancing act. We have to look deeper into each of these polarities to find an element common to both polarities and to the virtue itself.

This common element is the capacity of nurturing. Both self-abandonment and self-centeredness have a central component of an engagement in nurturing—either a nurturing of others, due to the great receptivity involved, or of oneself—self-feeling being essentially a form of attempting to nurture oneself. The primary difficulty inherent in both of these directions of nurturing is that the turmoil involved makes it quite difficult to sense this nourishing aspect, and thus to take it up in a conscious manner and develop it into the virtue we are considering.

The emotional turmoil of the extremes of self-abandonment and egotism consists of a compulsiveness in the need to feel, attained either through being vividly receptive to the feelings of others or vividly present to one's own self-feeling of oneself. Because of this compulsiveness, the capacity of nurturing has limited value, and is filled with conflict between desiring to be of genuine help to others, to selflessly nourish, and the need to be sensitive simply to have engagement in the feeling realm.

What is being sought in "the need to feel" is not just any feeling whatsoever. It is also something deeper than to feel our own existence or that of another as if it were our own, though these are symptoms of selflessness with no focus. The need involved here is to feel the actual presence of something divine, something holy, and this need is as great for us as the necessity for food when we are starving. We desire more than the idea of the holy. Our bones ache to *experience* the holy tangibly, as real, as palpable.

While the need for this experience may originate in a rather awkward place—with ourselves—these foibles of self-abandonment and egotism can actually get us oriented in the direction of selflessness, provided we wake up to the fruitlessness of both polarities and can develop the capacity to hold the polarities together, feel the discomfort involved, and begin searching around.

As the descriptions of self-centeredness and self-abandonment and how they must be worked with to awaken selflessness give an initial picture of this virtue, we can go on to say more concerning the action of the virtue itself. In order to develop an imagination of this virtue, it might be helpful to reframe the name. Selflessness, when put into action in the world, constitutes service. There are surely as many conundrums to be faced with this word "service" as there are with the word "selflessness." Nonetheless, if we are to deepen the sense of this virtue from its personal and individual sense out into a larger engagement with the world, with culture, with others, then it will be worth our effort to develop a new and fresh understanding of this overused word, "service."

Finding the way to selflessness has become exceedingly difficult due to the prevalence of a certain way of viewing service in the world. Providing service has become a huge sector of the economy. Now that it is commonplace for us to receive monetary compensation for serving others, it becomes much more difficult to imagine how selfless service can be enacted; it no longer has a place in the collective imagination. Even more, few forms exist in our culture for the practice of the virtue of selflessness. For those who do wish to develop capacities of serving in this way, the necessity of making a living looms like a great dark cloud, immediately obscuring the free exercise of selflessness. All selflessness seems now to be set within an economic framework.

While we can easily imagine selfless acts occurring within an economic framework, the demands of productivity, efficiency, and profit continually squeeze that framework tighter and tighter. We now expect compensation for what we do that helps others. These demands for connecting money with what we do for others have also fully entered into domains previously exempt from them, such as religious life, nonprofit organizations, hospitals, and all of the helping professions. It is not productive, efficient, or profitable to be selfless. Nor can the outcome of selflessness be measured; to the materialistic eye, it does not produce anything, and while cultural forms no longer support the practice of this virtue, a determination to do so individually typically meets with having to confront economic hardship.

What about the new interest in volunteerism? Many people offer their services—building houses for others, taking food to the elderly, helping the aged and the homeless, volunteering at hospitals. Just think of how much churches do. Are not these efforts examples of selflessness? None of these efforts is to be disparaged. Not in the least. They are all praiseworthy, and these good works have not been taken into the economic sphere.

It is not selfless, however, to help others according to what we think others need. If a group determines that low-income housing is needed by people who make little money and proceeds to develop a way to build houses for these people, that is giving to others what we imagine them to need. I cannot say that such people are not in need of affordable housing. These good works can be, for some, selfless, and for others they are not. Virtue does not have to do with the acts done. It concerns the way in which acts are done. What hides in most institutional structures organized to help others is our own need to satisfy needs we see that others have. Our need goes unrecognized, and the act seems selfless. If I say, I help others because I have so much and I want to give something back, that is not selfless. I am getting something from my act of helping others. Selflessness is something other than these kindly and important acts of giving something to others.

My aim of looking at the state of this virtue in culture is not to show how the practice of selflessness is nearly impossible; rather, it is to look at what is happening in such a way that the qualities of this virtue can be seen more clearly through the lens of cultural obscurity. For example, that selflessness does not fit very well with the kind of economic worldview we practice shows, first of all, that selflessness is a quality of time. Selflessness requires that we relinquish whatever time we may be living within and live within the time of those whom we are serving. Selflessness is not simply giving some of my time to someone in need. In selflessness we shift into the time of the other.

A mother must, for example, learn the time of the infant, or the child. This time is repetitious, loving doing one thing over and over without any outcome expected. It is not selfless to give some of my time to help a child. It approaches selflessness when I freely enter into a time frame that is not mine at all. A doctor learns something of the time the patient lives within, the time of pain and of suffering, to be able to enter into that time quality with his patients. A teacher learns the rhythms within which children live and learn.

If we went through all of the service professions in imagination, picturing the time qualities of those who are served, we would indeed find that selflessness concerns developing the capacity to imagine the tremendous flexibility of experienced time. The service industries, in following an economic model, completely ignore this element, flattening time into a single, measurable dimension. Lived time, on the contrary, expands and contracts, and selflessness can be understood as living in expanded time.

Everyone feels that time is contracting; we seem to have less and less of it. Thus, it would seem that we would rush toward selflessness, searching for a breath of freedom. You have to be able to feel a joy in spending time with another without feeling that it costs you money to do so. As the Chinese sage Lin Yutang once said, "If you can spend a perfectly useless afternoon in a perfectly useless manner, you have learned how to live." I don't think he was speaking about the virtue of laziness. The saying alerts us to the value of being free of our own concerns, and in our time, it alerts us to the value of time freed from becoming a commodity to be bought and sold. The saying also suggests that if we cannot practice selflessness, we are not really living.

The relation between selflessness and time is far more intimate than the fact that this virtue needs spacious time for it to be an effective action. To be selfless means no less than giving one's own time substance to another. What does a notion like this mean? We speak this way: giving someone our time. In fact, once it became noticed that serving others involved giving them your time, then this time became a commodity to be bought and sold. That was the beginning of the "age of service" and the promulgating of service industries. That time, however—the time that became an economic commodity—is a mere substitute, a double of our own time substance, the basic substance of our soul life, which can be given but can never be quantified, bought, or sold. Commodified time consists of billable hours, the time spent with patients that is clocked, with fees charged for service. Selflessness cannot work in this kind of time.

What is the time of the soul? We have to imagine soul itself as a temporal activity, not just the inner qualities of experience that seem to exist outside of time. Soul, in its temporal aspect, encompasses all of our individual past experiences as well as the collective past of all humankind, as well as all of our individual pasts over many lifetimes. In addition, soul is the temporal activity encompassing all of the future as open possibility, future as the not-yet nonetheless experienced in every moment, as anticipation, waiting, hoping, longing, expecting, desiring, wanting, wishing. Soul is also the continual experience of the overlapping of the personal and extended past with the personal and extended future, with the place of intersection being our usual and ordinary sense of the present, where we are conscious. The place of intersection, in fact, defines consciousness. Consciousness is the overlap between the time stream of the past and the time stream of the future.

Within this view of the temporal life of the soul, we can contemplate the question of what it takes to be selfless in a temporal dimension. We all know what it feels like to be in the presence of one who exhibits some degree of selflessness. Time opens up, it becomes a clearing, it has spaciousness. In this spaciousness, imagination can blossom, matters can be seen from all sorts of perspectives, a sacred dimension can be felt. All because someone has given you their time. These qualities certainly go out the window when someone says, "I can give you five minutes." It also goes out the window when you know you are being charged for each minute that you are taking or using.

Another cultural factor that hinders the practice of selflessness is of equal importance to time made into a commodity. Here, too, I will approach this factor by going beyond negative criticism, and instead let this factor reveal something of the essence of selflessness. Acts that in themselves would be selfless are thwarted from that end by virtue of the fact that instead of occurring through an immediacy of relationship, they become mediated through some kind of instrumentality.

For example, the selfless act of healing can be thwarted by the instrumentality of machines of every sort that now come between the serving act of the physician and the receiving patient. Or the selfless dimension of the act of teaching is deflected through the instrumentality of a computer in every classroom, or any of the other kinds of instruments that plague education. This instrumentality can also take the form of rules and regulations, so-called standards, that exist in every service profession. Or it can take the form of licensing requirements, competency testing, performance measurements, outcome testing. Or it can take the form of "professional" knowledge.

A host of arguments can easily be put forward extolling the value of instrumentality. I am not, however, speaking against these devices of mediation existing between an act of selflessness and the recipient of such an act. I want to draw attention to what instrumentality *does,* which will light up an otherwise obscure, essential aspect of the virtue of selflessness.

For example, it is certainly true that when an instrument of any sort is placed between one who serves and one being served, there easily arises the expectation that the instrument itself produces a result. We thus become enamored with instruments. In a strange way, of course, an instrument appears to be quite selfless, though, strictly speaking, it is a misuse of the term to apply this virtue to a piece of equipment. At the same time, instrumentality makes possible a kind of substitute selflessness; it inserts an objectivity into any apparent act of selflessness, attempting to assure that the transaction is not infected by personal desires, patterns, or investment in an outcome.

Technology often does for us what we, as individuals, do not yet have capabilities of doing. I am not referring here to technology in the sense of its technical capabilities. We cannot, in our mind, compute in a conscious way with the speed and accuracy of a computer. We cannot, with our senses, see into the stomach of a person. We have technologies that can do these kinds of things. But there is another, more invisible, aspect to technology. It seems to serve in ways that we are not yet inwardly capable of; it seeks nothing in return for its actions. We can learn from the intervention of instrumentality that exists in nearly all acts of serving that the virtue of selflessness can be effective only if carried out in an instrumental way. However, instrumentation has to be reimagined, put back into soul, revered as what we can learn to do and to be out of our own soul forces. When I act selflessly I am an *instrument* of spiritual intention.

The difficulty with technology, seen within this dimension of its substitute selflessness, is that, having such instruments, we can and do easily lose sight of any need to develop an inner quality of selflessness. For example, we can easily conceive of a narcissistic, self-centered, egotistic doctor who is nonetheless brilliant and highly skilled, able to use the advanced instruments of medicine in remarkably helpful ways. A kind of selflessness is brought about through technical instrumentality that is of true service to a patient. In a situation such as this, there is, of course, a great deal of illusion going on. The "selflessness" of the instruments can only bring about changes equal to their own level of being. That is, the "selflessness" of technology can only effect technical changes.

Medical instrumentation, for example, can be a valuable aid
in diagnosing and treating a disease—but it can never produce
healing. When this limitation is overlooked, we then become satisfied with getting rid of disease manifestations and lose sight completely of there even being a reality such as healing. Healing
requires more: an individual must become the instrument through
which a restoration of the soul of the ill person takes place. In all
places where we see a kind of selflessness occurring through the
intervention of technical instrumentation, the soul element is left
out.

Selflessness may seem to be brought about by taking ourselves
out of the picture, as it were, in order to allow something to take
place that is free from our interference. This view, however, is one
of technical selflessness, brought to an excellence through actual,
physical instruments. The practice of the virtue does not take us
out of the picture, but puts us more into it—more, in the sense that
more of us must be present to the situation than is ordinarily
required. We have to be awake and aware in our senses; we have
to be as awake and aware as possible in our feeling life, and in our
soul life and spirit life. Working to put these qualities into the picture can be far more helpful than working to take our ego sense
of ourselves out of the picture.

The intervention of instrumentality as a factor in producing
and yet obscuring selflessness points to another essential aspect of
selflessness. That instruments do function to bring about a kind of
substitute selflessness indicates that the virtue of selflessness,
when carried out in a direct and immediate manner, means that
we become instruments to be utilized by others; but not technical
instruments, lifeless instruments, instruments without soul or
spirit. So, what kind of instrumentality are we asked to become in
the practice of selflessness?

In selflessness, we stand in for creating and healing forces that
belong not to us, but to the spiritual worlds. However, with this
virtue, such forces do not work through us by our learning to stand
out of the way, as it were. Rather, the remarkable character of this
virtue is that it works through the individuality of our character,
our soul characteristics, our peculiarities, rather than bypassing

them. In this manner, selflessness is never something abstract. As we can be selfless only by being ourselves, so it is very likely indeed that we may not always know when we are being truly selfless and when we are not. Selflessness cannot be simplistically understood as doing something for someone else with no expectation of receiving anything in return. That definition is too abstract.

The relation between the virtue of selflessness and the ego is of particular importance to consider. We cannot bypass the ego to find selflessness. Rather, selflessness requires the presence of our ego, but a presence characterized by full and complete vulnerability. The substitute selflessness spoken about earlier has the defect of omitting this requirement of ego vulnerability due to the intervention of instrumentality, which makes it seem possible to be of help to others without having to feel anything oneself. True selflessness can occur only through vulnerability. We consciously hold back our thoughts, opinions, preconceptions, emotional reactions, knowledge, advice, experience, learning, in order to be radically receptive to the other person; that is selflessness. The question here, however, is what makes it possible for us to be oriented in this way? We seem to have to use our ego against itself. Is this possible?

In selflessness, the ego functions as everything it is not; we approach others unprotected, unguarded, defenseless, exposed, naked. We can perhaps imagine being present in this manner spiritually, where we can, for a time, put aside ego concerns and function according to higher motives. It is much more difficult to imagine how this might occur without attempting in any way to disengage our usual, everyday, self-centered, fairly egotistical being. But unless we can find that way, there is no vulnerability and the selflessness achieved may well be illusory.

The mere attempt to do something selfless, not by going through a great deal of inner spiritual discipline or taking up a spiritual practice, but in the most everyday sense you can imagine, sets up a current that goes beyond the ego and raises that act of the ego to a higher level. The initial phases of selflessness can be imagined as bootstrapping ourselves into a more spiritual sphere by acting *as if* we were acting out of the realm of the spirit. The "as if" here is important. We "play" at being spiritual in our most ordinary and mundane interactions with others. What results from such play is a new kind of feeling, one that we are not typically aware of as belonging to ego consciousness. We feel spiritual—a new and interesting kind of pleasure as far as the ego is concerned. This pleasurable feeling opens the ego a bit, makes it possible for us to be a bit less defensive, a bit more vulnerable.

Does this sound manipulative, something quite opposite what one would expect in addressing matters of virtue? Perhaps. But selflessness may well be the most human of all of the virtues. It is certainly the most painful one, for it works itself out right here in the trenches of our less-than-angelic humanity. Consequently, there is a strong tendency to make an illusory image of this virtue, imagining it to be a highly spiritual virtue, capable of being practiced only by would-be initiates who have gone through tremendous effort to rid themselves of all traces of the ego. Not so. We lose the practicality of the virtue if we take it out of the ordinary and make it falsely extraordinary.

Because selflessness works in close tandem with our ego consciousness, the process I have just described can easily backfire, and it does, all the time. The "good" feeling resulting from even a small act of selflessness, the play at being what we are really not quite capable of, can be used for personal gain. Being so open to others, we find in turn that they become open and vulnerable to us. The possibility of using vulnerability as a ploy to get what we want from others enters. The possibility of feeling that we are far more spiritual than we are also enters. What a risky virtue!

While the risk cannot be minimized, the nature of the current that operates when playing at selflessness cannot be ignored either. As soon as the act of playing at the virtue ceases and the kinds of selfless acts practiced become solely for our own self-aggrandizement, this current no longer operates. The particular kind of soul pleasure that comes from being within the spiritual current of this virtue ceases. While we may continue to utilize the now pseudo-selflessness, others, at perhaps only subconscious levels, perceive that this act is definitely not what it appears to be.

The virtue of selflessness itself is a vulnerable virtue. It relies upon giving us a taste of a different level of being from out of the practices of our most ordinary and usual levels of behaving. It leaves itself completely open to misunderstanding. This virtue, if we imagine it as if it were a living being, lives in the hope that we will become interested in the peculiar nature of the feeling of soul pleasure encountered as we open ourselves a bit and become oriented toward being genuinely present to the other person. If we do find that this pleasure catches us off guard, and penetrates, for a moment, the defenses of our ego, then there is an opening for further development of the virtue.

I like to think of selflessness as the "ordinary" virtue, and have attempted to develop here an imagination of that sort. Now, having looked into how this virtue becomes obscured in a technical world, but also having seen how this same world shows us something of the nature of the virtue itself, we can return to a pressing question. Is it possible to recover the virtue of selflessness in a world dominated by economic motivation? Is it any longer possible to serve selflessly? Well, perhaps, just perhaps, it is no longer possible to live this virtue surrounded and protected by forms explicitly oriented toward fostering the practice of this virtue. We have to look for the "little way" of selflessness much more now. Not big acts of selflessness, not institutions founded and oriented toward the practice of this virtue, and definitely not more or less bodiless and egoless creatures wisping around, acting completely in the interests of others, and doing so almost invisibly.

These days we can count it as being selfless simply to work at not going numb in the midst of a numbing world. We can count it as selfless when we manage, through inner effort, to remain embodied in a decidedly disembodied world. The mere act of attempting to stay in connection with the inner life of the soul, or to have a genuine spiritual life that we can call our own and is not imposed from the outside—these kinds of acts are the beginning of selflessness.

We might think of selflessness as the most silent of the virtues, going on invisibly, inaudibly, out of sight, not apparent to others. Perhaps this way of invisibility is necessary for the virtue, as if it does not like to be seen. When we see acts of selflessness displayed, this may, at least a good deal of the time, be a kind of literalizing of the virtue, taking it out of the domain of the soul, the only place it can thrive. When such display is not literalizing, it quickly becomes that by drawing attention to itself, becoming an item to be reported, sentimentalized, idolized.

Selflessness, if made into a project, stands out too clearly in the world and thus easily and readily becomes captured by the world. A special difficulty then arises. Those who are involved in the public display of this virtue will not recognize when they have been taken over into the selfish realm. To be recognized as being selfless is perhaps the most difficult trial for the virtue.

The other most difficult trial for the virtue of selflessness is not being recognized for our selflessness. We would have to have become completely egoless not to care whether others appreciated our selflessness, particularly those helped by such acts. Our ego takes great joy in saying, "Oh, it was nothing." If we do not have the satisfaction of being able to display this "nonacceptance" of what we have done, this delicious satisfaction of amplification of selflessness by declaring that what we have done is indeed selfless and wants nothing, it is likely that we feel quite hurt.

The trials of this virtue, it seems, are the very exercise of the virtue. If we cannot feel these trials acutely, constantly, then most likely we have taken a position of superiority, a position completely antithetical to the very nature of the virtue. We can think of selflessness as the slowest of all the virtues—or maybe it is that we are the slowest to adapt to its ways.

6 **The Virtue of Compassion**

Compassion forms a central aspect of Buddhist spirituality, so I want to begin by retelling the story of how Siddhartha came to compassion. Then it will be possible to form a proper relation between the Buddhist understanding and practice of compassion and the virtue. Determining this relationship will not be easy. We shall have to circle around, looking at the phenomenon from various points of view, only gradually seeing the likeness and differences between the compassion of Buddhist spirituality and compassion as one, perhaps the central, of the twelve virtues. Compassion as understood and practiced by Buddhism should not be wholly equated with the virtue. The virtue can be experienced in daily life without adopting the spirituality of Buddhism.

Siddhartha was born in 560 B.C.E. to the ruling family of the empire of Skya, on the border of Nepal and India. His childhood was accompanied by prophesies of greatness, even of divinity. The name Siddhartha means "one whose aim is accomplished," and it was given to the boy by eight wise men. He grew up in luxury, spending winter, summer, and rainy season each in a different palace. He could have spent his life in luxury, as intended by his father.

In his twenties, Siddhartha traveled throughout the region and was deeply moved by all the suffering he witnessed. At the age of twenty-nine, he gave away all his belongings and became a wanderer, vowing to seek out holy men who would teach him how to get beyond himself and break the endless chain of human misery.

He attained mystical states, but nonetheless remained unsatisfied. He entered into a severe regimen of mortification and fasting for a period of six years. This regimen nearly killed him. He said, for example:

> Because of so little nourishment, all my limbs became like some withered creepers with knotted joints; my buttocks like a buffalo's hoof; my backbone protruding like a string of balls; my ribs like rafters of a dilapidated shed; the pupils of my eyes appeared sunk deep in their sockets as water appears shining at the bottom of a deep well. When I wanted to obey the calls of nature, I fell down on my face then and there. When I stroked my limbs with my hand, hairs rotted at the roots, fell away from my body.

He experienced many horrible visions taking the form of Mara, the god connected with evil and passion. He endured these visions to the point that a dissolution of his psychic self occurred, which meant that he no longer possessed a psychic mirror in which the demons could take shape. It took a very long time to sift through the six years of experience, determining which of his experiences were true and which were illusion. The result of this time of discrimination was the forming of a union of his conscious and subconscious, and a melding of mind and body. At this point, he relinquished the austerities.

One morning he sat down and meditated beneath an *assattha* tree, determined not to rise again until he had achieved enlightenment. Within an hour, hordes of demons and monsters of a visionary nature attacked him. Siddhartha knew these were illusions and remained still in meditation. By evening, the armies of evil departed. Then the heavens opened up, and he saw how he had lived through multiple incarnations. He also saw the creative spiritual activity of the cosmos, and the laws by which reality comes into being. He said, "Ignorance was dispelled, knowledge arose, darkness was dispelled, light arose." So prepared was he that the whole process took but one day.

For the next seven weeks, Siddhartha reflected on his experience and reformulated it in terms that others could understand. He formulated the Four Noble Truths:

One, everyday human existence consists of confusion, conflict, dissatisfaction, and suffering.

Two, this tortuous existence is caused by our ego—the selfish craving for fame, fortune, and power over others.

Three, the only way to achieve freedom from worldly reality is to attain enlightenment.

Four, the way to enlightenment is the "middle way," between self-indulgence and self-mortification. This middle way is achieved through the Eightfold Path that consists of: right view, right thought, right speech, right action, right mode of living, right endeavor, right mindfulness, and right concentration.

By "right" is meant "in alignment with the divine." The practice of this middle way of the Eightfold Path leads to compassion, the capacity to be fully present to the suffering of another, without interfering or doing anything that would disrupt what the soul of the other needs to experience.

The purpose of telling this story is to alert us to the tremendous striving necessary to come to this virtue. We have to imagine a time when such a virtue did not exist and how it took the sacrifices of one person to bring it to the whole of humanity. This picture also suggests a most interesting line of research regarding all of the virtues. It is quite likely that each of the virtues required someone, an initiate, to bring the virtue to humanity, to do it for the first time, to accomplish an act that installs a new capacity into the soul capacities of human beings. We perhaps have not gone deep enough into imagining the source of the virtues if we consider them to be simply given, ready for us to take up, as if they have been in existence since the beginning of humanity.

Compassion stands out as perhaps the most central of the virtues, the virtue concerned with transmuting, or, we could say, turning all of the forces of our soul life outward, reorienting them toward the spiritual realms. The first thing we are able to say about the virtue of compassion is that it makes possible a spiritual outlook toward everything—everything without exception. Is this not the discovery wrought through the suffering and sacrifices of Siddhartha?

Before compassion is possible as an actual act and not just a conceptual notion that we may think we can live but in reality cannot, a purification process takes place. In our lives, this purification process happens through all of the suffering we have gone through—suffering of a physical, emotional, and soul nature. Such suffering does not purify if we go through it without much reflection, just waiting for it to be over. When, however, we allow our suffering to change us, then the process results in the capacity to experience a depth of love toward everyone and everything equally.

By purification I mean that desire is cleansed of fantasy, lust, greed, and memory. Our sufferings are like an alchemical fire that distills desire into its essence. The essence of desire consists of the inner soul's feeling-knowing and unswerving attraction to the spiritual realms. All our ordinary desires are like a refraction of this one desire. All desires are good because they refract, like light shining through a diamond, the divine source of desire. But even though all desire is good, it does not mean that the objects of our desire are necessarily good. We continually confuse our desire with the objects it gets attached to. Thus, a first step toward compassion, an unending step, concerns feeling desire more intensely without wanting the objects that draw it out. When soul life is purified, all our earthly activities are put under the glow of divine desire.

Compassion makes possible an intimate relating with others, even when we do not know them; it does not discriminate between personal and universal love. It does not differentiate between someone we are close to and someone we have not met at all. When we find we can feel something like compassion for someone with whom we have a connection but not for others, this would not be true compassion because it is limited only to those to whom we have some kind of a destiny connection; it is as if our heart can ray out only so far and no further.

Through compassion we are brought into intimate connection with all of humanity. Such a connection is felt deeply and does not exist merely as a concept, as the mere idea that we are each connected with each other. At the same time, compassion is practiced toward the individual, not to the whole of humanity. How can these two seemingly contradictory notions of being connected to the whole and to the individual come together?

Compassion involves a different kind of perception of another person than what we get through our usual sensing and thinking. It is a perception in which in each and every individual we also perceive the universal human. We have to develop this capacity of perception, for it is not naturally present, as is, for example, the capacity of seeing, hearing, or touching. For most of us, compassion of the kind attained by Siddhartha remains a distant goal, something to aspire to and work toward, but hardly an actuality. Through the complete purification of his soul life, he attained the capacity to perceive the other person as an individual spirit-being. He could see the spirit-being of the other person, the universal human, and see, in the confusion and suffering the person was undergoing, that unless the suffering person came to spiritual perception, that person would be condemned to one round of suffering after another.

Such a perception of the other person takes place through the organ of the heart. Compassion is the purified heart's perception of the other person, a highly spiritual capacity. The virtue as it can be experienced by us in daily life does not reach those heights and remains more in touch with the soul life.

It might be helpful to make a distinction between Compassion and compassion. The former is reserved for initiates. The latter is the way in which the rest of us participate, as best we can, in what has been brought to humanity by the initiates. We may not be able to sense the spiritual individuality of the other person, but we can develop the capacity to experience, in a direct and immediate way, the unfolding of the individual life of another person. This perception requires minimal purification of desire, for we have to be able to see another person for who he or she is, freed from our fantasies, conceptions, and assumptions. This perception, too, takes place through the heart. We can perceive others as in process. It is even possible to see how a person changes from one day to the next. We usually do not pay much attention to these changes, or we take them to be no more than changes of mood or attitude or outer behavior. But when we perceive such changes through heart-consciousness, we see a pattern, a soul development, going on.

The perception of this force is an inner feeling-perception of the unfolding of life. In order to feel compassion, it is necessary to be able, at whatever level possible, to sense that things are not fixed and static, but mobile, evolving, metamorphosing. I cannot possibly feel compassion for something that is fixed. I may feel empathy, or sympathy, or pity, but I cannot feel compassion for something that is incapable of change. As a corollary to this, I have to be able to sense something invisible, a core of movement, development, change, growth, in order to feel compassion. I have to have the actual experience of "This that I see does not have to be this way; I can see, in a feeling way, the actual possibility of what this person can become." This is a real perception, and not just a lofty or sentimental notion of what I wish for this other person. I feelingly perceive the dynamic coming-into-spirit-being of the other person.

The preparation for this kind of compassion-perception consists of the practice of developing a friendly relationship with human beings without any exclusion, an understanding and a tolerance without reservation, an absence of prejudice, the beginnings, at least, of an all-embracing love that can see deeper than the personality of the other and perceives something of the eternal individuality of the other.

A second preparation is also needed for developing compassion. Through our bodily senses we experience the physical world, and from that perception we have come to an understanding of the laws that govern the physical universe. Perception through the heart does not perceive the physical universe. The heart perceives the universe of goodness. Through the heart, we perceive the good that is the other person. Here also, I am speaking of something more direct, more tangible, than an idea of goodness or what I may think is good; it can be an actual perception. In order to perceive goodness, good thoughts and good intentions are necessary, though these qualities must here be felt as actual currents within the heart. We are able to perceive in the world only what is already active within us. The eye can see light only because the potential of light exists within the eye. The ear can hear only because the potential of sound exists within the ear.

In a time of materialistic biology, we are not accustomed to thinking of the sense organs as containing the potential of what they perceive. In earlier times, and in esoteric circles, this truth was known. It is depicted in much art and also in early anatomy and science. For example, there are many existent drawings showing rays of invisible light emanating from the eyes of a human being gazing out at a landscape. It would have seemed foolish to those early anatomists and physiologists to imagine that seeing consists only of waves of light energy coming from an object in the world, entering the brain, reproducing there an image of the object being viewed.

Each of the sense organs, it was understood, is also a force, a soul-force, projecting out into the world, meeting there with forces from the object being perceived. Actual perception, understood from this view, consists of the unified field between the perceiver and the perceived. This is the kind of imagination that is still necessary to understand what is meant by a perception of the heart. Without this kind of imagination, all that is said concerning the heart falls into mushy sentimentality having no substance and no actuality. By simply moving consciousness to the center of the heart and being present to the feeling-current there, we can come to experience something like a radiating warmth reaching out from the heart toward others. This is the basis of the heart perception through which compassion becomes an actual experience.

The force that rays out from the heart is the force of love. It is not a love for this or for that, for one person or another, but the force of universal love. Unless, however, we come into a direct and inner connection with that force, we cannot perceive others in their true goodness and individuality. To do so constitutes the major aspect of the virtue of compassion.

Compassion consists of something quite different than our usual conception of it. When we imagine compassion, we are usually imagining emotional compassion. Usually compassion is experienced with an accompanying desire to help, a desire based in a feeling response to the suffering of the other person. We feel compassionate when we see someone hurting. We connect compassion and hurting. This is the emotional level of compassion.

The function of spiritual and soul compassion, however, is not to alleviate pain directly, but rather to see the inner truth of the other person. Thus, compassion, in its spiritual-soul sense, leads others to see the truth of themselves. Compassion leads to self-knowledge, and it is self-knowledge that is healing. This seeing, by both the one having compassion and the one receiving it, is not an intellectual knowing or an intellectual insight, but rather, a heart-knowing.

With heart-knowing, we shift consciousness inward, away from its usual orientation toward the sensory world. When we do shift our consciousness in this way, we typically focus inwardly at the region of the head. This focus has to be shifted to the center of the heart. When we are able to still ourselves there, at the center of the heart, it is as if we can feel subtle currents in the heart. These currents are experienced as a direct feeling of the soul-spirit being of the other person. When we feel such a current in relation to someone, there is no doubt whatsoever that our heart is resonating to the heart currents of the other person.

Compassion makes it possible for the other person to bear pain, and helps make difficult experiences meaningful and tolerable. It does this by creating trust, which leads to seeing the truth of oneself. In suffering, this truth concerns the ways we can spiritually deepen through what we endure. To directly alleviate someone's pain can be a disservice to the soul and spirit of that person because it removes the possibility of seeing what the suffering is trying to tell us about ourselves.

Sometimes, of course, it is absolutely necessary to do something directly and immediately to alleviate someone's pain. We would not think it right, in the name of compassion, to let someone suffer intolerable pain if we know how it can be lessened. Usually, however, directly alleviating pain actually means only eliminating the outer manifestations of some deeper, ongoing soul pain. For this deeper pain to abate requires that the person come to significant self-knowledge, and here the virtue of compassion is the greatest aid toward the possibility of healing.

The difference between emotional compassion and soul-spirit compassion has to be emphasized. For example, if someone who is dear to me is unhappy, then it is quite difficult for me to be happy. If I feel and experience the unhappiness of that person, feel it as if it were my own, then I cannot be happy as long as the other person is unhappy. This is emotional compassion. With soul-spirit compassion, we perceive the spirit aspect of the other person, and no matter what that person may be going through, we do not lose sight of their spiritual being and do nothing that might interfere with the spiritual destiny of the person.

While emotional and soul-spirit compassion are different, it is also true that the former can and often does lead to the latter. Suppose, for example, it becomes necessary for me to take care of someone who is dying, someone going through a great deal of pain in the process of dying. If I am with that person and do not cut off my feelings, then I too will go through a great deal of suffering. Through knowing this person who is dying, I am learning compassion, and the person whom I am caring for is also learning what compassion is. The experience can stay at the level of emotional compassion, but it can also open the heart and lead to a different outlook in life. Opening of the heart can move from a deep emotional experience to a spiritual experience.

The virtue of compassion lies on the border between emotional compassion and spiritual compassion. Because the region of the virtues belongs to the soul realm, it is necessary to keep in connection with the emotional element without getting caught there. When compassion becomes wholly a matter of the spirit, we have left the circle of the virtues for something higher. So, while we can have the utmost admiration for the practice of compassion in Buddhism, that is not where we are seeking to go with the practice of the virtue. Nor, however, are we content to remain wholly within emotional compassion, which can lead to numerous psychological maladies, such as codependence. We have to remain on this border to remain in and with the virtue, adhering to virtue itself as simultaneously belonging to the sphere of the soul and the sphere of the spirit.

To remain on the border between emotional and spiritual compassion can be quite difficult. A special relation obtains between the virtue of compassion and that of discernment. Compassion is always in tension with discernment. When we feel the impulse toward compassion, if we are sensitive to the soul level, we will also feel the necessity of discerning whether our emotional engagement with another person helps them toward self-knowledge or is merely soothing. An inner desire to come to clarity can be felt in the midst of feeling compassion, a desire that pushes us to observe the feeling of compassion closely and yet in an engaged way. This inner observation helps us to gradually come to clarity concerning where we are in the continuum of the emotional-spiritual aspects of compassion.

When we encounter someone who is suffering, we are automatically in a position of power. We are not suffering, or are suffering to a lesser degree than those we see. This position of power can mean that a cheap kind of compassion can creep in before we are even aware of it. It is easy to feel sorry for someone, and in fact, seeing the suffering of another affirms our own power to ourselves. To be truthful, we need the presence of a suffering other in order to experience our own sense of power.

For example, if I am a psychotherapist or a doctor, or a lawyer, or anyone who works in service to others, I need the suffering other in order to affirm the power of my being the "professional" person. This is just the way this archetypal tandem works. There are no helpers without those needing help. What usually goes unnoticed, however, is that the helpers need those who are in need. People come to me in need. I can then approach them with compassion. This rather grim picture seems to be a far cry from the way our understanding of compassion has developed thus far. Nonetheless, it is a true reality, one that must be faced and worked through.

It is far, far more difficult to feel compassion for another when I am in the throes of suffering myself. Remember, when Siddhartha was growing up, he had all the luxury anyone could want. Through his travels he encountered the immense tragedy of people. He then relinquished his riches and went through immense suffering himself, and only after this could speak of compassion. This sequence is highly interesting.

He began as a person of tremendous earthly power. We cannot, however, neglect the fact that it was this very power, taking the form of riches, that allowed him to see, in contrast, the tremendous suffering around him. With all of those riches, he could have surely done much to lessen the suffering of those he encountered. He could have given them food, clothes, built schools, hospitals. To do so, however, would have kept him in a position of power. The lesson in this is that we need power in order to see, but then power, if it is to turn into compassion, must be given away.

The giveaway of power necessary for the enacting of compassion does not have to be literal. I do not have to stop practicing medicine, psychotherapy, or another service to break the power-weakness relationship. It does, however, seem difficult to wield power and practice compassion. For each of us, living in the kind of world we do, where we have gifts and wealth and jobs and professions, the practice of compassion, if it takes place at all, takes on a subdued form. Can, for example, a doctor have compassion in the way in which it has been pictured thus far in this writing? Is it possible to work in a large medical practice, make a six-figure income, work under the constraint of managed care, and practice compassion? Is it possible to have all of this power and enter into the virtue of compassion?

This virtue makes clear that the soul's path of virtue requires a turnaround, a conversion, a metanoia, of our way of living. Once we recognize it here with the virtue of compassion, it becomes more clear that all of the virtues place our lives, our ways of living, into question. At the same time, I am not suggesting that the soul path of virtue requires that we step back and away from the present world. If anything, virtue ought to mean that we enter more deeply into the actual realities of our time. We can indeed do so.

We do not need to give away all of our belongings. However, we do have to relinquish certain aspects of the way the present world works. We can work, be professionals, make money, but the need for security has to be loosened. The soul path of virtue requires that we release the need to hold on to anything. In this manner, particularly with respect to the virtue of compassion, we go a long way toward the necessary relinquishing of power, a release that is necessary for the practice of the virtue.

When Siddhartha relinquished his riches and began his time of fasting and sacrifice, he was confronted with his many inner demons. We can well expect that if we can come to the point of starting on the soul path of virtue, we also will, at our own levels of development, confront our many inner demons. These demons are likely to take the form of fears: fears of not being able to survive in this competitive world; that as we grow older we will not have a stock portfolio, a large bank account, a retirement fund to take care of us; that we will look unsuccessful to others. In truth, these little fears are nothing like the order and magnitude of the demons that attacked Siddhartha. But then our level of compassion can hardly be compared to his.

Here is an example. A number of years ago, I met a Jungian analyst, Irwin Vassavada, who worked in Chicago. He was very concerned about how to morally practice psychotherapy. He was acutely aware of the power involved in doing psychotherapy. He made the decision not to charge patients for therapy, as he felt that charging money for such work conflicted with the soul resources needed to be a compassionate presence. He did allow people to give him money if they wished, but he never set a fee; sometimes it was food, or other things, that people gave him. He was not considered a part of the world of professional therapists. He also lived simply. I would say he lived deeply into the virtue of compassion. He also suffered a great deal, feeling in a way I had never experienced, the suffering of his patients, and he was continually concerned about the moral nature of his work with patients. He removed certain "cushions" of comfort in his life in order to be and remain fully present to the movements of his own soul in relation to those with whom he worked.

This point may be the most essential one in relation to experiencing compassion in the kind of world in which we live. Our comforts easily dull the sensitivity of our soul life. We may be engaged in some kind of work or profession that seems to involve the virtue of compassion. When we are with the people in times of serving, we may even feel emotional compassion. But unless we are changed in our own soul life through what we experience, the compassion has remained on the side of emotion only; it was only a momentary reaction. The spiritual side of the virtue takes longer to work into the life of the soul, and cannot do so if the soul is numbed through comforts.

As the movement from the more emotional dimension of compassion to its more spiritual dimension takes place, a feeling of conflict arises. As we move from the soul and toward the spirit, an unbalanced spirit orientation can make us feel guilt concerning the way we live, as if compassion is not possible unless we also change our relation to the way we live and work as did Irwin Vassavada. The result is that the things and comforts we possess begin to be viewed in a literal manner as standing in the way of experiencing the spirit aspect of others because adherence to having things can dull our sensibilities.

From the point of view of spirit, it seems necessary to relinquish things in order to practice compassion. If we notice how our balance is going overboard, however, it is possible to adhere to the imaginative side of soul life while refraining from getting caught in the emotional side, which does not mean shutting off emotion or feeling, but being able to hold emotion while being present to spirit. If the imaginative side of soul life can be retained, then we come to a different sense of a necessary condition for the practice of compassion.

We do not have to literally give up our comforts in order to feel compassion for others, but we do have to give up any inner *hold* they might have on us. This condition, needed for the practice of compassion, is something, then, that has to be done over and over again. If we live imaginatively, in soul, but soul that is reaching toward spirit, then relinquishing comforts, a necessity in order to be able to feel compassion, becomes ongoing inner work, not something necessarily literalized. We have to continually release the hold things have on us, not necessarily let go of things.

How we work through the manner in which we live the soul path of virtue and still remain connected and engaged with the world is something to be considered by each individual. There are no rules saying that it has to be done in one way. However, it would be false to suggest that the soul path of virtue is something that can be simply added on to the way that we live without it bringing out major changes in our existence. I do not wish to suggest that people go out and change their lives in order to engage in virtue. Rather, I suggest taking up attention to virtue as living in harmony with the whole of the Earth and cosmos and then watching with great interest how life changes. It will change. Of all of the virtues, it is perhaps the virtue of compassion that will launch the biggest changes of our lives.

Compassion has enormous strength. Through it, we can meet any and all suffering, no matter how great, and not be defeated. It can take someone who has, through their suffering, been removed from the community of humanity and bring them back, heal them, make them whole again. Think, for example of Saint Francis of Assisi, a true knight of compassion.

In the medieval world of Saint Francis, people found to have leprosy were taken through an elaborate religious ceremony that, in effect, removed them from the human world. The discovered leper was brought into the hospital chapel and forced to kneel before the altar. The priest then performed a ceremony of separation, saying to the leper:

> My brother, dear poor little man of the good God, by means of great sadness and tribulation, of sickness, of leprosy, and of many other miseries, one gains the kingdom of heaven, where there is no sickness or sorrow, and all is pure and white, without stain, more brilliant than the Sun. You will go there, if it pleases God. In the meantime, be a good Christian, bear with patience this adversity, and God will be merciful to you.

The people responded:

> My bones tremble, my soul loses its way. Alleluia.
> Have mercy on us, O Lord. Keep us from evil.

The priest then said:

> My brother, take this cloak and put it on as a sign of
> humility and never leave here without it. In the name of
> the Father, the Son, and the Holy Spirit.

Francis lived in this environment, and like Siddartha, was the son of a wealthy individual. One day, as he was riding near a hospital on his way to one of his father's estates, his horse suddenly shied, and Francis saw a leper standing directly in front of his path. As though drawn by a power he could not resist, he dismounted, walked up to the leper, and took his hand into his own. He pressed a gold piece into the palm of his hand and gazed into the man's face. He embraced the man, and kissed him. Francis did not understand his own actions. When Francis looked up, the man was no longer there. He had vanished. Francis had opened his heart to what, until then, he had rejected with utmost horror. In that single instant of meeting this man, a new quality was born in Francis, the quality of compassion.

Francis continued to work with the lepers. Compassion was so strong in him that many lepers were healed simply by being in his presence. They were healed because they came to the self-knowledge that they too belonged to the wholeness of creation. The compassion of Saint Francis brought them to be able to experience that. Here we have an image of the strength of compassion. With Saint Francis, we are given a way of understanding the source of this strength. The form and structure of *The Canticle of the Creatures*, an exquisite lyric poem by Saint Francis, reveals the source of the strength of compassion. First, the poem:

The Power of Soul

The Canticle of the Creatures

Most High, all power, all good, Lord!
    All praise is yours, all glory, all honor
    And all blessing.
To you alone, Most High, do they belong.
    No mortal lips are worthy
    To pronounce your name.
All praise be yours, my Lord, through all that you have made,
    And first my lord Brother Sun,
    Who brings the day; and light you give to us through him.
How beautiful is he, how radiant in all his splendor!
    Of you, Most High, he bears the likeness.
All praise be yours, my Lord, through Sisters Moon and Stars,
    In the heavens you have made them,
    Bright and precious and fair.
All praise be yours, my Lord, through Brothers Wind and Air,
    All fair and stormy, all the weather's moods,
    By which you cherish all that you have made.
All praise be yours, my Lord, through Sister Water,
    So useful, lowly, precious and pure.
All praise be yours, my Lord, through Brother Fire,
    Through whom you brighten up the night.
    How beautiful is he, how gay! Full of power and strength.
All praise be yours, my Lord, through Sister Earth, our mother,
    Who feeds us in her sovereignty and produces
    Various fruit with colored flowers and herbs.
All praise be yours, my Lord, through those who grant pardon,
    For Love of you; through those who endure
    Sickness and trial.
Happy those who endure in peace,
    By you, Most High, they will be crowned.
All praise be yours, my Lord, through Sister Death,
    From whose embrace no mortal can escape.
Woe to those who die in mortal sin!
    Happy those She finds doing your will!
    The second death can do no harm to them.
Praise and bless my Lord, and give him thanks,
    And serve him with great humility.

In this simple and beautiful poem we see the extent, the depth and the height of the imagination of Saint Francis. Here we have an extension of compassion by another initiate of compassion who stands as equal with Siddartha. Something new is brought in. We experience in *The Canticle of Creatures* an intimacy on the part of Saint Francis with the whole of the cosmos, from the farthest reaches of the galaxy to the smallest of creatures.

There is a tendency, because of the Buddhist understanding of compassion, to connect compassion with detachment. Then Saint Francis comes along and says, in effect, that if we understand compassion that way we would be mistaken. Detachment is not what Siddartha meant. Rather, full engagement is necessary for compassion, but it has to be more than engagement with the suffering individual. It has to be full engagement with the whole of creation, felt through and through as personal, as living. Each and every thing of the universe is our friend, and each of us is friend to the universe. The healing of compassion invites the dispossessed back and puts Siddartha and Saint Francis alongside each other.

We have to realize that Saint Francis did not think all of these things out through logic. He was present, in soul, to this fullness, and it is this imaginative fullness that gives compassion its healing power. When, for example, a leper was excluded from the human community, that meant that it was not possible for the people in general to imagine a person with such a disease as belonging to the human world. The compassion of Saint Francis was able to look upon such a person and see this person as belonging with the whole of creation. Such seeing, again, was not intellectual knowing, but a deep emotional-spiritual realization, one with great power that healed the ill person.

Finally, we can consider some of the expressive characteristics of enacting the virtue of compassion. Knowing something of how this virtue expresses through the person can be helpful because we can also get a glimpse of how the virtue can be easily thwarted. There is, for example, something aristocratic and royal about the compassionate person. In the stories of Siddhartha and Saint Francis, we see how royalty was central to their lives. When they opened to the path of compassion, this royalty to which they belonged did not disappear, but took on a spiritualized form. Compassion is a kingly and a queenly virtue. It is majestic. The task given to those practicing compassion is to remain within the soul-spirit practice when devotion comes their way, when they find themselves being treated like royalty. The moment such devotion becomes expected, the virtue is lost.

The person of compassion is also characterized by calm composure and poise, a serenity that can look like detachment but is actually an imaginative engagement rather than simply a reacting to suffering or horror, that looks like engagement but is a way of gaining distance. This composure is a radiating of the very joy of life itself. The heart is all-embracing. However, these same attributes can be used to win approval and praise, a love of honor for its own sake. The truth-seeing essence of compassion can thus be lost, for if we need honor, we are subject to all sorts of lies and flattery. Thus, a second task involved in the practice of compassion is to be conscious enough to refrain from using the qualities of this virtue for one's own purposes, to remain the servant and not turn into the politician. The person who practices compassion has to learn to stand alone.

Lust for vanity, for honor, for praise, for power, are the shadow qualities that have to be encountered when entering the path of the virtue of compassion. The virtue of discernment comes along as the help here, as well as patience, both good antidotes for the fiery heat of untempered compassion, which so quickly turns into the exercise of power.

These warnings concerning the possible ways in which compassion can be thwarted show us something about the nature of virtue itself. All of the virtues have their shadow side. The practice of each of the virtues certainly involves confronting their shadow aspects. But even more, the shadow aspects can come to dominate only when we imagine that we have mastered the virtue, or have come to the point where it seems to be a habit in our lives. Each virtue is a creative act.

Thus, we are off the mark when we think that we *have* compassion, or *have* courage, or *have* patience, or *have* any of the virtues. They are not to be *had*, but, in each and every instance, to be *created*, at the precise moment each is needed, according to the circumstances necessary at that moment.

7 **The Virtue of Courtesy**

In relation to the other virtues, courtesy may seem to stand almost as something secondary, a behavior that does not seem at an equal level with the other virtues. In comparison to courage, or love, or compassion, courtesy seems close to trivial. In some ways, courtesy is indeed quite small. This quality of seeming cosmically insignificant may actually make courtesy one of the most important of the virtues; it introduces us into the small way, the way of little things rather than large, high, and lofty imaginations.

Courtesy adds an extremely important tone to the whole of the circle of virtue; it keeps our imagination from soaring into heights that have nothing to do with our daily lives, or our ongoing relationships with others, or the mundane events that, in truth, occupy us most of the time. Courtesy is the virtue that removes the illusion of loftiness that can infect our imagination of the virtues and locates their action in the heart of the smallest deeds of our lives.

All virtue, we might say, begins with the declaration, "Be courteous to one another." This act holds together the extraordinary with the commonplace, and the performance of it places everyone within the great circle of the virtues. Thus, it is an act worth looking into, worth contemplating and meditating upon to see its essential character. Further, it is an act worthy of learning how to do in proper and healthy ways. If we find it difficult to approach another person with reverence, then certainly the performance of the other virtues will be impossible.

We cannot get along with each other very well without the help of some intervening forms that make our connections with others have an ease about them, bringing moments of pleasure into the functional and mundane aspects of life, and smoothing the rough spots where the possibility of friction occurs. When courtesy is absent, rules have to be introduced to do the work of the virtue. For example, in the functional world of our work, there are generally outer constraints that dictate what kind of behaviors toward others are deemed acceptable, and which are not. Corporations, businesses, schools, and even charitable enterprises now promote internal training that has to do with treating others with the proper respect. These trainings concern matters such as racial relationships, sexual conduct, and customer relations.

The presence of such training indicates the absence of the virtue of courtesy in the world. We are not brought up with an education into the ways of this virtue. While the gestures of trying to add an education into manners later on in life are certainly important and often do a great deal to change attitudes and prejudices, they are finally inadequate substitutes for far deeper soul qualities. Further, since these gestures take the form of training, of "how to do it" workshops, they easily degrade into a kind of conditioning reliant on external pressures or external rewards for their continuance after the training ceases.

Courtesy concerns something more than a code of behavior. When a code of behavior tries to stand in for the deeper qualities of the virtue, it is easy to tell that the deeper qualities of soul life have not been touched. A kind of overlay of proper actions can be perceived, while the depth of the persons practicing the code remains veiled. In a place of work, for example, you can readily tell when people have been instructed in how to behave. They all perform their instructions quite well, and an outer respect toward others is evident, but it has the quality of turning the people into abstract functionaries. A place of work where training into how to behave has occurred exudes a very eerie quality because the spirit of the people has often been effectively shut off, or only shows up in the tiniest of ways, through a mechanical-like covering. People of many races, sexes, backgrounds, and histories may seem to be working together wonderfully, but there is a plastic look about them, or they all take on the "look" of the enterprise for which they work.

If we observe the ways in which something like the virtue of courtesy enters the world these days, it becomes evident that this virtue cannot be enacted in a collective way that has little or nothing to do with the individuality of the persons involved. Often, two layers of covering can be perceived; there is what might be called the corporate layer, where people take on the "look" of the enterprise they work for. Then, on top of this first collective layer, a second layer often consists of the evidence that the people have been through some abstract training concerning how to behave to stay within the bounds of the laws of the workplace. The perception of these coverings can be quite alarming, because often nothing can be seen beneath the surface of these imposed behaviors.

More and more frequently these days, we see the dire results of trying to live and work together in ways that bury the individual expressions of soul and spirit. When expressions of individuality are obscured, psychological pathologies are created. In their mildest form, the soul maladies are expressed as ongoing stress, gradually entering the body as diseases such as heart attack or ulcers or anxiety. In their strongest forms these pathologies are expressed as violence in the workplace—a person coming back after having given up his or her soul for a job for many years, and shooting everyone in sight, or threatening some kind of violence toward the impersonal nature of the workplace.

While these observations focus on the way in which a substitute for the virtue of courtesy is enacted in the world of work, it is not hard to see that a similar substitution goes on in many other aspects of daily life. Codes of conduct are enforced in schools, from kindergarten to college. In spite of laws, forms of courtesy in relation to driving are becoming more and more difficult to enforce. Codes of conduct also govern public gatherings such as city council meetings and community gatherings. Such codes, no matter where they are found, are important and necessary. The difficulty stems from the fact that, more and more, such outer codes have come to replace the individual virtue of courtesy. The lack of this virtue cannot be filled in by regulation, and as this substitution occurs, collective behavior replaces individual care.

A cynic might respond that it makes no difference whether good behavior toward others occurs as a matter of outer rules or inner desire; the result is, after all, the same—an orderly social realm. I have already given a picture above of how collective conformity differs in kind and essence from individual initiative. I have known several places of work, small to be sure, where courtesy rather than codes of behavior governed the interactions of the people. From on onlooker's point of view, such places look unruly and chaotic. Seen from within, however, as long as there was an ideal that the place stood for, people there were far more effective and creative than in a "socially governed" setting. Such places are the exception.

Organizations of every kind—from the large corporation to the nonprofit service organization—tend to fear individuality, and certainly will not let go or loosen their sense of the need for collective rules of conduct. Thus, I want to first give a phenomenological description of the virtue of courtesy, one that will bring out what this virtue brings into the world that can never be present through outer organization alone.

We do not act alone, and the spheres of our interactions with others often collide. Friction inevitably results, and often irritation and anger. Our individual purposes seldom, if ever, exactly match those of others, and we find ourselves at cross-purposes even when we seem to have the same ideals or the same goals, and even when we work together with others in order to be of service to the world. Is it not highly interesting that our first impulse is not to fall into line with each other and carry out our tasks? For such behavior to occur, to simply and spontaneously act cooperatively, whatever constitutes individuality would have to be forgotten or ignored. In contrast to the collective cooperation visible in creatures such as ants or bees, we quickly make a mess of cooperative action by asserting our uniqueness into whatever we do.

This characteristic individuality of expression, which constitutes an essential dimension of being human, does not have to do merely with egotism, getting what I want at the expense of others, though it can go in that direction quite easily. At a deeper level, what is being expressed is a living out of the problem of how we each can fulfill our individual destiny in the midst of others who are trying to do the same, coupled with the fact that each person's destiny is unique. How can we do this together?

Courtesy enters when the plight of finding our destiny in the midst of others who are doing likewise can be felt. The virtue concerns recognizing and honoring something beyond someone else's egotism. When we are truly courteous and not just enacting a social habit, we are doing something more than stepping back so that the other person's ego can shine. What that "something more" consists of, however, has to be looked for; it is not immediately apparent. Actually, we have to develop a certain capacity for seeing this "something more" in advance of what and how the other person presents himself or herself. If I see others only in their most outer aspects, then I only see the ego dimension of the person. When I step back to give the ego dimension of the other person more room for self-display, this cannot be called courtesy.

Everything that was said earlier concerning rules of conduct concerns setting up the conditions under which people can work and be together in proximity and live in a social manner while at the same time have a healthy sense of the ego level of soul life. The regulated life allows for the multitudes to associate and receive a certain degree of consideration from each other. The regulated life allows us to perform our tasks with minimal hindrance; it, however, goes no deeper than ego and the recognition of ego-identity.

How does courtesy differ from mere good social conduct? The will to give others room has to originate freely from within our soul for an action to be one of courtesy. It is not something demanded or even expected. Courtesy goes beyond being a social form. We have the capacity to recognize the good in others, and it is this quality of the good that we honor in courtesy. The good that we recognize does not have anything to do with what the person has done. That kind of honor does not require very much in the way of perceptual capacities.

If one has done an honorable deed, is recognized for some accomplishment, or holds a station of honor, then courtesy takes place readily and easily. It is not quite so easy to approach a stranger on the street and treat that person in the same manner as one would treat an honorable public figure. It is even more difficult to treat someone at work in this fashion when perhaps we feel in competition with that person, or feel irritated when we are forced to work together.

To honor someone, in effect, is to bow before that person. The word "courtesy" originated as a term describing proper behavior at court, before royalty. It was recognized that a person holding a position of royalty was an earthly representative of something larger, something of a divine nature. For a long time the royal person was considered divine. Later in history, the person was not considered divine, but the office was. To bow before the royal person was recognizing the holy office of that person. Now, in our time, to express courtesy toward another person requires recognizing the soul-being of the person. We step back, hold ourselves back, in order that the soul-being that is the other person be given room for expression. For the act to be the virtue of courtesy and not just an outward behavior, however, it is necessary that we be able to perceive the soul-being of the other person.

Stating the central concern for the starting place of courtesy as the capacity to recognize the soul-being of another person poses a certain difficulty concerning the nature of soul life. In the tradition of depth psychology, soul is considered only in its form as the factor in-forming individual existence. Indeed, this notion of soul—as a wholly individual factor of existence—can be found in every philosophy, from Plato through Aristotle, Aquinas, Descartes, on up to the present. Thus, the imagination of soul as wholly individual is very strong.

The study of the psyche—from which we get the word "psychology"—however, was not originally considered the center of the self, the center of personality. For example, in the *Iliad* of Homer, psyche (*psukhe*) meant "breath," which referred to life and to soul. The psyche was the soul *breathed into* the person by the life and love of others—by family, by tribe, and by those for whom the psyche was to be responsible, ultimately by the Spirit of the universe. This sense of the psyche is understood by Jung's psychology and its later developments in archetypal psychology as soul breathed into human beings by the gods. But the early usage went further, and included other persons. Psyche was a gift from others. Only later did the psyche come to mean the center of the private personality.

The sense of our soul as being generated by others, and the soul of others being generated by the treating of them as soul presences, is central to the deepest sense of the virtue of courtesy. We cannot get to a soul sense of courtesy by starting with the imagination of the soul as private, unconnected with others. It is one's soul, when truly open to the other person, that breathes the life of soul into the other person. Soul is not self-generated, nor is soul wholly a generation of the gods, or in more modern psychological parlance, generated exclusively by the archetypes.

The metaphor that soul is "breathed" into others conveys the sense that our soul life is not self-generated. I do not make my own soul, nor do I activate my own soul. The inherent good of the other person brings out the soul-being that characterizes my individuality, and this is something we, in turn, do for others. The gift of soul occurs only through relationships that are open and loving. This gifting of soul, however, can be lost.

We can become utterly forgetful of this level of our existence and proceed in our relationships with each other without a semblance of soul. When we become forgetful of this level of existence as a culture, law and regulation have to then stand in for the respect that otherwise would be there on its own accord. We cannot restore this level of existence directly, because it is not under our direct control. We can, however, become aware of the conditions under which the soul life that is generated between ourselves and others takes place. Courtesy is one of these primary conditions.

As with all the virtues, it is important to imagine courtesy not as something added on in exterior fashion to who we are as human beings, but as a quality essential to being human in the first place. This imagination, this attitude of realizing there are qualities essential to our remaining human, is even more critical for courtesy than for the other virtues since it is so easy to take

111

courtesy to be a bit of social refinement, something that makes life more enjoyable, more bearable, and in the present world, something belonging to the elite. We have to first work to rid ourselves of this commonplace notion of courtesy.

The act of courtesy makes the space, the psychic room, for perception of the soul-being that is the other person, and simultaneously for the expression of soul-being by the other person. But what does this mean? Courtesy strives to keep conceptual understandings of the other person at bay. Typically, we do not see, are not truly present to others in their utter otherness. We perceive others through, by means of, conceptual understanding, though we are not aware of doing so.

We see someone as, for example, a teacher, or a mother, or a child, or a boss, a lover, a friend—any number of innumerable categories that bring some kind of order to our perceptions. This ordering, which occurs without our realizing it, hides, covers, veils the mystery that is the other person. This ordering gives us a sense of knowing the person, where knowing something about the person stands in as a substitute for knowing the person. Knowing the person directly and with immediacy, actually, is not possible—at least in the usual sense of what we mean by knowing. Actual knowing of the other person consists of coming into the ineffable space of mystery.

Initially, we can imagine courtesy in this way: we give the other person the space to be present as unknowable, uncomprehendable, uncontrollable, and unconsumable. We cannot approach the other person in this manner from the place of our ordinary ego consciousness. This consciousness immediately categorizes, seeks to seize a certain degree of control, a certain degree of power, and to retain self-identity. This last point is essential, for it suggests that if we are present to the essential unknowableness of the other person, we, at the same moment, cast ourselves into the same realm of being unknowable, even to ourselves.

This notion of entering into a relationship with another, in which the other is essentially unknowable and at the same time so are we, may seem a far cry from what we think of as ordinary acts of courtesy. To hold a door open for someone, to step back and let another speak instead of immediately stepping in to fill the space, to be, for a moment, wholly oriented toward the other—all this seems to have very little to do with this deeper ground of the mystery of the other person. If these acts are carried out simply on the basis of having learned "good manners," then, certainly, the depth of experience possible in the act of courtesy is missed. If, though, in the midst of such simple acts, it is possible to let that split-second moment of doing something for another with kindness open up for us, then much more can be perceived as going on in the simplest of interactions.

The quality of courtesy, understood in this deep way as the perception of the mystery of the other person, in our time, seems wholly superfluous. In life determined by science, technology, functionality, and material objects, proceeding directly to the matter at hand seems primary. No time for qualities that seem to have no functional purpose. Time cannot be squandered basking in the mystery of others or of ourselves. No time for such luxury.

Courtesy cannot be argued for in terms of how it might benefit us. We are too skilled in knowing how to go about satisfying our own needs and comforts to relinquish these skills even a little to give honor to the soul-being of others when there is nothing in it for us. I do not mean or intend to put forth a cynical view, but simply want to keep in mind the actual circumstances of present cultural life and the enormity of what is being asked by even suggesting that courtesy requires putting our self-concerns aside. While there may be no benefit to us for attempting to hold back ourselves, there is, I believe, a basic and fundamental desire to do so, and this needs to be explored.

Courtesy celebrates the fundamental dignity of the person, of what it is to be a person. We defer our own affairs for a moment, not to dignify the affairs of the other person but to honor the person as a person. Courtesy operates, however, according to different laws than the laws of functional life. Courtesy takes detours, it squanders time, it lingers, it delays, it engages in the extravagant, the superfluous. Courtesy takes these detours because life itself, in its essence, consists of these seemingly extraneous qualities. Life never goes directly from A to B. Life itself is more like the movements of a ritual, an improvised ritual, where each and every thing we do is highly meaningful, highly symbolic, but it may seem as if we are wandering around, lost.

Try to think, to imagine, how our soul-being must have a difficult time with existence in this world. For, after all, soul has its home in the spiritual world; there soul knows how to navigate, how to get around. Here, no matter how long soul has inhabited our body and the world, there must be a feeling of strangeness. When someone shows us the smallest act of courtesy, it is as if our soul, for a moment, feels relaxed, comforted, recognized as a spiritual being just a little bit lost; in fact, in this highly materialistic world, soul must be constantly confused. Courtesy says, even for just a moment, "I recognize who you are. Welcome to this world. I am deeply honored by your presence here. I thank you for your sacrifice of coming into the world. You bring a sense of the holy, which makes me feel whole and complete and reminds me that I too am a soul-being." This is courtesy as everyday reverence, as religion without walls.

Without everyday reverence, our democratic life in which everything has the quality of being basically the same as everything else is nothing more than imposed order holding back chaos, which tries to erupt every moment, to revolt in the wings. Remember the Greek tragedy, the *Bacchae* of Euripides. This play takes place in a world overcontrolled by structure. Pentheus, the king, is all order and structure, and the result of this overlay of rigidity is that Dionysus breaks through and demands to be honored. As levity, renewal, and regeneration have been kept out of the Saturnian order of doing things by the book, by the law, Dionysus returns with revenge, bringing violence, blood, and chaos. Life without the virtue of courtesy—courtesy felt in this deep manner and not just as a superficial, clean style of behavior existing at the same level of other functionality—becomes more and more structured, holding off the radical forces of renewal and regeneration.

Here, then, with the imagination of renewal and regeneration, we begin to have a sense of what the world of courtesy offers to us. What seems to be a deviation from getting on with things, with efficiency, productivity, and product, actually is what is most necessary for experiencing life in all its complexities and levels.

To understand the depth of courtesy, it is necessary to realize that this virtue, not unlike the other virtues, is not something that we bring preformed into situations and then put into operation. Because the nature of courtesy so vividly involves the presence of the other person, this virtue amplifies for us something concerning the essential character of all of the virtues—we develop them not as habits but rather as *capacities* of our being.

The difference between a capacity and a habit lies in the fact that the former exists only as a kind of schemata, an orientation, an open possibility, while the latter consists of a specified content. We can be taught the contents of manners—what to do in the presence of a lady, how to sit at a table, when to speak and not speak. These contents, when learned, form a habit of action that makes relationships take on a certain beauty. Courtesy does not consist of such predetermined contents we then bring to situations. We can develop a capacity for courtesy, which is the capacity to be present to, to face the ineffable otherness of, the other. When the mystery of the other person opens to us, courtesy is present. The forms that the virtue takes are not therefore predetermined but will be exactly right for the moment of such openings.

Here is an example. The other day I drove to town to go to the post office, which I often do. This day, however, the first real evidence of spring was showing. The sky was a pure, deep blue, a blue going into infinity. In early morning three large turkeys strutted in our front yard. When the largest of the birds walked in the sun, its feathers shimmered with copper. As soon as they left, a red fox appeared, repeatedly jumping for its tail, thinking, I suppose, that it was some other creature. A golden finch walked through the grass. All of this beauty was already in my imagination as I got to town. Walking up the steps of the post office, I breathed in the beauty of the day. An elderly man was coming out the front door, and out of habit I stepped back and held the door for him. He looked directly at me, right in the eyes, and said a simple, "Thank you." His manner of expression took me aback, made me present to the moment. It was not my holding the door for him that was the act of courtesy; it was his "thank you" that was courtesy in operation.

In that split second his "otherness" broke through, disassembling the imagination that I was living in, making it possible to experience, for a moment, the wonderful strangeness, not of the stranger, but of the soul-being that is this person. His ruddy face, his curly gray hair, his gentle, gruff manner, his blue eyes that were even deeper than the blue of the sky that day, still live on within me. Strange the effect of this person whom I do not know, but whom I met in a moment of *his* courtesy.

Is courtesy reserved for moments of intrusion into the ongoing functionality of our lives, or can this virtue be extended in time? Perhaps we should not be greedy, hoping for the possibility of living extended moments in the atmosphere of courtesy. On the other hand, the kind of instances we are most familiar with are perhaps no more than impressionistic scenes of a world we can enter more fully once we discover the discipline needed to keep the door open.

What, then, is the discipline or the practice of courtesy? It seems that it is a matter of becoming more and more able to be present to what is going on that is other than the immediate content of what is going on. I do not mean looking behind or beneath what happens, as if something is hidden that has to be exposed. This kind of imagination invites us to be interpreters of our daily relationships with others, which removes us even further from the immediacy of the moment. No, what goes on in the presence of another person besides the content is to be found right there, in the visible. But in order to find ourselves present beyond the content requires what at first may seem a rather strange, even disagreeable, attitude on our part. We must freely take up a radically receptive stance toward others—one in which, in effect, we become hostage to the other person.

We can be radically open to the other person only by forgetting ourselves, by giving ourselves over to the other person, but in a very particular way, a way in which by giving ourselves over we do not lose ourselves but find ourselves. I mean to imply this particular kind of giving over when suggesting the necessity of becoming hostage to the other person in an act of courtesy.

116

By losing ourselves, I in no way mean losing our consciousness. In fact, an intensification of consciousness occurs. I also do not mean becoming egoless. Rather, by becoming hostage to the other person, I mean that we come into radical proximity to the other person in the act of courtesy. In this position of radical proximity, the goodness of the other person calls out the act of courtesy in recognition of the goodness of this being. I do not think about it in advance. I do not self-generate the act; it is called out of me, but only under this condition of radical proximity. Of course, this kind of act can and does become schematized into language, concept, and formal behavior. Then, however, courtesy is on the way to becoming a habit and from there to being excluded altogether.

The key term to expand, and to try to describe something of its practice, is "radical proximity." We do not, in fact, go out of ourselves, leave ego behind, as it were, and find ourselves more or less merged with the other person. Radical proximity is where we are, how we are, the very activity of our soul-being in its usual and ordinary state. Radical proximity is the primary condition of being a soul-being in the world-with-others. It is not a matter of practicing radical proximity per se but rather practicing being present to this primary level of soul-being. To be in soul in the presence of others is courtesy.

The best access to the experience of radical proximity may be to engage in those formal acts of courtesy that take the form of good social manners. However, it is necessary to bring a new quality of consciousness to those acts. Think of these ordinary acts of courtesy as magical acts that make radical proximity appear, not as something we can know, but as a sensible, tangible reality, a bodily knowing occurring before the self-reflective act of knowing. The simple reality is that courtesy concerns some bodily action whose meaning lies completely in the action itself. The act of courtesy does not in itself intend to accomplish anything. In fact, it is an act that moves against the notion of accomplishing anything. Courtesy is not something that brings about an honoring of the other person; it is that honoring. So, it is only in the act itself that we can experience the radical proximity of the other; again, the act does not bring about this proximity, it exposes it.

117

The formal acts of courtesy, the good manners, which we can indeed practice and learn, can be thought of as the secondary act of courtesy, the outer motions, that can, if done in an attitude and an imagination of openness, expose the primary act of courtesy, a letting-be-present of the soul-being of the other in radical proximity with our own soul-being. What is exposed is not that there are two soul-beings, but rather that there are two beings-in-soul. The doing of courtesy and the receiving of courtesy are the two necessary polarities for exposing the most radical fact that soul is not first and foremost "in us" each individually, whole and complete, but that we both together are in-soul.

The act of courtesy exposes the scandal that soul is present only when two or more are together, really together, in radical proximity. It is a kind of scandal to recognize this ontological ground of soul. We are accustomed to holding the view that soul individualizes us, that it is the factor that makes us each uniquely who we are. To imagine that this sense of soul depends on the presence of others can appear scandalous. Are we not, potentially at least, whole and complete in ourselves? There is also a way in which soul is indeed individual, but this more commonplace sense of soul is "soul within soul." We have to exist with others, in soul, before we can experience the individuality of our soul. What has been described here as the act of courtesy is the soul that is necessary for individual soul.

A clear example of what I mean might be seen in the work of psychotherapy. If we put aside notions of problem-solving, or trying to get to the root of someone's problems, and look at the act of therapy itself, we have a good picture of courtesy extended in time. Through radical proximity with another person, being-in-soul is discovered, which leads to the possibility of coming to one's individual soul. It is interesting, indeed, to reframe psychotherapy, putting it under the rubric of courtesy.

If I am forever analyzing, it is impossible to engage in courtesy. On the way to courtesy—as, for example, with psychotherapy—it is quite possible to get stuck in analyzing. In daily life, this kind of intellectuality takes other forms. In relation with others, for example, I might get stuck in wondering what is the right thing to do: should I do this for the other person, or should I do that? What would be the best thing?

I said above that courtesy concerned the little way. However, this little way has to be carried out with imagination; if it is not, little becomes literalized and falls into characteristics of fastidiousness and concern over detail. These are certainly positive characteristics, but only when accompanied by a sense of wholeness. Otherwise, courtesy becomes a plethora of empty manners, a concern for doing things right rather than doing things compassionately.

This smallest of virtues, courtesy, turns out to be the virtue that makes virtues a matter of communal soul concern. Without this virtue, the practice of all of the virtues would be oriented only toward one's individual soul development, having little to do with or concern for others. With the other virtues, there is indeed a strong sense of communal quality. When we do experience that communal quality, it is the reverberating of the radical nature of courtesy.

8 **The Virtue of Equanimity**

What is it like to be perfectly balanced in the realm of emotions? Typically, our emotional responses are one-sided. We are either happy or sad, angry or glad, exuberant or withdrawn. When we are not bouncing between these polarities it is because emotion is hardly present at all. Equanimity does not mean absence of emotional quality. It does not mean feeling the same all the time, neither hot nor cold. Nor does equanimity mean a mixture of emotions from either side of the polarity—a little bit of anger mixed with just the right amount of love with a dash of joy thrown in for seasoning.

Equanimity also cannot be imagined as the point of balance between polarities that are established in advance. If something wonderful happens and we feel overjoyed, to find equanimity in our joy does not mean to balance this feeling with just the right amount of sadness, because we know that to let one emotion dominate would be a loss of equanimity. Such a view would require that we have within us a quantity of every emotion and that we could learn to draw upon the right one at just the moment needed to bring balance. To be able to draw up emotions in this manner would require taking a standpoint outside of our soul life, being detached observers of our own emotions, mixing them to the right proportions.

Many spiritual practices place equanimity at the top of the list of attributes necessary for spiritual development. These practices often speak of equanimity as if it is something that can be controlled through our will. It is spoken of as something that we can come to by modifying the extremes of our emotions. We do have to find equanimity, but it is not the result of alteration of other emotions. It has its own soul life independent of other emotional qualities.

It is helpful to remember an actual instance of a strong emotional experience. Suppose I am at work and I have asked someone to do a task. When this person comes back three days later and shows what was done, suppose I find that the task was done incorrectly. A flame of anger arises within me. What would make it possible to feel the force of this anger and yet not be taken over by the anger and explode at my colleague? The object of virtue here would not simply be to refrain from anger in order to keep good social relations, but to see that in this surging up of anger there resides a bit of unrefined material that can be transformed into a spiritual gift. If I can feel the anger as a force freed from using it to be hurtful to the other person, if it can become a force for exuberant engagement with the other person that helps us focus on the needed task, and if it can also be a force for the sharpening of thinking, then I am on the way to equanimity.

In a work situation, particularly with our supervisor, we learn quickly not to explode, but what usually occurs is suppression of the anger, which then shows itself in all sorts of indirect ways. Suppression of anger is possible by applying the force of thought to what we experience. In this example, I may feel the force of anger, but at the same time I am thinking that I may lose my job if I let this anger explode, or that I will be seen as an inadequate leader, or any number of other dire thoughts. The thought alone cannot push the anger down. This must be done by an act of will, but it is an act of will stemming from the thought. Suppression of an emotion can outwardly look like equanimity. There are differences, though, perceptible even in the countenance. A person who is suppressing an emotion looks emotionless, flat, almost psychotic. Equanimity does not look flat, for it is not an absence. The person of equanimity bears a countenance of buoyancy accompanied with an inner light that shines from the soul, lighting the eyes, expressed as engaged interest in all that one encounters.

From this picture of working with anger in an unhealthy way, by willful suppression, we get a better picture of what equanimity requires. How do you come to it? If you are seeking this virtue, where inwardly do you look, and how?

Equanimity concerns balancing the relationships among emotion, thought, and will. We have to try to feel the connections among all these to be able to feel into equanimity. It is not an emotion alone, or a thought about an emotion; nor can it be simply an act of will. We cannot directly alter our emotions, for there is almost no freedom in the realm of emotion. Once an emotion is present, it is something that we go through, whether the emotion is pleasant or unpleasant. Our emotions have us, we do not have them. It is probably not possible to establish equanimity from within an emotional experience itself. The practice of this virtue involves consciously coming to be able to establish the right relationships among emotion, thinking, and will.

When emotion takes us over, it is as if it functions separately from thinking and from our will, and in fact, at that moment controls both. A healthy respect for the force of emotion is the beginning of equanimity. Emotion is the life force of the soul. We do not and cannot control life. We are simply in it. Thus, there is the constant background of the life force of emotion. It is always there and can always come to the surface in powerful ways. No amount of spiritual development takes away this life force of the soul. Any spiritual path or work that purports to rid us of emotion is dangerous because it mistakes suppression and repression for freedom from this oceanic tide that constantly brings us into the life of life.

We can readily recognize when thinking predominates, when the force of thinking seems to dominate even our emotional life. We call it "being in the head." We readily recognize when someone is taken over by the will, which expresses itself as dominating, controlling, and being in power. So these three functions of the soul can and do separate and go their own way. In ordinary life, when it is not so possible to see that one function predominates over the other, then all three are more or less mixed together. This mixing together of emotion, thinking, and will is not equanimity.

Equanimity does not consist of balancing these three soul functions so that no one of them gets the upper hand. The mixing together of these three soul functions has the result of keeping us on an even keel, but it also means that we do not realize when our thinking is being dictated by our emotions, or when our emotions are being held in check by our thinking, or when we do something out of sheer will without rational thought or without realizing how willfulness hurts our emotional life. In those times when we are simply functioning and don't seem to be out of balance in any one of these three directions of feeling, thinking, or willing, we are not thereby living in equanimity.

It seems as if equanimity cannot be worked on directly. From what interior place do we have to establish evenness that has within it the quality of buoyancy and spiritual light and interested engagement with others and the world? We can get control over our emotions, but if you have seen someone who has such control, it is evident that this is not the kind of relationship entailed in the virtue we are concerned with here. Perhaps we need to look more carefully into the example presented earlier concerning an instance of anger.

When our emotional response to someone is anger, or for that matter, any strong emotion, our attention is no longer focused on the task at hand. We become totally occupied by the emotion, and even though it seems to have something to do with the situation at hand, it does not. For example, if I start raving at someone who has, according to my evaluation, done something wrong, the raving becomes the focus and what is at hand gets lost. The person on whom I am venting my anger looks at me wondering what in the world has gotten hold of me. We have left the immediacy of what is going on, and now something else has our complete attention.

Equanimity involves being able to hold our attention to what is at hand. I am suggesting that the practice of equanimity first of all concerns developing the powers of attention so that they do not get diverted. If our attention gets focused on the anger, then the anger grows and swells and takes over. So, when anger arises, we can learn to feel the anger and at the same time keep attention focused on what we are engaged with outside of ourselves. This capacity is the beginning of equanimity, but it is not enough to establish it.

We can imagine many situations in which keeping attention focused on the task at hand would not bring about equanimity. The situation may become colored with anger, so thinking must also be brought into consideration. What happens to thinking in a situation that evokes anger? The anger can take over; then thinking disappears. When it comes back, if the anger is still present, our thinking becomes harnessed by the anger, and the intellect is used as the instrument of anger to lash out at others. With other emotions, even pleasant ones, essentially the same thing happens, though with more pleasant emotions we tend not to be able to see that here too our thinking becomes the instrument for the execution of the emotion in an indirect manner.

We can begin to see that individual variations exist and that it is necessary to have insight into each person in order to proceed in developing the virtue of equanimity. One individual may have to work on strengthening capacities of attention so that when a strong emotion rises up, its presence can be felt without taking over. As long as, in the presence of an emotional response, we are able to keep focused on what is before us, the emotion will not take over. For another person, it may be that the power of thinking needs to be strengthened so that through thinking it is possible to gain adequate distance from the press of the emotion without leaving the emotion altogether and hiding in thinking.

What is entailed in strengthening either capacities of attention or capacities of thinking? We might imagine that these capacities are fixed. We think and we attend to one thing or another. That is all there is to it. There does exist some flexibility, though, in our soul capacities. The strong power of emotion can be seen as a kind of gift that can show us that our capacities of thinking or of attention are not equal to that of emotion. Or, if we seem not to be able to have much of an emotional response at all in a situation that is clearly emotional, then it is likely that the capacity of thinking is too strong and we are removed from emotional life. The lack of emotional response may also indicate that we are so focused in our attention on what is going on before us that we do not even notice the presence of emotion.

If it is not possible to either strengthen or moderate attention and thinking, then equanimity cannot be achieved. I am here concerned with the conscious soul life of relatively healthy (psychologically) individuals, in whom there exists the flexibility of soul necessary to modify capacities, at least somewhat. Let us consider thinking first.

By modifying thinking, I do not mean that one works at, say, becoming more intelligent if this capacity shows itself as weak, or becoming less intelligent if this capacity shows itself as being too strong. Rather, I mean that it is of importance to become acquainted with the process, the activity of thinking as it occurs within us. We have to learn how to become aware of the act of thinking itself, which is something different than thinking about things, in order to be able to find equanimity.

To attempt becoming aware of thinking is an interesting process, something that we can do only by looking at thinking as if out of the corner of the eye. We cannot observe the act of thinking directly because the primary characteristic of all consciousness is that consciousness always intends an object. When we think of something, we take the object we are thinking about to be the thinking itself, which is not, strictly speaking, true. The term "intentional" does not have anything to do with willful intent. It is a term that describes the fact that when we think, there is always something that we are thinking about. This object might be something very concrete and practical, as, for example, what food one has to buy at the grocery store; or the object can be something very abstract, such as the nature of a circle. We are aware of what we are thinking about but not of the activity of thinking itself. The activity of thinking is submerged in what we are thinking about.

Suppose that you are in the situation mentioned earlier in which the emotion of anger comes pouring over you at work. You find that you can suppress the anger, but it boils up within. You also notice that when this anger comes like this, for a while it is not possible to think, and when you can, your thinking has become the instrument of your anger and all you have are bad thoughts toward the person. At that moment, try to be aware of the act of thinking itself and not what you are thinking about. You can do

125

this by *noticing* that you are thinking bad thoughts of another person. You don't just take the bad thoughts as the thinking, but you realize that these are *what* you are thinking, but they are not the *act of* thinking.

You can then get a kind of intuitive sense that thinking is creating the object of thought you are focused on. This noticing is not analytical; it is a kind of noticing that takes but a second. That short time is all that it takes to have a sense of the act of thinking. This noticing will not stay, but once you have experienced the act itself you are freed from the emotion of the anger. Being able to shift focus in this manner is a major step toward developing equanimity.

To be able to get a glimpse at the activity of thinking, it may be necessary to do some exercises specifically oriented toward this end. We may have to learn to concentrate on thinking for a while in free situations of meditation before it becomes possible to feel the quality of the thinking act in everyday matters. One way to practice such thinking meditations is to take five minutes each day and inwardly concentrate on a neutral object; for example, picture a pencil. Then begin to form thoughts about the pencil that have to do with the pencil and nothing else—such as its length, its color, what it is made of, how it is used. Continue to think all things connected with the pencil. Then, when that seems exhausted, stop and reside in the emptiness.

This practice, adapted from the spiritual science of Rudolf Steiner, will help in developing the capacity to be present to the act of thinking. We can also practice becoming aware of our thinking in everyday situations, and doing so brings a meditative quality to what we do every day. In this circumstance of anger, for example, in which we have angry thoughts about another person, when such thoughts come, we can go off for a few minutes and think not just about what happened, but about our thinking as it was going on. What will come to light is that our angry thoughts were not thoughts at all; we will see that emotion had taken on the guise of thinking.

Now let's concentrate for a moment on the act of attention, which is the other way in which we get thrown off balance in the presence of a strong emotion. One may also have to work on attention in developing equanimity. In the example we are working with, if anger comes and what seems to happen most strongly is that we lose connection with what we are doing and cannot get back to it quickly, then it is helpful to work with the process of attention. It is likely that it will be necessary to work with both thinking and attention. Of the two, attention functions more subtly. If your attention is distracted by the anger, try as immediately as possible to return your attention to what you were doing. As you do so, you can try to be aware of the act of attention and not just to what we are attending to.

Trying to describe the quality of attention requires language that may seem a bit unusual. When we turn our attention toward something in the world, it is as if something streams out of us and attaches itself to the world. This quality of a kind of force streaming from us can be either narrow and focused, or it can be broad and comprehensive.

We have a great deal of difficulty experiencing the quality of attention because our attention is not very free. Things get our attention, grab it, take it, and once this has happened it is impossible to be aware of the act of attention itself. The situation of captured attention looms particularly strongly in this world of technology, manipulation, media, and consumer consciousness. Thus it takes quite a bit of experimentation to become aware of the current of the force of attention just described. Such experimentation can be done by deliberately focusing on one of the senses as we consciously engage and disengage that sense with something before us. For example, shift your attention from reading to something in the room where you are sitting. Notice how your vision goes out and meets the object. It is something very subtle, but perceptibly present. We do not just receive from the world. We go out and meet it through the act of sensory attention.

Begin with sight. Look at a common object, something that is before you. As I sit here writing, for a moment I glance over at the lamp on the table. I try to be aware of what happens in this act of looking. If I place my concentration more on the act of looking than on what is seen, this subtle current can be felt that moves from the region of my eyes toward the lamp. I do not want to call this current "energy," for that seems to be too quantitative a term for something that is more subtle. This current is so subtle that it is almost immediately submerged by the object that we attend to, and we are thus typically only aware of the object before us and not our bodily relation with the object, with what exists between our body and the object. Once you catch this quality, though, it is unmistakable, and its recognition becomes the way to reestablish your attentional relation with the world when it has been disrupted.

We can practice being aware of this soul current as it functions through other senses besides sight. Hearing, for example, does not consist only of sound entering the ear; a current of attention also can be felt in the region of the ears that goes out and *meets* the sounding object. Similarly, we can be aware of how, with touch, the soul moves out to the periphery of the body to meet the kind of material that we may be touching.

Having experimented with the realm of sensory attention, it becomes possible to notice that when our attention is diverted from what we are doing by the presence of strong emotion, the stream of attention withdraws; it goes inward. Further, we cannot say that now the strong emotion captures our attention. Our relation to our emotions does not have the same quality at all as our attentional relation to some external object.

The difference concerns more than the fact that emotions are internal while sensory objects are in the world. It is much more that when we experience strong emotion, this emotion is not the object of our attention but rather becomes the force of attention itself. You do not have to give attention to a strong emotion; it gives its full and complete attention to you. Due to the way that emotion functions, depth psychology came to speak of the surging up of strong emotion as complexes. This psychology points out to us that emotion has an autonomous character to it; it is as if emotions are living beings. In the presence of such beings we become more the objects of attention than people capable of attending to others or the world.

The usurpation of the capacity of giving attention seems to indicate that working toward equanimity is more difficult coming from this direction than from thinking. We have to be able to come to the point of realizing that other people do not cause our emotions. It is not other people who make us angry, or make us happy for that matter. Other people make us aware of our emotional complexes, not by pointing them out to us or telling us about them, but, in effect, by drawing them out from deep within our soul life for us to experience directly. However, it is certainly not necessary to go into analysis to learn how to retrieve the capacity of attention that is needed to bring about equanimity.

Once an emotion is recognized as having an autonomous character to it, a bit of the capacity of attention returns and becomes available for use. With this bit of attention, now freed up, we turn it to the emotion itself and give it due recognition as an almost independent being within us. Once this occurs, the emotion no longer has its hold so strongly. Then, loosened in this way, more attention is freed up and it is possible to reestablish our attention to what is before us.

This description of the relation between emotion and attention depicts a process that occurs nearly instantaneously. Describing the process required slowing it down, almost like looking at it through a slow motion camera. We do not go through the process described in the linear fashion in which I have just presented it. Rather, I have translated a soul event into language that can be more readily understood. If you work with this description, it will not be what you see when you try to observe your own soul when it lacks equanimity, but it will help you to see what's going on.

We have come to the point of realizing that three soul factors are involved in equanimity: emotion, thinking, and attention; or feeling, thinking, and willing. Think of these three soul qualities as scales trying to come into balance. There are three points to scales: two pans for weighing and the balancing point. We can imagine thinking on one side of the scales, feeling on the other, and attention at the fulcrum point. This image of the scales goes back to the Egyptians, who depicted the weighing of the soul after death. The soul is imagined as being placed on one side of the scale, with a feather on the other side, and if these do not balance, the soul cannot move on to the spiritual realms.

In relation to the virtue of equanimity, the image of the weighing of the soul shows us something even now concerning what we are doing when we engage this virtue. We are working toward a more spiritual activity within our soul. The emotions sit in our soul as heavy lumps, which, from time to time, become active and leap out at us and others. Equanimity, as pointed out, does not mean just learning to hold these back, but to get a kind of participatory look at them through the activity of thinking and to restore a healthy connection to the tasks at hand. At the same time, if the scale happens to be more weighted on the side of the feather, this does not mean that purification of soul has occurred, but rather that emotion was taken off the scale altogether, and the feather-like quality of thinking suddenly becomes a leaden mass.

A further aspect of this image of the weighing of the soul concerns the fulcrum point, which we have identified with attention. This point not only serves as the midpoint from which balance can come into operation, but it also is a point that draws up or holds up the scales. This aspect of the image indicates that attention is more than a particular psychological function; it is also a spiritual function, and thus operates at a different level than do emotion and thinking. Implicit in all that has been described concerning equanimity has been the invisible but most necessary factor of there being a capacity of observing our emotions, our thinking, and our attention to work toward equanimity. This point of observation is not completely exterior to soul life, something outside, where we become a detached observer. Attention is a psychological and a spiritual function. In the terminology of spiritual practices, this point of attention is called the "witness." It is that capacity of being able to be completely engaged in something while also observing the engagement. Attention consists of this duality of spiritual and soul function.

The spiritual aspect of attention, as you can imagine, is subtle, but unless this aspect of attention is discovered within oneself, everything that I have said concerning equanimity will not prove fruitful. In order to discover this aspect of attention, it is necessary in one's life to be engaged in some sort of meditation practice. I do not propose one practice as better for this than others. In meditation we are building the capacity of attention because that is what we have to do in meditation: sustain attention. Further, the things we meditate on are of a spiritual nature, and thus, through meditation, the psychological function of attention becomes oriented toward spiritual matters and these spiritual matters in turn enter into the process of attention itself.

We can visualize two currents or forces operating within the imagination of the scales with the fulcrum point being soul attention/spirit attention, and one pan holding the emotions, and the other holding thinking. Attention is the highest of these three psychological functions. Emotions and thinking exist at the same level, which means that we can be thrown off balance either by emotion or by thinking. Attention, as a psychological function, can help restore balance, but the difficulty is that it is able to do so only when balance has been disrupted. Through meditation practice, attention begins to recognize its own spiritual character, and as this happens, a current of spiritual force begins to flow from the fulcrum point into emotion and thinking, so that, gradually, our psychological functions become infused with more spiritual qualities. Practically, this infusion means that we are no longer so susceptible to being caught by emotions or one-sided thinking. Nonetheless, whatever emotion may be present is felt, and thinking is enhanced.

When we consider establishing equanimity in the triad of emotion, thinking, and feeling, it may seem that it is either unpleasant emotions or abstract head-thinking that can make us lose our equanimity. Pleasant emotions and concretistic thinking disturb equanimity just as much, and in many ways pose deeper difficulties because these qualities are likely to be seen as qualities to be sought after. Someone who goes around angry all the time will be feared, while someone who is exuberantly bubbly is more likely to be thought well balanced. Someone who thinks abstractly is likely to be considered strange, while someone who thinks concretely may be seen as highly practical. If we find ourselves in these states, then the same kind of efforts as those already described can be useful in finding equanimity.

While the exploration thus far can help in practicing equanimity, it seems important now to try to give a picture of what this quality feels like. It may seem that an evenness of emotional life can be compared to flatness of affect; it cannot. Nor are we trying to establish high and low limits to the expression of emotion, thinking, and attention, with anything outside that range considered to be lacking and out of the range of equanimity.

Equanimity counts as a virtue because through it, spiritual qualities begin to be experienced within the soul. A kind of ongoing inner stillness results from the practice of this virtue, no matter what the outer circumstances may be. The soul requires such stillness to respond to the subtlety of currents from the spiritual realms. Practice of the virtue also results in a capacity to experience the soul and spiritual qualities of others, even in the surrounding world. This happens because spiritual activity begins to characterize soul life, meaning that interest toward purely material matters lessens, though it is not a matter of turning away from the physical world and engaging in ascetic practices.

We now engage with vitality in what we have to do in the world, but more for spiritual reasons than getting something for our own satisfaction. We begin to recognize that the presence of emotion gives us material to work with, to refine, over and over.

Equanimity can become a habit, but that does not mean that once established we have it from then on. Quite the contrary. What can become habitual is the practice of being able to be a witness to the soul process of emotions and thinking as they tend to each want to take over. This act of witnessing becomes the primary tool with which to exercise the virtue. Thus, we become able to hold ever stronger emotions without them adversely affecting us or those around us.

What does the practice of equanimity do? It is one of the processes of soul purification through which the sludge from past emotional experiences gradually gets cleared, and as such constitutes an ongoing therapeutic experience occurring in daily life. Equanimity purifies the soul and brings soul into an initial conjunction with spirit, so that we begin to live from the place of soul in a spiritual manner. Rather than leaving behind the soul, as can happen with many spiritual practices, or rather than leaving the spirit, as can happen with many psychological practices, equanimity holds these two qualities together. We feel the depth of experience while being open to receive what the spiritual worlds have to give us.

Equanimity also becomes a gift we bring to others, and thus brings about a purification of the life of the community. To get a feeling for how equanimity affects others, try to recall someone you know who works at practicing this quality and how it feels to be in the presence of such a person. At first, it may be unsettling to be in the presence of someone who is so poised, composed, dignified, serene. These qualities are gifts to us that allow us to stumble, fumble, hesitate, and perhaps realize how out of balance we are. While it may not feel very comfortable being so out of control, in the presence of a person of equanimity we feel no fear of reprisal for revealing our lumpy souls. The alchemical operations necessary for the purification of soul life cannot even begin until we become aware of our own mass of confusion.

While we may expect, for example, someone who belongs to one of the therapeutic professions to pour forth this quality of equanimity as an aid to our own soul discovery, it is far more amazing and community-transforming when we come across such a person, say, in our work. By working with this virtue at work, we can become that person at work who silently brings about a transformation of the whole operation without any need for organizational restructuring. However, such a possibility needs to be imagined in realistic terms. Practicing this virtue does not mean that everything at work begins to go our way, the way we imagine things ought to be. What we hope to accomplish in community through the practice of equanimity is to put the work of a group of people under the auspices of the spiritual worlds.

The person of equanimity can appear to be one who has trouble making decisions. When emotion, thinking, and attention all have equal value, it is indeed hard to make decisions. However, equanimity does not rule out making decisions. This difficulty arises only when the capacity of attention remains solely a psychological function and its dual aspect as being both psychological and spiritual is not developed. When attention develops in this dual way, then decisions come much more easily and quickly because it is as if we are aided by forces and currents from the spiritual realms. The hesitation usually characteristic of having to make decisions seems to disappear. This freedom in the midst of making decisions is one of the great gifts of equanimity.

9 **The Virtue of Patience**

Patience is an enduring quality of consciousness that has to be formed and shaped into a habit of soul for it to be a behavior that has any meaning. There can be acts we do that look like patience that are nothing more than behaviors inculcated in us by others. These kinds of behaviors, which certainly have a social worth, might be better termed manners than virtues. We may have been taught by our parents, or in school, or as a part of our religious training, that patience is a good practice. Such practice may indeed be salutary for our relationships, but it would be only the most outer shell of the virtue itself.

The most central aspect of the virtue of patience concerns the quality of what can be described as a "plentiful void of expectation." If you meditate a bit you will be able to locate a current of feeling, a soul current, that has this characteristic, not just now and then, but as a constantly flowing current with this particular feeling quality. What does it feel like?

This quality may be somewhat difficult to experience if you are in the midst of an expectation surrounding a particular event in life. For example, if someone who is very dear to you, someone you have not seen for a very long time, has arranged to visit, an active expectation of that visit may be so strong as to overpower the more subtle current that we want to describe here. Indeed, our lives may be so filled with little expectations of every sort that a deliberate stilling of the soul life is required in order to feel the current of patience.

This plentiful void of expectation can be described as a feeling of tension in which the soul life experiences a constant, ongoing pull in two directions at the same time.

An unknown factor pulls soul life outward toward expression, though what is to be expressed remains veiled. At the same time, another, also unknown factor, pulls soul life inward, producing an uncomfortable suffering, but one that can be endured without the interference of severe pain. This ongoing tension is in fact responsible for the capacity to feel the inner experience of life; that is to say, the current of life force moves through us and is perceptible as an actual experience, the inner perception of this tension.

In one way, then, patience can be described as the very experience of life. We are patience! Patience, then, is far more than an act of deliberately holding back when we want to experience or accomplish something. Such moments express and bring to awareness the presence of a deeper, ongoing activity; here the virtue can become available as a conscious feeling.

The term "life" is so broad and pervasive that it may seem that we have not gotten very far at all by discovering this relation between patience and life. Nonetheless, more is involved in relating these two than juxtaposing the two words, "patience" and "life." Life as experienced has a dynamic to it; our life is in the constant process of coming to be and dying away. We do not just live or have life; life is not simply there the moment we are born into the world; that moment is just the beginning of the process of life coming-to-be and passing away. The tension of this process can be further described as occurring between two polarities—the polarities of dying and regeneration.

What exists between the polarities of dying and regeneration is the virtue of patience—when, that is, the dynamic of these polarities is actually a felt experience. Patience has to do with exactly experiencing the realms between these two polarities. As we move toward one side or another of the polarity, a different kind of inner experience occurs: the experience of desire. The direction toward regeneration intensifies the realms of desire connected with sensation and passion, while the polar direction toward dying intensifies the realm of desires connected with spiritual matters, which in its most intense is felt as the desire for God.

Desire, felt too strongly in either direction, upsets the current of patience and turns it into a task to accomplish rather than an ongoing state. No judgment is implied here, no suggestion at all that desires are to be avoided, not those desires that are specifically bodily, nor those desires that tend to pull us away from earthly existence. The conscious development of the virtue of patience, though, has to do with coming to tolerate the tension of being between the extremes of desire. The importance of developing this capacity must indeed have something to do with there being an intimate relation between desires in a spiritual direction and those in a bodily direction. We need patience to keep these polarities in ongoing connection, as one is apparently necessary for the continuance of the other.

Without the tension between desires of both sorts, we exist in the absence of the feeling life, or alternately, are overcome with either religious feeling or bodily feeling and sensation. The question then arises: how is it possible to consciously develop the capacity of patience?

From time to time, we can force ourselves to be patient; maybe with someone at work, or with a partner, or with a child struggling to learn a task that we take for granted. Does developing patience in a more ongoing way require this kind of deliberate force? When we force ourselves toward patience with another, it usually means that we are suppressing some desire. The two polarities of desire mentioned above have decidedly different valences, and this difference must be taken into account with respect to the question of force. When we force ourselves to be patient, to wait, to stand between what we want and what is needed in the moment, the different qualities of desire that have to be attuned to are ignored. We may indeed be able to force ourselves to wait, but we will not feel the soul quality of patience.

The desire for God is typically not nearly as impetuous as the desires connected with sensation and passion, although, under certain conditions, it can certainly become just as strong. We typically experience great impatience when the fulfillment of our desires in the direction of sensations and passions is thwarted. To try to develop patience by deliberately holding back desires in this direction can bring about momentary acts of patience, but not the virtue. Suppression of desires can also result in a false movement to the other side of the polarity, expressed as fanaticism. Such holding back, or suppression of desire, will usually increase the felt force of the desire.

The desire for God, on the other hand, in order to be felt and not just be a matter of belief or of having been instructed by religion that this desire needs to be present, requires facing the fact of dying. The fact of dying needs to be faced with equanimity, that is, without fear. Only then can we feel the pull of God on us. The fear connected with facing death assures that desires remain out of balance, weighted in the direction of sensations and passions while the desire for God is ignored.

We cannot get very far with the development of patience as a virtue of the soul without an engagement with death. In this image of the polarities of desire, death resides as the figure of fear. We typically cannot feel this side of the ongoing polarity of dying and regeneration because of fear. We do not see that this fear is a mighty illusion. We have to do battle with this illusion, which does not mean that death itself does not exist, but rather that the sting of death does not exist.

Here I want to be careful to remain within the sphere of spiritual psychology and to avoid moving into a theological discussion. It is helpful to keep our initial image in mind—patience as the dynamic of felt life flowing between the polarities of dying and regeneration. We have to think of patience dynamically, not statically, and such dynamic flow requires the full force of both polarities. The fear of death or of dying blocks the experience that the vivaciousness of life originates in the eternal vivaciousness of some divine creating force in whom death has no part.

If we have come to terms at all with death, then impatience that is often connected with spiritual matters also becomes more vividly experienced; we recognize our great impatience with the spiritual realms. We wonder why our prayers do not seem to be answered, or answered promptly and in the manner expected. We wonder why we do not have vivid spiritual experiences after perhaps having spent ten or twelve years developing a meditation practice. We begin to discover that our desire for spiritual experiences of one sort or another can indeed be as strong as our desire for sensations and passions.

This vast realm of impatience, for the most part, does not express itself in the clear forms outlined above. Rather, impatience expresses itself in all of the ongoing little ways we experience being too sharp with others, too quick to criticize, the ways we flare up in anger, express frustrations, become angry with ourselves. However, any of the innumerable ways you can imagine being impatient, if looked at carefully, will be seen to be related to the two polar directions described. Our impatience takes place somewhere along the dynamic between spiritual desires and bodily, earthly desires concerned with sensations and passions.

Do we not always think of a patient person as calm and serene? It is impossible to imagine coming to patience through the act of withholding of desire or trying to get rid of it; ultimately this direction can only result in violence. On the other hand, unbridled delving into desire takes us to the depths of pride, jealousy, wrath, and vengeance, to all the excesses of desire in the direction of sensations and passions. It is just as impossible to imagine coming to patience by jumping fully into desire as it is by withholding desire. On the other side, once we have worked very hard to come to terms with death, the desire for spiritual experience seems to be a good from which we would not want to withhold ourselves. Here the excess of fanaticism as spiritual impatience looms on the one hand, while the impatience connected with not having spiritual experiences when we think we ought to looms on the other hand.

There seems to be no way to come to patience except through enduring our impatience without self-judgment. Perhaps, though, coming to patience is not so much a matter of a corrective movement, of trying to put on the brakes, as it is a matter of what we learn from our excesses. If we can attend at all to what goes on with our soul during times of impatience—impatience in any direction whatsoever—we notice that something more happens than trying to get our own way quickly. Something, a particular quality of consciousness, is also shoved away. We know this quality more by its absence when we have acted hastily. This quality can be described as a kind of fecund time existing in and of the soul.

Rather than trying to learn patience directly, it might be better to focus on how to go about feeling the presence of this quality of time. Patience, then, becomes a matter of protecting this quality of soul time. This practice gives us something tangible to work on, whereas otherwise we have to work on restricting ourselves in order to develop patience. Restriction alone seldom works as a strategy for accomplishing anything.

Imagine acting impatiently with someone. Say I am sitting, writing, trying to concentrate. My friend comes into the room and interrupts. I try to act interested in what she says, but I am irritated. She leaves, and I get back to work, but I have lost the train of thought and have to search around to find the contemplative state that I was in. Just as I do, she comes in again. This time I blow it and almost scream at her; an act of impatience, one in the direction concerned with the satisfaction of my own desire, which here is a kind of sensation, the good bodily feeling of writing something well.

Let's look at another example, from the other direction. Say I am meditating. I can't seem to find the kind of space, a particular inner quality that one goes into when the flow of meditation goes right. I keep looking for this inner space but find myself becoming anxious. Then, finally, I do find it, but in the midst of meditating become dissatisfied, wanting something more, like the direct and immediate and clear presence of a spiritual being, standing there, talking to me, giving absolutely clear guidance, just like you read about in all the pop-spirituality books. But really, there is nothing, and I am unable to stay with this absence and stop the meditation.

In each of these instances, what may be most important as the act of impatience was shoving away a particular inner quality of experience, one that cannot be described as having a content, which makes describing the quality difficult. At first, we have to approach description in a negative way. This quality is one that can be characterized as the absence of ego. Impatience is a shoving away of force or quality within that is other than my ego. Impatience is not so much egotism as it is this shoving away of all

140

else. That is why impatience has a power to it. This dimension of experience—the felt quality of there being far more to us than our little sense of ourselves—is always there, always present, even when there may be strong ego-feeling.

Alongside ego-feeling—or more accurately, it feels as if it runs right beneath the sense of ego-feeling—is another current, vast and deep. If I try to picture this current, make it for a moment into a content of consciousness, it takes on the image of an intricate weaving, a many-threaded weaving. Further, while ego-feeling is centered more in the region of the head, this current is felt most strongly in the region of the chest. This is the current of patience that we have to learn to dip into rather than shove away.

I notice that whenever a particular kind of thought intrudes, this current disappears. Without exception, the character of the thought concerns my impatience with someone, including myself. I may, for example, have a thought of how it seems to me that my colleague has not been working very hard. Or I may have a thought of all that I need to try to get done in the next month. The moment these sorts of thoughts intrude, the current of patience is shoved away. If I try to pay attention to what specific quality of consciousness has changed when this current is shoved away, I see that it is one of a continual blessing, or a kind of mantle that lightly covers all that I think and all that I do. It is a current of blessing.

Is it necessary to interrupt this current, this mantle of blessing, whenever we want to get something done? If so, all of our actions are without blessing. Without this current of blessing, this current of patience, our actions, no matter how noble they may seem, are actions from an ego-centered consciousness. The content of what we do does not matter, it will be ego-centered when this feeling current is shoved aside. We may think that we are doing something spiritual because we are operating out of a spiritual idea or motive or context. But if this current is interrupted, we are executing only a spiritual idea, not a spiritual action. Impatience is impiety; it is acting without the felt presence of spirit, without the inner quality of soul, even though what we do may have a soul and spiritual content.

The quality of the current of patience described above gives a clue concerning the kind of practice needed in order to stay present to this current in spite of all the internal and external interruptions that come along and break the threads of our patient weavings. We have to develop the practice of becoming perpetual weavers. Watch someone knit, weave, or crochet, and you will see the act of patience in operation. Weavers do not apparently do their work with an end in view, a goal toward which they strive. The moment such a goal would come in and become the reason for weaving, at that very moment the task would begin to be filled with errors.

A weaver may set out to create a particular object, with a particular design in mind, but has to quickly put aside the vision of its completion in order to do the work of repeating the same act over and over, for days, weeks, maybe even months. A certain rhythm is employed, a great skill is involved, and a continuous act of concentration needed. The concentration is of great interest because it apparently does not necessarily involve the mind. I have seen people knitting a sweater while listening to long lectures and apparently comprehending what is being said, as now and then I have also seen such people look up for a moment to ask rather penetrating questions. Weaving on a loom may require more mental attention, but the act of concentration even here certainly does not issue from the mind. Patience is continually weaving into our lives; the virtue is learning to attend to this beautiful silence.

If you watch an accountant place numbers in various cells of a spreadsheet all day long, it might seem that patience can be mental. Patience may take place at the mental level, and also at the emotional and the physical levels. Patience, however, itself does not issue from any of these, but may interweave with them all. Better said, patience interweaves the multidimensional aspects of our being—the spiritual, mental, emotional, and physical. We experience impatience when one dimension seeks to do business on its own. For example, if at work, you become impatient as you explain to a colleague the way in which to carry out a particular financial procedure, at that moment, there are dimensions of the relationship that have been left behind. Perhaps at that moment the spiritual sense of the relationship is obscured, or the emotional dimension.

When we put aside our wholeness to carry out a specialized function, the situation becomes ripe for the explosion of impatience. We cannot exist in the world without closing down certain aspects of our being at times in order to do the tasks required of us. Impatience threatens to enter either when we must put aside aspects of ourselves in order to do a particular task, or when we have become accustomed to doing that task and are called back in a rather sudden manner to function as more complete human beings.

Central to the disruptions we experience in going either toward a specialized task or away from it is an alteration of the experience of time. If you are in the midst of a task that took an effort of concentration to come to the point of being solely with that task without distractions, and then suddenly someone interrupts you, it is as if the kind of time that had to be woven that matches the particular task at hand suddenly collapses. In a related manner, when you move into a certain specialized task, it takes an effort to weave the time you are living before beginning the task into the kind of time characteristic of the task. These transition points become the most vulnerable points in which we may find ourselves becoming impatient.

It would appear from what has been said thus far that the development of patience requires the weaving together of the various worlds in which we constantly participate, going into one for a while, then another, then perhaps back out into the everyday life world. How can the relations between our experienced worlds become more smooth and harmonious?

We certainly can conceive of someone developing patience by learning to stay with one world of experience. Not only does this restriction account for the holy person who has moved into a life of prayer or meditation; it also accounts for the workaholic. The only difference between these two lifestyles is that they exist within differing experiential times. While we readily evaluate the workaholic as missing something essential, we certainly tend to evaluate the individual who goes off to the monastery or ashram as having made a high and noble choice. We might, however, do well to question the kind of spirituality that comes from relinquishing what may be the true spiritual task of our time—developing the flexibility of soul needed to move in and out of worlds.

The kind of spirituality that holds to the spiritual worlds existing in one time realm—sacred time, eternal time, timeless time—perhaps represents a spirituality from the past more than that of the present time. It may well be atavistic to hold to this singular view of spiritual experience, an adherence contributing to the lack of patience in the world. Patience, as we have seen, does not originate from any of our psychic capacities. We cannot get to patience by means of the mind or intellect, or by means of the emotions, or by physical means. We cannot think our way into patience, though we may think about it. Patience itself also does not seem to be an emotion, though it leads to the emotional quality of calmness. And if we try to act patiently, we may be able to enact the outward behavior for a while, but it will lack the inner qualities of the experience.

The quality of patience, we have seen, involves experiencing a certain quality of time that is different than the time we ordinarily live within. Calling this quality timelessness would be descriptively inaccurate; it is not outside of time. However, we may be more precise if we speak of patience taking place in a different time rather than saying that it involves a quality of time. When we are patient we seem to have plenty of time. We mean by this that ordinary clock time recedes and another time becomes more prominent. We now experience duration. Duration feels like ordinary time stretched out. We are still in this world, very present to ourselves and to our ordinary surroundings; we are not out of body, or outside the sense of place, and in fact, we feel even more securely located as belonging here where we are.

In patience, time become spacious. Living impatiently as we typically do, time lacks this quality of spaciousness—something that you feel that you can live within, can inhabit. We are not friends with time, and this lack of friendliness manifests as constant impatience. There does not seem to be enough time, but we typically think that if we had more of the quantity we would be qualitatively different. Not so. If we did have more time of this sort, we would either fill it with the same kind of actions we already engage in, increasing impatience, or have time on our hands, but the same kind of time that is already so troublesome, which would now be felt as boredom. Empty ordinary time is boredom.

Duration, then, differs from having more of the quantitative sense of time. Duration feels more like time stretched, time felt from within rather than being pressed, shoved, and ruthlessly moved about by it. When we feel more the quality of duration, time feels plentiful; it is filled with that mantle of blessing. What strikes me as most interesting about the virtue of patience is that with this virtue, this durational quality of time enters into the activities of everyday life. We can and do experience the quality of duration, seek it, need it, but usually find it by leaving our typical activities and entering into situations where time can be experienced in this way. We go on vacations, or wait for the weekend for a chance to renew ourselves, take up golf, find ways just to pass time unencumbered. But then we have to return to situations where we have no time, and we have not developed patience in the interim.

Developing patience involves consciously drawing duration into the folds of clock time. Many spiritual platitudes urge this direction without giving a clue about the actual process—slowing down, savoring the moment, being present, and so on. Such instruction tends more to foster self-absorption rather than the virtue of patience, for patience always involves an imagination of an other. We do not just have patience. We are patient *with* someone or patient *about* something. As with all of the virtues, we develop this virtue and the virtue is also the gift we offer to others. We develop patience, and it is a gift we offer to others and to the world. Both aspects are needed for the presence of the virtue.

We always experience patience or impatience in relation to someone. We may become impatient with ourselves, but when we do so, we have become objects to ourselves, onlookers who are dissatisfied with what we see. The someone need not be another human being; we also experience patience and impatience in relation to spirit beings, including God.

That this virtue takes such an apparent relational form can instruct us in learning the process of weaving spoken of earlier. With patience, a commingling with the soul life of another takes place, and the process of weaving concerns such communing. Patience counts as one of the primary communal virtues, an absolute necessity to any community. However, what needs to be recognized most is that when we act patiently or impatiently, we do so in relation to the soul life of the other person. Patience blesses the soul of the other person, while impatience aggressively crosses the boundary, imposing one's ego onto the soul of the other person. Soul, I suspect, knows no other way to relate than through the durational time of patience. Ego, on the other hand, knows no other way to relate than through the hastiness of ordinary clock time.

Patience thus educates us into becoming conscious in our soul life. Here, time and timing are different. In fact, time changes into timing, the awareness that the rhythm with which we move, act, and relate to others is far more important than the specific content of what we may be doing. *Festina lente* was the way the importance of timing was recognized by the alchemists. "Make Haste Slowly"—that was their dictum and the discipline they developed to transform ordinary metal into gold, or, we could say, to take something transitory and make it into something with great duration.

Making haste indicates an intense engagement in life, the recognition that we are here to do something and that we have a relatively short time to accomplish what we are to do. At the same time, what we are here to do—a spiritual task, not simply living, working, having a family, and so on—requires careful attention, astute inner observation, the right moves at the right time. A hasty move without the right slowness of perception may result in losing the interior sense of what we are doing.

The timing of the soul and everyday time are not the same; the task of patience concerns coordinating these two times—the time of slowness, of contemplation, brooding, mulling things over, seeing deeply, feeling intensely, with the time of getting something accomplished, getting on with the work, moving to what needs to be done next, being effective and out there in the world. Is developing patience a matter of establishing a rhythm, of moving inward for a while, being quiet and deep, and then moving outward, getting things done? Such a rhythm can work only if one phase overlaps into the other and this motion goes both ways. Something of the mood of contemplation has to overlap into the action, and something of the action has to overlap into the contemplation. Then each aspect has to gradually come closer and closer to the other such that eventually both rhythms go on simultaneously. Then we would be "making haste slowly."

What does patience accomplish in the world? The emblem "Make Haste Slowly" can be found in a sixteenth-century alchemical engraving by Heinrich Kunrath. The engraving is entitled "The Amphitheatre of Wisdom." The picture shows the interior of an alchemical laboratory. A number of things are going on.

The alchemist kneels beneath a prayer tent, with two books on the altar before him. One book is the Bible and the other a book of geometric drawings, apparently drawings of the movement of the heavenly bodies. A work table stands in the middle and up front; it is cluttered with all sorts of instruments, and in the midst of the conglomeration it is possible to see three musical instruments—a violin, a harp, and something like a mandolin. At the right of table, on the floor, stands an alchemical furnance, the source of the fire. Writing on the furnace vessel carries the dictum referred to, "Make Haste Slowly." At the far end of the vast room, which is drawn according to geometrical perspective, at the vanishing point there is an arch, and a sign over the arch reads, "While asleep, stay awake." A sign in the smoke of the incense burner indicates the necessity of sacrifice. Much more goes on in the engraving, but these are the essential elements.

The alchemical laboratory of our life, the work of transformation from ego life to soul life, is the place of the conjunction of labor and prayer. The three musical instruments on the work table indicate that laboratory work, making work also prayer, brings into harmony three aspects of our being: the mental (the violin is played in the region of the head); the emotional (the harp is played in the region of the heart); and the willful (the mandolin is played in the region of metabolic processes).

147

The laboratory work involves seeing the universe as divine work, working in prayer, and it also involves the heat of the furnace, the right application of fire, or of love, the timing of the heart, which must be applied with patience, as patience. In all alchemy, the furnace is said to hold the secret of the work. Through patience we live and work in the world, with the interior qualities of everything of the world. We work wholly, meditatively (the meaning of the sign "While asleep, stay awake"), for the sake of the world.

The alchemical laboratory I am describing demonstrates to us what patience does in the world. The alchemical laboratory is the whole of the universe, experienced from within. What patience accomplishes is the development of the capacity to perceive the world as soul, the whole world as interior qualities in the constant activity of transformation.

It takes the virtue of patience, a change in the way we perceive the time of the world, and sensitivity to timing, to experience this world as the spiritual world. We are accustomed, from the traditions of the past, to imagining the spiritual worlds as elsewhere—certainly not here, not in the physical world. But there is no "elsewhere." Looking elsewhere is an act of impatience, the incapacity to be here in full and total joy and desire and also to be here in full and total spiritual fulfillment. We do not experience here as the spiritual world because we do not have the patience required. Each little instance in which we are asked to slow down, enter into ourselves, be truly present to others, is a spiritual practice. We are training ourselves in patience, which is also a training of ourselves to experience this world as spirit and soul-filled.

10 **The Virtue of Truth**

In order to get a sense of truth as a virtue, we must refrain from any notions of the possibility of having the truth, possessing it, or, in any particular instance, knowing in full what constitutes the truth. Truth as a virtue concerns not the metaphysical aspects of this reality but rather how truth lives within the soul of the individual and expresses itself through the actions of the person. Metaphysical and epistemological approaches to truth would take us into concerns of how judgments are made and also into the question of how the mind can come to conform to reality. The virtue of truth does not concern these matters directly.

The poet Novalis speaks of "natural truth," and this is where I think we need to locate the virtue. There are many noble individuals who live in truth without a notion of metaphysics or philosophy. They have come to experience truth through applying attention to their inner lives, slowly elevating a natural instinct for truth to a virtue of the soul.

Does the virtue imply being true to oneself? Does it imply being well rounded, like a circle or a sphere that is true, that is, perfectly round? We also speak of someone as being a true healer, or a true teacher, or a true politician—is this the quality entailed in truth as a virtue? In all of these instances, and, I suspect, in any that we could name, a quality of idealism or an inherent notion of an ideal of some sort is conveyed with the word "truth." We typically feel frustration and resentment toward someone who pronounces "the truth," but admire and respect someone who seems to be seeking, searching, looking for truth as a central part of life. When we engage in such searching activity ourselves, it always carries the character of not exactly knowing what we are searching for; but we always do know when we have not encountered the mysterious truth that we seek, and we know when we get a glimpse of it.

Philosophy carries the connotation of being a search for objective truth, so it might be helpful to convey the more bodily side of the virtue of truth in order to remain grounded in spiritual psychology. In giving attention to this side of the virtue, we also avoid the pitfall of conceiving of truth as a strictly intellectual virtue.

When our idealism is engaged, or perhaps it is better said, when idealism engages us, no matter the particular content it may take, an urgency can be felt, and it is felt in a most bodily manner. A fire burns within us. The intensity of such fire ranges from a mere smoldering to that of an actual soul quality that can be strongly felt to that of, in some instances, actual physical sensations. The virtue, in large part, entails remaining close and in connection with this fire. Perhaps this fire can be called desire, but it is an objectless, bodily felt yearning, both a heat and a light, although the light, because it exists more in the spiritual domain, cannot initially be seen.

There is, though, a longing for truth that, when felt, can be every bit as strong as a longing for someone we love. This subtle light cannot at first be seen, so where we are going, the truth we seek, cannot be clearly known. When we do not feel this burning fire within ourselves, we see it in others, and indeed often say that such a person is "on fire." However, in this realm of deep truth, having to do with soul and spirit life, everything that we learn from the truth of others has to be assessed and then relearned from the particular point of view of one's own individuality. In doing so, we do not at that point have the truth, but we have become engaged with the virtue of truth.

As a starting point, one that is never left behind but has to be returned to over and over as a base, the virtue of truth is founded in a felt quality of desire. This quality has to be distinguished from other desires such as sexual or emotional or material desires. Its distinguishing characteristic is that we feel this desire but do not know what its object is or could be. This desire lies right on the border between bodily desire and spiritual longing. Thus, it is often confused with the press of other bodily desires, but it does not wax and wane as those desires do. It is more of a permanent inner urging. We might even consider the strong possibility that all the ways in which desire comes to be expressed are but variations of an aspiration for truth.

Thus, none of our desires, absolutely none, can be suppressed or denied without harm being done to the vitality necessary to know the presence of truth with us. On the other hand, any thoughtless spending of one or another of the infinite variations of desire without consideration given to them as a base of the search for truth, and the need to nurture it in right and healthy ways, harms the capacity for truth. To live in truth, do we not always need to consider what our desire seems to be seeking at a soul and spirit level, rather than simply seeking satisfaction of our desire?

An answer to the question of what desire seeks certainly does not always appear, nor does it tend to appear on schedule, that is, at the moment the inquiry is made. Quite often, we do go on and carry out actions oriented simply toward the satisfaction of desire. I am not putting forth a moralistic stance. Rather, I am convinced that the slight act of inhibition—a pause that poses the inner question, what does this desire *want?*—which gives attention to desire's autonomy, is sufficient to activate the virtue of truth inherent in the urge of desire. If we pose the inner question of what desire wants each time its presence makes itself felt, that serves as a sufficient starting engagement with the virtue of truth.

An emphasis on desire as basic to the virtue of truth is also necessary in order to feel the sense of truth as a form of action. Typically, we imagine truth as concerned with knowing, beauty as concerned with feeling, and goodness as concerned with action. The virtues lie in the realm of actions with ways of doing the good. It is not sufficient to know the virtues, or to just feel them; they must be done.

Truth, as a virtue, then, also belongs to this realm of acts. Doing truth is something different than knowing the truth and then seeking ways to act in accordance with such knowledge. What is the specific mode of action that could be called a doing of the truth? Is it not when there is a complete resonance in which the vital life of the body exists in sonority with the life of the individual soul and with the life of the individual spirit? Accomplishing this virtue, we can readily see, is not so easy. Often our instincts go one way, our feelings another, and our thoughts, aspirations, and goals and spiritual intentions yet another.

The connections among desire, truth, and action can be clarified by giving attention to a side of desire that is usually not seen. One side of desire is that it is a kind of push, an urging felt deep within the body, probably originating in the very tissues of our corporeal being. Desire has another side, however. It is not only, as it were, a push from within; it is also the felt quality of being drawn toward something, though what it is drawing us toward is no more known than what is pushing us from within our bodily existence. For desire to be foundationally connected with truth, both these aspects of desire have to be felt. Both aspects, indeed, are present all of the time; they are given with our existence as human beings. However, the side of desire that is the push, the urging, the impulsive—that side is more strongly felt. The other side of desire, its pull, is far more subtle, not nearly so apparent, and thus we easily sweep it aside without our even knowing we have done so.

We can go a bit further and name the desire felt as the push of our existence as fate. It is fate in the sense that we feel compelled by this side of desire; this push ranges from strong impulsiveness to needs and persistent interests. The other side of desire, more subtle, felt as being drawn toward something, that is our destiny. It is not that we know our destiny with the clarity of rational knowledge. Rather, we feel oriented toward doing something, pulled toward accomplishing something in life, though often we do not know exactly what it is.

I do not mean outer accomplishment, for this pull is felt more as the pull to be who we are, knowing that we have not yet found ourselves. Daily life takes place between these two forces, and we are living in the virtue of truth when both can be felt and vehemently adhered to. Typically, however, these two sides of desire are lived as a kind of tension of opposites. Getting these opposites to face one another is the primary work of truth.

The approach I am taking to the virtue of truth may seem to conflict with our ordinary understanding of truth, and as well the understanding of truth spoken of by philosophy and also that practiced by science. In all of these more usual ways of considering truth, truth is thought to be something objective, an altogether independent reality. The virtue of truth, however, runs through our lives, though by making such a claim, I do not reduce the virtue of truth to anything strictly personal. Here is what Novalis (*Philosophical Writings*) says of this kind of truth: "Man has his being in truth—if he sacrifices truth he sacrifices himself. Whoever betrays truth betrays himself. It is not a question of lying—but of acting against one's conviction."

In this view, truth is not something to be discovered external to ourselves, but lies rather in acting in accordance with our convictions. Conviction here does not mean faith or belief or personal prejudice, but rather means confidence, or even better, certitude. This certitude is the certitude of one's being. Thus, to act in this manner, to act in truth, it is necessary to be in deep connection with the fundament of our being.

Certitude of being cannot be experienced through ordinary ego consciousness. This aspect of the psyche, the ego, through which we function and have a minimal sense of control in day-to-day existence, operates according to an intrinsic principle of opposites. Within this mode of consciousness, for example, life and death are separate and opposite; love is the opposite of hate; one image, idea, concept, excludes another. The ego knows by making divisions, by standing against something, and so does the intellect. We cannot come to certitude of being intellectually.

Truth as a virtue can never be abstract. It has to find its way into the blood, the breath, the pulse, the very processes of life. Ego consciousness can only know about truth, just as in all ego-bound things, we do not know with immediacy, but always we only know about things. The virtue of truth is a kind of knowing in which we become what we know. It is the Self that can know truth by becoming it. Ego consciousness is like an eye that looks at something; we see with the eye. The Self is more like a mode of consciousness that sees through the eye, the emphasis here being on the "seeing through."

We utilize the ego as a tool to know and somewhat control what surrounds us. The Self sees through things, including itself, to the spiritual realities that are the creating forces of all things. At the same time, the Self, which is usually considered the spiritual aspect of our being, here, with the virtue of truth, must be always imagined as the embodied Self.

Two pressing questions arise. The first is how to get from ego to Self, and the second is how to embody Self. These questions are eminently practical and necessary for anyone interested in developing the capacity of the virtue of truth. We have to encounter these questions because in ordinary living we are dissociated from the Self as an actual experience and are also dissociated from a spiritual sense of the body as an actual experience. Further, as we proceed to enter more fully into these questions, we will see that neither spiritual nor psychological practices typically enter into the processes required for the awakening and sustaining of the embodied Self.

We can approach understanding the embodied Self better with the help of images. Two images that express the reality of the embodied Self are the Greek myth of Chiron and a mythical story from the Indians of the American Northwest.

The ancient Greek god-hero of medicine, Aesculapius, carried a staff along which two serpents entwined, ending at the top with their two heads facing each other. This symbol is now used by the medical profession, though it is confused with Mercury's staff, the caduceus. These two snakes facing each other symbolize the lower and higher self facing each other. Aesculapius had to learn the art of coming to a truthful certitude of himself in this way. Chiron, a centaur who had been incurably wounded by a poisoned arrow, educated Aesculapius in this knowledge of himself. He initiated Aesculapius into the truth and mysteries of the body; he taught Aesculapius the healing power of herbs and the mysteries of death, how to live the fullness of life, how to experience death as always accompanying life. This deep and mysterious experience is the basis of the truth of our being.

The place where Aesculapius learned these mysteries was a cave with two openings. The front of the cave opened out to Pelathronian, a valley containing every healing herb in the world. The back opening of the cave was an entrance to the Underworld. Aesculapius resided in this double-edged place where healing and death occurred together, one not opposed to the other. The double-headed serpent image, the healing staff of Aesculapius, symbolizes the embodied Self that can reside in these opposites that the ego cannot embrace, so this image is worth meditating upon to gradually understand what is required in entering into the alchemical process of moving from ego to Self and also into the embodied self.

A vivid representation of the configuration of opposites that must be faced to awaken to the certitude of ourselves is found in a myth from the Kwakiutl Indians of the Pacific Northwest. This myth deals with Sisiutl, a god who is a double-headed serpent, a dangerous sea monster. The myth tells how to face this mighty monster:

> When you see Sisiutl you must stand and face him. Face the horror. Face the fear. If you break faith with what you know, if you try to flee, Sisiutl will blow with both mouths at once and you will begin to spin. Not rooted in the earth as are the trees and rocks, not eternal as are the tides and currents, your corkscrew spinning will cause you to leave the earth, to wander forever, a lost soul, and your voice will be heard in the screaming winds of the first autumn, sobbing, pleading, begging for release. . . . When you see Sisiutl the terrifying, though you be frightened, stand firm. There is no shame in being frightened, only a fool would not be afraid of Sisiutl the horror. Stand firm, and if you know protective words, say them. First one head, then the other, will rise from the water. Closer. Closer. Coming for your face, the ugly heads, closer, and the stench from the devouring mouths, and the cold, and the terror. Stand firm. Before the twin mouths of Sisiutl can fasten on your face and steal your soul, each head

155

must turn toward you. When this happens, Sisiutl will see his own face.

Who sees the other half of Self, Sees Truth.

Sisiutl spends eternity in search of Truth. In search of those who know Truth. When he sees his own face, his own other face, when he has looked into his own eyes, he has found Truth.

He will bless you with magic, he will go, and your Truth will be yours forever. Though at times it may be tested, even weakened, the magic of Sisiutl, his blessing, is that your truth will endure. And the sweet Stalacum will visit you often, reminding you your truth will be found behind your own eyes. And you will not be alone again. (Cameron, Anne, 1981. *Daughters of Copper Woman.* Vancouver: Press Gang Publishers, 45-46.)

This story tells us the way in which the virtue of truth must be approached. The opposites within ourselves must face each other. The facing of the opposites is also at the beginning of every alchemical process. For example, the alchemical work known as the *Rosarium Philosophorum,* upon which C. G. Jung based his understanding of the transference phenomenon in psychotherapy, begins with an engraving with a two-headed serpent, each head facing an opposite direction at the top of the engraving but coming together in the bottom of the engraving. A similar image of opposites is given in the alchemical document known as *Splendor Solis* and also in *The Book of Lambspinck.*

Different images are utilized to depict the facing of opposites, but the initial stages of alchemical transformation always involve this process. The images are a way of conveying that the truth of one's being must be found before further transformation can take place. The truth of our being lies in the experience of the opposites of life and death as coexistent. This certitude of being forms the ground for the virtue of truth.

Ego consciousness is only the surface starting point for entering into the virtue of truth. The ego must voluntarily relinquish its position as the aspect of our psyche that knows, in order to come to realize that its way of knowing is but one way, a highly restricted way. But do you know anyone who would voluntarily relinquish their personal sense of power, control, knowing, personal sense of identity? Not likely.

Giving up this mode of consciousness is not quite so altruistic in alchemy either. A stage of alchemy precedes the facing of the opposites. This earlier stage is always characterized as chaos. Something we encounter in life throws us into the state of not-knowing. We typically do all sorts of things to recover from this state of not-knowing and regain the control of ego consciousness. It is only if we have some inkling, an inner sense that there is some sort of mysterious purpose in our losing our moorings, that the possibility arises of attempting to continue with the process that has begun rather than to cut it short. The factor that accounts for the possibility of having some minimal awareness that ego consciousness is not all there is can only be grace. The alchemists were well aware of this factor, and thus virtually all alchemical writings begin with prayers, an indication that they realized the process was not ultimately under their control. The virtue of truth, too, often comes as grace, but usually under the circumstances of coming to the end of our rope, where life and death meet and we are no longer in control, but thrown into chaos.

This beginning of the process of moving from ego into Self as pictured throughout the tradition of alchemy shows us that the virtue of truth is not something that is automatically given; it must be sought. However, we encounter all sorts of inner resistances to facing the truth of our being. These resistances cannot be dissolved through our own application of will alone. There is nothing within us that will or could voluntarily put aside ego consciousness. Even taking up various forms of spiritual practice does not in the least assure that ego consciousness will be relativized, not even if it is clear to us that this is what we want more than anything.

Once again, Novalis understood that the truth of one's being was something different and prior to any other sense of truth and involved inner transformation. The certitude that we can experience within our being, what Novalis termed "conviction," is not something that we can arrive at exclusively through our own efforts. He says:

> All conviction is independent of natural truth—it refers to magical or miraculous truth. One can only be convinced of natural truth—to the extent that it becomes miraculous truth. All proof rests on conviction, and is accordingly only a makeshift where comprehensive miraculous truth is lacking. Therefore all natural truths rest equally on miraculous truth. (*Philosophical Writings,* pg. 64.)

The virtue of truth is different than the belief in objective reason. The correspondence theory of truth, that truth is when the mind is in complete conformity with the object of consideration, has little to do with the virtue. Further, objective truth always rests upon the inner conviction of truth. Truth cannot be arrived at through logic. We feel the truth, and when it is not felt, all arguments trying to prove truth are pure sophistry. Unless some unknown factor turns us toward facing the opposites within the psyche, the possibility of coming to an inner sense of conviction cannot exist.

The beginning of developing the virtue of truth, then, seems to be more or less out of our hands. In the midst of chaos, though, if we do have some sort of intimation that falling apart may be not just a breakdown but a breakthrough, at that moment, we are called upon to respond in a certain specific manner. If this response does not occur, then the process goes no further and we must wait for another opportunity. The specific response required is one in which we do not try to recover from the breakdown but rather refrain from taking what feels like death as any sort of literal end.

In alchemy, this phase of the process is often pictured as an individual with a sword who is about to cut the head off a dragon. The dragon images our literalistic way of experiencing, of seeing rather than seeing-through. But we must slay our own ego consciousness; we must, so to speak, cut off our own heads. This act does not mean the end of ego consciousness; rather, it means to begin to be aware that there must be more to soul life than that little part through which we have been functioning.

The indication that we have begun to touch upon the possibility of the truth, the conviction of our own being, is the intense presence of fear that arrives the moment we relinquish the thought, the hope, the fantasy, that with a little bit of repair work we will be the same as we were before suffering entrance into the realm of chaos. This fear is expressed in the Kwakiutl myth cited above. The question now is whether we can bear the horror.

The myth states that truth consists of one half of self seeing the other half of self. Ego consciousness, the consciousness that functions by way of division, separating, dividing, is in fact a splitting of the self. Facing the disowned parts of our self fills us with terror. We are all we have rejected, turned against, viewed as wrong, scorned, disliked, hated, seen as evil.

Does coming to the conviction of our being, the virtue of truth, always require going through what seems to be breakdown? No, not if an inner urging can be felt, and so strongly felt that it cannot long be turned away from or forgotten without our feeling that something essential has been lost. Strangely though, the conviction that constitutes the truth of our being cannot be known directly; it does not fall into the province of rational knowledge.

We often know such conviction more by its absence; that is, at times when it is forgotten or put aside, we lose the sense of being ourselves even though we may not yet have developed a real, living sense of the soul and spirit aspects of ourselves. On the other hand, when such conviction feels present and strong, it still remains mysterious in its intent. What the truth of our being wants or is for may not be at all clear. Other ways of knowing the truth of our being are required than rational or intellectual knowing.

In order to shift usual knowing to the imaginal knowing necessary to come into conscious connection with the virtue of truth, it is first necessary to be able to hold, to contain, the fear that enters when ego consciousness begins to be relativized. By containing or holding the fear, I mean refraining from letting the fear take over, on the one hand, and on the other hand, refraining from letting the fear drive us back into ordinary ego consciousness. It is not a matter of avoiding fear but only of not allowing fear to have its way. The question here is what within us can meet fear in this necessary way of containment?

Fear separates, tears us apart, divides us, dismembers us, so there must be something, some psychic factor, that remains invulnerable to attacks of fear. That factor is our individual spirit, what Jung called the Self. In the presence of strong fear, if we are able to stay with and in the fear without being overcome, our staying ability indicates a first though often unconscious connection with the Self. From this newly won point of view, it begins to be possible to observe the attacks of fear without becoming overwhelmed.

Even to come to this point in the discovery of the virtue of truth, something else must occur. The relativizing of ego consciousness results in experiencing ourselves as weak, vulnerable, naked, and utterly human. The omniscient perspective of the ego crumbles, and we find that the entry into the truth, the conviction of our being, lies far from any godlike point of view. In alchemy, this initial phase of the process of coming to truth is spoken of as the *nigredo*. It is often experienced as a deep depression, which, if the ego identifies with this state, can become clinical depression.

What about the disowned or undiscovered aspects of the Self, the other half of Self spoken of in the Kwakiutl myth of Sisiutl? The truth of ourselves is not found alone in the discovery of our vulnerability as an individual human being, or even in the kind of darkness that it can bring about. The other half of Self that we must meet and encounter, not simply know about, is our madness. To come into the virtue of truth, we have to meet the psychotic parts of our Self. Certainly, this encounter does not imply becoming psychotic. I need a sufficiently strong enough word, though, to convey coming into relation with the side of madness that is indeed present for each of us, and "psychosis" is the one that is right to describe what we meet. The Greek word *psychosis* means "soul-animation."

The split-off parts of our Self, then, are the psychotic parts of us as sane people and do not here signify going psychotic or going insane. I want to avoid using more usual terms such as the "unconscious" or even "soul" in referring to "soul-animation" in order to stay with and in the given experience of the terrible difficulty of coming to the virtue of truth. The current romanticizing of soul that has become popular in the many books using the word haphazardly tends to miss entirely the pathos involved in encountering the life of the soul in a conscious, embodied manner.

The forms madness takes vary considerably from individual to individual. Difficult aspects of our early lives are often the gateways to these split-off areas. I am not suggesting that the only way to come into relation with the split-off parts of ourselves is to go into therapy or long-term analysis of one sort or another. Those parts often announce themselves through bouts of despair, rage, panic, anxiety, and feelings of abandonment. Some kind of soul work is usually needed, and it can take many forms. Some ways we can do our own soul work include: paying attention to dreams (remembering them, holding them throughout the day, taking them seriously); paying attention to body symptoms (honoring them, not immediately seeking to medicate discomfort, paying attention to what inner images might accompany the symptoms); paying attention to our relationships (trying to catch hold of the beginning moments of conflict and working to realize that our complaints about the other relate to our own split-off parts); paying attention to inner images (noticing them, developing the ability to look upon them as autonomous activity rather than something we think we are doing); and developing image-based meditation practices. Such practices include active imagination as described by Jung, and the heart exercises described earlier. Simply making a daily practice of moving the center of consciousness from head to heart makes a big difference.

All of these practices share one common point: taking psychic or soul imagination seriously. Whatever practices one might develop that would lead toward viewing and participating in psychic imagination—not as some sort of subjective state, but as, on the one hand, a deep mode of consciousness, and on the other hand as the accessing of imaginal worlds—will be helpful in "soul-animation."

Coming to the virtue of truth requires a great deal of the deepest levels of patience, and there can be no better preparation for courage than having entered the regions of truth. What can be the expected outcome of following the process described thus far? First, two extremes of the virtue—making rash judgments and having rigid opinions—begin to drop away. Judgment attempts an intellectual declaration of the truth that occurs far too prematurely, and similarly with opinion. Both of these stabs at truth bypass the psychic and the somatic unconscious, which the process just outlined in alchemical terms brings awake. Second, an amazing and unexpected outcome results from entering into the process of discovery of the virtue of truth. We are changed in our physical being. Let us now look at what that change entails.

Coming to the point of being able to live within the conviction of our soul strengthens the body. We feel more solid in our embodiment, though at the same time, our embodiment is more transparent. By more transparent, I mean that we become aware that we do not, as perhaps previously assumed, have a body, but rather we are a spiritual body. We become aware that the body that we are cannot be identified only with physical, material processes. We know this now from within; it is not just a New Age philosophy. It is as if there is a second person within us and this second, subtle person is more us than we know ourselves to be. Living with soul conviction awakens this second person.

The spiritual body that we are cannot be neatly divided and separated from the soul that we are and the spirit that we are. The whole point of the alchemical process, in fact, was to enter into conscious, embodied, soul/spirit life. As long as we are dissociated from the interior sense of our living body and also dissociated from soul and spirit, the virtue of truth can only exist as an abstraction. The awakening of this virtue that is attendant upon going through the trials and difficulties spoken of thus far means living in a different body.

This "new" body cannot be described in materialistic terms. The alchemists and other spiritual traditions have always utilized the imagination of the subtle body to speak of the unity of body, soul, and spirit. It is possible to go further than this term and begin to describe the actual manner of function of the subtle body without resorting to terms such as the chakras, the etheric body, the astral body, and other esoteric concepts. Such esoteric concepts can be extremely valuable for providing a tradition and a language to describe the finer aspects of embodiment. What, though, is it like to live these finer dimensions of body?

To live the virtue of truth as the body of conviction, the inner certitude of being, of the embodied Self, is experienced as a living "field," an imaginally whole situation in which the "substance" of body is felt within and around and between ourselves and others and even the wider world, all at the same time. The body, understood in this manner, is an encompassing, infusing, interactive field rather than a thing, an object of physical matter only.

The word "field" used to describe the body of the virtue of truth is somewhat different than the way the term is used in classical physics. In classical physics, a physical body, for example, the Sun, or the Earth, generates a field, an actual modification of the space surrounding these physical bodies. This field contains energy and exerts forces on bodies like the planets placed within it. While these fields are invisible, they are substantial, since fields carry energy and momentum and have measurable effects. The electromagnetic field also falls within this way of thinking; a pair of protons generates electric fields around itself that mediate their mutual repulsion. In this understanding of fields, the object, thing, substance is first, and these entities generate fields around them.

In speaking of the embodied, conscious Self as a field, I am drawing not on classical physics but rather on the outer edges of depth psychology. If I were speaking of the body-field in the way physics does, I would say that the unconscious is invisible, pervasive, and continuously influencing the body and consciousness. In turn, our conscious position affects the unconscious. The language here is all substantive, and we imagine a field as a kind of surround. The body-field is not in ordinary spacetime or directly measurable, and thus, the language of "energy" or "energy exchange" and all such notions does not apply.

Here, a view opposite to that of classical field theory holds: field first, substance as secondary manifestation. With respect to the virtue of truth, coming to experience this kind of field would mean that we do not "know" the truth, or "have" the truth, but rather, we live *in* the interactive field of truth, which is a very specific kind of experience.

For example, here one lives in a clarity of awareness that at the same time can only be characterized as a quality of "not-knowing." This region is a zone of indeterminacy, where events and experiences unfold, rather than our usual way of going through experiences, which is characterized by a kind of "knowing-in-advance." This region can also be characterized as a realm of acausal connections. When Jung began to explore this realm in his studies of the transference phenomenon of therapy, based upon his conversations and friendship with the physicist Wolfgang Pauli, he termed the experience of acausal connections "synchronicity." This region, then, is much more fluid than that experienced through ego consciousness, and this fluidity does not result from the generation of a field by the physical body. Rather, the fluidity takes precedence; it occurs first, and out of this fluid medium, the sense of the body as an object is the result of a mental objectification of the body.

To be fully in the field requires an openness to fantasy, feelings, intuitions, sensations, and images. This openness is won through the very difficult work of searching to discover the certitude of our being, from finding the way into the virtue of truth. I have to emphasize that truth, understood in this soulful way, does not by any means lead to a subjective view of truth. While the independence of truth from the observer or knower that characterizes the intellectual way of knowing truth has been left behind, a new objectivity emerges.

This objectivity is one in which the participant becomes included in experienced truth, along with the object experienced. The site of this mode of knowing, however, is not within the person on the one hand, or in the conformity of the mind of the person with the known on the other hand. The site of living the virtue of truth is the region of activity that has been described by Jung as the "numinous" field.

To speak of the numinous or the etheric may sound abstract or perhaps mystical. One knows the virtue of truth by being within this region rather than by knowing about something. While engaged in this region, bodily vitality intensifies, but in such a manner that heightened attention is not drawn to the body, as it is with other forms of intensification, such as eroticism. This intensification encompasses our perception, so sensing is more awake. This heightening, while it makes the surroundings appear more vivid, does not result in our becoming more immersed in the materiality of things. Rather, the heightening makes the regions between things nearly sensible.

The result of this heightening is that there is a region of activity that nearly supersedes the substance of things; there occurs a kind of reversal of figure and ground. Whereas in usual perception the things, the objects perceived are figural and what they are within remains invisible; with the kind of heightening I am describing, we become aware of the spaces between things as substantial rather than empty. The substance is, of course, quite subtle.

While I have employed a perceptual example to describe the experience of the field of the virtue of truth, what was stated above applies equally to, for example, our thinking and feeling. While we typically think from one thing to another thing to another, in the heightened state we are more present to the continuous flow that characterizes the act of thinking. The "space" between thoughts is where the truth is found, more so than the content of the thoughts. Similarly with the realm of feeling. In all instances, what I want to emphasize is that our sense of embodiment does not decrease or disappear, though the strictly material sense of the body does diminish.

Experiences of moving in the field of the virtue of truth are not our usual mode and cannot be sustained in everyday life. However, it is possible to gradually develop a kind of "side-by-side" consciousness in which this mode of experience lives alongside our more usual and habitual ways. This dual mode of consciousness is not to be thought of as a deficit or a concession, or a retreat back to something outmoded. In fact, the virtue of truth, the actual experience of living within this virtue, consists in maintaining the polarity. It would be quite foolish to become enamored with experiencing the numinous realm. The result would be that, at some point, the ego, which certainly has not disappeared or dissolved, would identify with this new mode of consciousness, with tragic consequences. This identification is what Jung spoke of as inflation.

11 **The Virtue of Courage**

The virtue of courage is not to be confused with acts of heroism. Typically, the two—courage and heroism—are put together. Heroism, however, is more of an outer designation, made by others, not by the one engaged in the acts themselves. No one would call himself a hero, unless caught up in extreme egotism. Those individuals who do act courageously are most likely surprised if, afterward, they are designated as heroes. There is, of course, a more ancient meaning of the hero than that of someone to look up to as having accomplished difficult deeds.

In the Greek world, for example, the hero was a human being who performed deeds that rivaled those of the gods and was thus deemed to be part human and part god; or the hero was from birth part human, part god. The dimension of the hero as partaking in immortality is still today a central aspect of our imagination of the hero in sports, military, or even entertainment. Today's heroes are not immortal, but we imagine them as if they were.

The virtue of courage, however, does not require imagining the courageous person as immortal. If there exists today a prevailing sense of the loss of heroes for young people to identify with, or indeed, for our nation to identify with, what is missing may not be heroism, but the virtue of courage. We perhaps find ourselves disappointed with our heroes time and time again because what we seek in the wider culture is not heroism, but courage.

The tragedy of the terrorism of September 11, 2001, has restored a national image of courage. We have heard innumerable stories of acts of courage. Fortunately, while the stature of police and firefighters has been elevated, they, for the most part, have not been turned into heroes. They exist in our imagination as courageous human beings. Attempts to turn them into heroes have not worked because of the many individuals who died. We are unable to imagine these people as immortal. The two images nonetheless remain confused if we focus only on deeds performed. A hero and a person acting with courage—both go beyond the boundaries of what seems possible and perform some act for the sake of others. We need to describe the actual soul process of courage in order to get a clear picture of this virtue.

Consider dance as an imaginal prototype of the virtue of courage. Dance gives us a helpful analogy through which we can develop an imagination of the soul quality of courage. If we can imagine what is involved in dance, we are well on the way to a deeper understanding of courage.

For example, we do not just use the sense of balance in order to move in the rhythmical ways of dance. Dancers give themselves over to the sense of balance and in so doing, go beyond what the sense of balance is able to do in ordinary bodily life. The capacity to go beyond the ordinary sense world constitutes a distinctive mark of courage, too. In fact, this capacity to go beyond the ordinary accounts for the confusion that can exist between our imagination of courage and of heroism. Sometimes, the two function as one, but they are two distinctly different ways of going beyond the ordinary.

Stretching beyond the ordinary capacities of balance involves the ability to find orientation in the absence of familiar landmarks. It marks a certain intensification of life. Classically, the hero was often drawn more to death than to life. Even today, it is perhaps the death-defying dimension of actions that draws us to the hero and the antihero, while courage often goes unnoticed. The death-defying dimension is not present in acts of courage; in fact, it is all too true that large acts of courage involve putting one's life on the line for the sake of others. Such acts, though, are not a challenging of death. The hero challenges death, acts as if he or she could outwit death.

When one goes spinning through the air, moving rhythmically, in full control at every moment, then one not just is dancing but has been taken into the form of dance itself. This kind of expansion of the sense of movement does not happen accidentally; it requires long, hard, patient, repetitive practice. In a similar way, courage does not just happen. Heroism, of course, also does not just happen. With the latter, however, the given preparation, more often than not, is something given in one's bodily constitution. In ancient times, the archetype of the hero was one who had one mortal parent and one immortal parent. Today, we call such a gift genetic inheritance.

Michael Jordan, for example, may be a basketball hero, but he is not necessarily courageous. Much of his ability to hang out in the air is due to what he was given, such as his height, his ability to move, his natural talent. All of these gifts, it is true, have been honed to a high degree. Even though his capacity to move and jump and fly through the air extends the sense of balance beyond the ordinary, the term "ordinary" here refers primarily to physical abilities. When we expect our heroes to have exemplary moral attributes, as we do, then we are set up for disappointment; for that, courage is needed.

The virtue of courage, we could say, is always heroic, but heroism is not always courageous. Heroes and heroines go beyond the ordinary, but it may well be that they are so endowed that such expansion is a given in their lives, or certainly given as a potential. The virtue of courage requires the awakening of a spiritual dimension in one's life, even if this is but for a moment. Courage is much more spiritual than heroism alone. The particular nature of this spiritual dimension, then, must be explored.

We might get to the spiritual dimension that defines courage more easily by noting how this virtue has, in large measure, gone the downward slope where it is now expressed in the degraded form of a lust for power. Therefore, in areas where we might expect expressions of courage—for example, in leadership, politics, business—instead we find rampant ambition. Ambition is one of the extremes of the virtue of courage; the other extreme is timidity. Courage finds its way between these extremes.

For example, a person who stops at nothing to get ahead and be on top may look courageous, but the spiritual act of courage has here been invaded by the ego. In timidity, we have the opposite. The timid person often has strong images of doing courageous acts, but does not have the ego strength to bring these imaginations into reality. We need to give ambition particular attention since it is so prominent in our time; doing so will give helpful insight into courage. Our strategy is to examine the manner in which courage shows up so strongly today as a kind of symptom instead of its vibrant spiritual form, and to look deeply into the symptom to see if we can locate the stirrings of its healthy form.

Ambition concerns the desire to gain power in any form. Ambition has been defined as "reach exceeding grasp"; here we see its connection with courage, which in its essence also involves going beyond one's reach. But with ambition there is a vaulting pride in one's own capacities; no need for the gods, or counsel, or even for others except insofar as they can be used for one's purposes. The word "ambition" is related to "ambit," meaning circuit, or circumference. This sense of the word indicates that ambition concerns going to the outer edge, finding and testing one's limits. Ambition conveys an outer movement, practical in nature, that takes us to the verge of the farthest possibility. Ambition calls for risk—you don't know where the edge is, and you keep extending it and extending it, never sure when you will be thrown into the abyss. Sounds a great deal like courage, doesn't it?

There is an excess to ambition, necessary to the very definition of ambition. We cannot be truly ambitious as long as we practice restraint, control, carefulness, always needing to be sure of where we are and how far we can go. It is necessary, with ambition, to be over the edge, engaged with the unforseeable, out beyond our better judgment.

These aspects of ambition are all also shared by courage, so wherein does the difference lie? I think the difference shows up in a different relation with fear. The highly ambitious individual has the ability to instill fear in others as the primary way of exercising power. Perhaps that is why ambition is both admired and despised. But this kind of exercise of power is what most differentiates ambition from courage. The courageous person does not instill fear but rather has the ability to face fear, not due to having any personal power, but through completely relinquishing personal power.

If we are connecting power with both ambition and courage, the question arises whether courage carries or exercises any kind of power. The person of ambition at least recognizes, owns up to, the need for power. If there is no power in courage, then how can it possibly accomplish anything? At the very moment a person sets his or her own life aside for the sake of someone else, personal power is relinquished. We go beyond the edge, go to the very outer limit, take an enormous risk, do not seek anything in return, and do not know or even think about whether we have the ability to do what is needed or not. Here, with courage, we use our power to give up our power. With ambition, we use our power to gain more, for no other purpose, ultimately, than this gain.

Before making any suggestions concerned with developing the virtue of courage, it seems particularly necessary with this virtue to ask why anyone would want to do so in the first place. No gain comes from it. Once we have a living sense of the truth of our being, we are compelled to face the realm of courage. Developing courage is not a matter of choice, but rather of having come to a certain inner level of development. When the truth of our being is experienced, then the soul quality of courage will emerge. Further, the virtue of courage is not a quality that just comes forward at times of extreme need or duress on the part of someone else. We have to take the notion of courage away from one of being a momentary act and extend it into the very manner in which day-to-day life might be lived.

Living for the sake of the world and for the sake of others, going beyond what we know, living on the edge, on the verge, might well be called practical spirituality. Practical spirituality is a good synonym for the virtue of courage. The practicality of the courageous personality is well known; it is someone who perseveres, keeps going, maybe plodding, but never moving backward. While there is this earthly, practical aspect to the virtue, the direction of movement is not only forward, it is also to the heights, to the summit, in the direction of the spirit.

The description of courage as practical spirituality may seem quite the opposite of what we imagine as practical. Practical spirituality, it would seem, would be better defined by something like the marriage of religious fervor and success in the world. Plenty of people these days engage in this kind of practical spirituality. Alternately, practical spirituality might mean keeping your spirituality separate from your everyday concerns. Go to church on Sunday and hope that it has an influence the rest of the week, but by all means do not allow what went on in church to influence your next big business deal. Today, practical spirituality tends to mean keeping your spirituality separate from the main goals of life, believing it will not contribute to the bottom line.

By equating courage with practical spirituality, I mean something different than the kind of materialistic pragmatism of the spirit that characterizes our national character at the moment. By practical, rather than how to use the spiritual to gain advantage with the earthly realms, I mean it as how to work with the earthly realms as a reaching toward the spiritual realms. Or how to stay alive and help others and see spiritual significance in all things, all the while responding to the moment-to-moment actualities as humanly as possible—that is practical spirituality. And not to just stay alive, to survive, but to stay intensely alive. This task, I think, constitutes the new realm for the virtue of courage. Further, the practical spirituality of courage entails not only intensity of life, but also intensity of soul.

The aspects of courage that have to do with being on the edge, going to where there is no outer support, the spiritual realms, have to be supplemented with an understanding of the depth of courage. This dimension is more difficult because it concerns the will, the most unconscious aspect of our being. We hardly know anything about the will in the most simple of actions, let alone the action of courage.

Suppose I want to open the window in my room. I have the thought of doing so, but this thought has to be transferred to my limbs in order for me to get up and do it. What goes on in an inner way in order to carry out this simple action remains covered, mysterious, virtually unknown. Purely physical explanations in terms of centers of the brain, motor nerves, and such do not take us into an inner understanding of the event. Further, such explanations are always trapped in a outmoded dualist imagination. The thought is something of a spiritual nature even if it is so that the trace of the thought is registered by the brain. The brain and the motor pathways are material. How in the world can the two interact?

What we can say with descriptive accuracy, however, is that our body, in executing the thought, engages in an act of doing. Will does not exist in the realm of thinking. I can think about closing the window, but the body must do it, and will is in the doing. Will, seen from the viewpoint of its execution by the body, shows us that our bodies are extraordinarily generous without seeking much in return. We may, in our inner consciousness, want something from the acts of the body—pleasure, for example. Strictly speaking, it is not our body that experiences pleasure, but what our body is subjected to may be experienced in a pleasurable way.

Here, with the question of will, we have to try to imagine the body itself in its very action; there is no more accurate or descriptive way of saying what the body does than to say it courageously does almost everything it is asked to do. Our body does its actions with incredible wisdom, uncanny accuracy, and impeccable integrity.

Having located the basis of courage as a fundamental act of the body engaged in the execution of will, we now need to see that there is courage, and then there is the virtue of courage, and the two are not quite the same. The virtue of courage concerns the alignment of the actions of our body and the will with the higher consciousness of our spirit individuality. In the virtue of courage, our bodily actions, our consciousness, and our spirit-being are one. We act in wholeness in courage.

Developing the virtue of courage, while not easy, does not involve any special kind of knowledge. It has to do with working with the will. In the example above, thinking about opening the window moves within the very tissues of the body setting an act of self-sacrifice in motion. For a moment, rather than wallowing in self-absorbed processes such as enjoying the world, digesting lunch, hearing beautiful sounds, the body gets up out of the chair, goes to the window, moves the lock to the open position, pulls up, bangs on the ledge to loosen the sticking, pulls again, and accomplishes the task.

Certainly, to do an action such as this does not seem to us to be anything we could call courageous. But looking strictly at the flow of what happens, from the thought to the act, that flow is what has to be kept open in those larger acts that we recognize as courageous. A continuity is established between what is seen as needed and the swift execution of the actions required. We may think that courage involves leaving the realm of thinking altogether. Because courageous action is swift, the cognitive dimension seems obscured; it is nonetheless present, and when it is not, we have not courage but foolhardiness.

Instead of the act of opening a window, imagine seeing that someone needs your help. Imagine whatever kind of situation you wish, from something simple to something serious. To do something requires an act of will. To the extent that you get caught up in thinking about what might be the right thing to do, what might be the wrong thing, how to go about doing what you think will help, courage is thwarted. This blockage, which occurs often with the most simple of situations requiring courage, becomes even more serious in the instance of the virtue of courage, where an alignment of body, will, and spirit is required.

The virtue of courage exists within the same framework I am trying to picture. Except, with the virtue of courage our thoughts are attuned to the spiritual realms along with the realms of our usual perceptions in life. However, a different kind of thinking is involved than the usual sort of materialistic-bound thinking that characterizes most of what we do.

We cannot have a spiritual thought with our usual ways of thinking. We can think *about* spiritual matters with this kind of thinking, but that is not spiritual thinking. From thinking about spiritual matters, it is not possible to enact the flow from the thought to the act of the virtue of courage. We try to do this all the time and are constantly thwarted and disappointed and feel that we have failed to do the good in the way we think it should be done. Between what we know is the spiritually right thing to do and doing it lies a huge abyss.

We conclude that, after all, we are weak, but that is not it. The difficulty lies in our thinking. We think *about* the spiritually good thing to do and then imagine that these thoughts have to be brought into the world. No courage can come from this form of thinking because there is too large a gap between the thought and the action. They are not of the same character. A thought, after all, has no force, yet we are expecting that forceless thought to provide the impetus needed to carry out an action in the world.

When we see people who are able to transfer their thoughts into swift action, it is because the thinking happens without the typical self-examination of the thinking that usually characterizes the way we think about doing something. Developing the capacity of courage requires that we close the gap between thinking and doing by learning to refrain from the secondary act of thinking—thinking about our thinking before we act. This secondary act has become so habitual for us that we do not realize it happens.

A more spiritualized thinking that can flow into the act of the virtue of courage to be carried out by our body does not consist of thinking about our thinking. That is to say, spiritualized thinking is not just another content—thinking of spirits, angels, God, the dead, or any other kind of spiritual beings. These thoughts are still secondary thinking. All such thinking is thinking from the outside, and is like the husk of the vitality and power that are needed for the virtue of courage. An apt way of describing spiritual thinking is clarity with immediacy, presence of mind. With this term, I have something deeper in mind than absence of confusion, or good logic.

Clarity means "transparency to itself," a kind of thinking that bears its own inner significance and does not need to refer to anything else in order to be comprehended. We know immediately what to do.

The virtue of courage, that is, practical spirituality, requires developing the ability to move in soul horizontally and vertically at the same time, to be in relation with the world and the spiritual worlds simultaneously. This form of soul movement also adequately describes balance. Movement, here, is also an image, and thus indicates something other than our literal notion of movement.

The balanced movement of the virtue of courage occurs when we are able to live in the perceptual experience of the ordinary world while we simultaneously live in the soul experience of the spiritual realms. Not one and then the other. Not one as more privileged than the other. Not one in service to the other. Moving courageously in the world can become a way of acting in daily life. Courage is no longer reserved for the momentary actions of emergency. Indeed, to live in the world, consciously attempting to do so spiritually while bringing spiritual vision into the practical affairs of life, is the new courage.

Courage requires that we develop the capacity to do two radically different things at the same time: to be in this world and the spiritual worlds simultaneously. To do so necessitates a kind of double vision on our part, a kind of dissociation in which two different things are going on at the same time. Dissociation, however, is not neurotic unless it is the form that is dissociation with denial.

For example, doing two things at the same time is not neurotic. Doing something different with each of our hands is a skill, and in order to do so, what I am doing with the left hand has to be dissociated from what I am doing with the right hand. But if I deny I am doing something with one hand while doing something different with the other, that is neurotic dissociation. Similarly, to hold that this earthly world is the only world there is, even though we are in constant relation with other worlds, is neurotic dissociation. Materialism is a neurotic dissociation. To hold that the spiritual world is the only world there is, that this earthly world is in fact the spiritual world, is also neurotic dissociation. Spiritualists of every sort live this neurosis. Neurotic dissociation cannot live in the ambiguity of holding contradictory things, both of which are true at the same time.

I develop this complex picture to do justice to the virtue of courage. We have to face the contradictory nature of this virtue. On the one hand, we need to be able to imagine two orders of existence, earthly and spiritual. On the other hand, we need to be able to imagine these two orders of existence functioning, not in tandem, but as one, without collapsing the one into the other. We have to be able to have the simultaneous imagination that the two (orders of existence) are the one (the fullness of the act of courage).

Our ordinary ego consciousness cannot function in such a state of contradiction. It strains at the prospect; for the ego, it has to be one *or* the other, one *then* the other. To practice the virtue of courage, we need to have stepped already into a different kind of consciousness. With courage as we usually know it, not the virtue of courage as developed here, there occurs a kind of automatic and immediate stepping over the threshold into a different mode of consciousness. People who do courageous acts find themselves, momentarily, on the other side of the threshold, in a new and different kind of time and space. When the act is completed, then ordinary perception returns. With the virtue of courage, a further step in consciousness occurs. Both ordinary perception and spiritual consciousness are required to be going on at the same time.

What courage accomplishes in the world—if we can even legitimately think of it in such terms as "accomplishment," which tends to be an exclusively ego-oriented word—is genuinely creative spiritual action in the earthly world. With spiritual courage we no longer act strictly out of personal desires, motives, urges, impulses, ideas, and ideals; but rather we allow ourselves to be vessels through which spirit works through us, radically changing us and our surroundings, and affecting others in unpredictable ways. Simultaneously, our actions in the world are a reaching toward the spiritual worlds.

Through the practical spirituality of courage, our experience of the spiritual realms becomes real and right here because we "see" their action within the perceptible world of our senses. Someone else, standing right next to us, who has not worked at this virtue, would not see the same thing we are seeing. An inner seeing accompanies an outer seeing for the person of spiritual courage. But this inner seeing is not to be confused with clairvoyance as clairvoyance is usually understood. Typically, one imagines this capacity as a kind of leaving of this world and an entrance into visions of other realms. Not so for the virtue of courage. For the person of spiritual courage, a kind of double vision exists.

The ordinary realm of perception and thinking goes on, but everything is also seen as corresponding to something of a spiritual nature. One might, for example, see another person and at the same time see in a nonphysical but real manner the spirit activity that is the essential being of that person. We see more of the person than can usually be seen. Or one might see how devastating the technologizing of the world is to the human spirit, but instead of withdrawing from it, or trying to attack it, or working against it, one sees in a concrete manner that what is being spiritually asked for is to develop an inner life that keeps pace with outer, technical development. The specific ways the virtue of courage appears in action are endless. In all instances, though, the virtue works toward the spiritual intensification of life.

Since courage works toward intensification of life, no action is taken in opposition to what may be harmful to life. We see, for example, the harmfulness of certain forms of technology, or the excessive use of carbon fuels, or multinational corporations. In the face of such things, the courageous move is to also work toward simultaneously perceiving the spiritual things that can balance such harm. This kind of courage is a new form of soul activism. This activism works only positively; it never stands against things; it seeks always to enact the necessary balance. Thus, with respect to harmful influences, the act of courage involved in relation to them is to have enough presence of mind to present to others clear ways of bringing balance to those harmful factors. This balance is first and foremost of an inner and spiritual nature.

For example, rampant electronic technology has the dire effect of cutting away the depth of human life and experience. Through the computer, Internet, cellular phones, or digital television, a certain harm is wrought in the soul; surface information and speed render the needed time and space of the depth of soul obsolete. The silence needed to come into connection with soul life is also taken away. Soul life loves repetition, slowness, contemplation, memory, dreaming, drama, and circuitous inefficiency. Once this is thoroughly understood, a stance of courage is needed to respond to this situation in the world where soul life is being depleted. A response of courage would not be to oppose what is going on in the domains of technology. To respond in opposition would be a heroic stance, not a courageous stance. Instead, two acts would characterize a stance of spiritual courage. The first would be to be able to clearly see the difficulty of technology, rather than to just respond emotionally or to get involved in dialectical thinking about technology, arguing for its good and bad points. A clarity is needed in which it can be understood that electronic technology can harm the soul. Following that, the task would be to develop inner technologies of spiritual imagination that keep pace with the outer developments of technology.

Naturally, keeping pace does not mean to invent a new meditation technique every time a new and faster computer system comes on the market. Rather, it means that runaway technology, more than anything, shows the need for individuals to consciously take up inner work to balance this outer mania.

Many additional examples of the act of spiritual courage could be presented. Personal, individual, daily instances of being asked to respond out of the virtue of courage follow the same basic pattern. As with all of the virtues, the task in thinking them through is not to come up with all the instances in which they can be applied. The intention, rather, is to develop a true imagination of the virtue that opens the possibility of not just knowing about it, but being claimed by it. Only then can the virtue work.

12 The Virtue of Discernment

The virtue of discernment holds particular importance for a deeper consideration of all the virtues. We might think of discernment as the "meta-virtue." By the term "meta-virtue" I mean to convey a sense of an overarching virtue that backs everything of its kind. I do not propose a metaphysics or an ontology of virtue, but simply want to emphasize that the relevance of the virtue of discernment extends beyond its own character. All of the virtues bear a particular relation to discernment, which is both a virtue in its own right and the quintessential *spiritual* virtue.

All spiritual traditions have recognized the importance of discernment of spirits, the capacity to know the precise nature of spiritual influences, for what can seem good can in actuality be something harmful. The virtue of discernment elevates all of the virtues onto the spiritual plane. Think of discernment as a kind of "gateway" virtue, one characterized by a quality by means of which all of the virtues take on a spiritual dimension while retaining the practical relevance necessary for action in the world. Through the practice of discernment, the level of consciousness necessary to living all of the virtues shifts to a different level.

We all have a sense of what it is to be a discerning person. It is the capacity to determine the important from the superficial, the true from the false, the helpful from the harmful. Discernment is not a matter of thinking through all possible alternatives and possible consequences of choosing one thing over another. It is more like a spiritual instinct that operates without the intervention of intellectual reflection. All of the virtues require discernment, the discernment of discovering what is needed in any given moment of action. We do not go through all of the virtues in our mind before applying the right one in any given circumstance. We know what to do intuitively. This intuition characterizes discernment, a mode of consciousness that orients us toward virtue and into the virtue needed in any given circumstance.

Each virtue is dependent upon the others, and only exists in light of those others, never on its own. At the same time, each virtue bears its own unique characteristics and equally stands on its own. When the unique quality of a virtue is grasped and entered into, a deepening of understanding and practice of all the rest also occurs. The autonomy of each virtue, while existing within the circle of the whole, necessitates the capacity of discernment, whose primary aspect consists of combining the sense of the discrete with the sense of the continuous.

The usual sense of the word "discern" has to be extended. Typically, this word signifies a capacity to separate things that may be confusedly seen as one. Discernment enters to tell how one experience, idea, perception, or inner state differs from another that may be similar in kind. The virtue of discernment, however, retains the relation between similarities at the same time that it determines the differences.

An example of discernment: I go into work and find a huge backlog of things that need to be done. Many of these things require making judgments and decisions that will affect the lives of others for many years. I feel pressed and am about to explode emotionally. I need to be able to think of what others need and not just the inconvenience this work is causing me. There are a number of virtues needed here—balance, selflessness, compassion, courage, patience. How does each virtue enter as a mode of consciousness at the exact right time and way it is needed?

I certainly do not think which virtue to apply. But, if I have made a decision in my life to live the virtues, then the virtue of discernment will be present and will make possible my doing the tasks that need to be done in relation to the virtues required. It will not be necessary to think about which virtue I am applying.

The spiritual instinct of discernment is the guiding consciousness. Discernment founds the soul's capacity to hold many different soul qualities together without contradiction or confusion.

Once a sense of the continuous universe of virtue is put forth, there exists the danger that the particular, discrete character of each gets dissolved into an undifferentiated field or flow. The reason these two kinds of thinking—discrete and continuous—cannot be held together very well is that they do not exist at the same level. Discreteness characterizes physical reality—one thing or event is separate from another. Continuity characterizes soul and spirit reality. Here, for example, one image, feeling, thought, imagination, intuition, overlaps with others. Discernment has a strong continuous dimension to it; it is a way of getting around in realms where one thing overlaps, folds into, includes, nests in another. Discernment gets us around in the virtue realm.

Our ordinary consciousness and the kind of thinking stemming from it operate at the level of empirical things and events. At this level, one thing, one event, one experience, is felt as different and separate from another. If there seems to be an influence of one empirical happening on another, the reason for such an influence is sought in the realm of a narrow view of causality, such that one realm exerts an influence on another and does so as a discrete, empirical event acting externally on another discrete, empirical event.

Our thinking concerning virtue has tried to avoid this type of empiricism, but we have to face the actuality that in daily life we still rely upon this type of consciousness.

We are required to hold two soul qualities together if we wish to have a valid sense of the quality of the virtue of discernment. Containment and openness at the same time—that is an initial quality of the act of discernment. Not one and then the other, but both simultaneously. Ordinary consciousness cannot conceive of such a contradictory reality. Not just containment and openness, but radical containment and radical openness at the same time.

For discernment to operate, we are required to locate within soul life the simultaneous feeling of containment and openness. To do this is simple. Go into silence, deep silence, so deep that it becomes a palpable, objective quality, not just being quiet. Being quiet is only the necessary condition for finding silence. It may take several months of meditative work, spending twenty minutes each day trying to find this profound silence. Once it is found, there will be a darkness. Then work at entering the darkness ever more deeply until the darkness is experienced as a "cosmic" darkness; that is, enter it until it can be experienced as a realm and not just an absence. When profound silence and profound darkness have been found, then you are in the interior of soul. This inner space will be experienced as having the two simultaneous qualities of containment and openness.

If you go into something deeply enough, and allow yourself to be contained by that one thing, you come to a point where the severe limitation opens up and the whole universe is found in this single thing. Artistic sensibility works in this way. The artist is always concerned with the particular and accepts the containment of the particular. But by going so deeply into a particular painting, poem, music, or other art form, the universal is achieved. Radical containment results in radical openness, and if someone is radically open and lets their full being take in what is presented, then the particularity of what is perceived, felt, or known is experienced.

We cannot experience the true particularity of something if we approach it with preconceived notions; we perceive only our notions projected onto the thing. If we work at the concepts of containment and openness from these characterizations, we realize that when we experience the fullest sense of containment, that is an experience of openness; when we experience the fullest sense of openness, that is an experience of containment; or, we are contained by openness and opened by containment. Getting a feeling for the play of these contradictories operating as one is a primary experience of discernment.

These permutations of the two words "containment" and "openness" are more than word games. They are intended to shift us out of the ordinary mental image we have of containment and openness as two separate and unrelated qualities so we may begin to get a true sense of the *experience* of discernment. When we put the two words and experiences together and stay true to this binding, then we begin to have intimations of the quality of the virtue of discernment.

When we are contained within ourselves, we seem to be separated from the realms outside ourselves, that is, the spiritual realms. This containment is necessary. It gives us a sense of the true transcendence of the upper or spiritual realms. Containment guarantees that our experience of the spiritual realms will not be just a subjective experience. The spiritual realms are objectively real, even though they are experienced as within. In this manner, we are most open when most contained, and when we are deeply contained, the spiritual realms can work through us. To be contained thus does not mean to be closed off from others or to be closed in on ourselves. It means to be *in soul,* to feel the innerness of things, to see things from the inside rather than outside as a spectator.

This extended description of the process, the activity of discernment, has attempted to remain at the level of the activity itself. It is important to get a sense of the process in its independent quality before inserting a more subjective element. The descriptions have kept the ego out of it. We can now go on with the inquiry, asking what the process is for, what does it do, whom does it serve?

Approaching discernment in this fashion, first viewing it as a process on its own and then seeing how it enters into individual life, is a necessary sequencing because the realm of virtue has to be approached before enacting a particular virtue. If there is not a sense that we are entering another layer of reality, then our attempts to practice virtues will be done without any development of consciousness. The result would be that virtue becomes a moralizing about life rather than a living in harmony with the more subtle dimension of the universe.

Can we say anything now concerning how the virtue of discernment operates within individual experience? We can say that it operates instantaneously, like electricity; it operates like a moment of illumination. Boom! It is there, then it is gone. You cannot hold on to it; it appears and disappears in an instant. A moment of pure openness to the spiritual realms and an equally brief moment of containment. Such moments can occur when we are the most contained, when we make an interior vessel of the whole of our being. Such moments occur when our inner containment operates in rhythm with moments when we are the most open, when we are way "out there" in our wildest spiritual imaginings.

What are we discerning when discernment operates as a virtue, not as, for example, an ordinary act of differentiating one experience from another? For example, a kind of discernment is often needed to tell when a particular emotion is ours and when what we are feeling is someone else's feeling. If, in the presence of another person, I suddenly feel a wave of anger—is that mine, or does that belong to my partner with whom I am trying to have a calm conversation while she is very upset? This kind of experience is a kind of discernment process, but it is not the virtue of discernment. Discernment operates as a virtue only when a specifically spiritual dimension of a moment of experience enters. We could say that discernment always involves a discernment of spirits. But what does that mean?

When we suddenly and unexpectedly have a bright idea, is this an illumination of a spiritual nature, or is it just my bright idea, carrying the intent of furthering my own desires? Should I follow this idea, take it up and develop it, or, seeing that there is a great deal of self-centeredness in it, let it drop by the wayside? How in the world do you tell the first kind of experience from the second?

Both occur as seeming flashes of insight. Both usually occur following a prolonged period of going inward, of concentration, perhaps of meditation, the containment necessary for the openness. Thus, one aspect of the virtue of discernment concerns the interior differentiation concerning what kind of insight we have been given. Another aspect concerns the process of letting the insight develop into an actual act in our lives and in the world. What can be said concerning these two moments of the virtue of discernment?

The first aspect of the virtue of discernment, considered in an individual manner—how it touches us individually—concerns the determination of the nature of the insights that come to us. These insights can be received as spiritual, or they can be as if they were produced by our own "brilliance." When they are spiritual insights, they are more like visitations, and we, in our containment, are the receivers of this open offering from the spiritual worlds. However, spiritual insight does not involve becoming a medium for the spirits. Spiritual insights occur with more intensity of consciousness. Mediumship requires loosening the intensity of consciousness.

When insights are "brilliant," we take the illumination to be of our own doing; we try to possess and hold on to them, and make use of them for our own purposes. Or when a "brilliant" insight comes, we take it to mean that it was meant for us and we are supposed to take it and run with it. Often, however, the egotism in "brilliant" ideas is not this clear. The bright idea may seem to be one that can be taken into the world to bring some good to others.

The "brilliant" ideas of scientists are very often of this nature. The first moment of the virtue of discernment asks us to be able to tell the difference between being an illuminated person and a brilliant thinker. One might think that this virtue, then, applies only to those who have to contend with the gifts and defects of strong intelligence, but that is not so. We all have to suffer this question of the difference between illumination and brilliance in one or more arenas of our lives. Brilliance is characterized by the capacity to combine thoughts in a way that makes everything conform to the way I want to see it. Illumination is interested only in serving the spiritual intelligence that is the source of the insight, that serves what it wants, not what I want.

The second moment of discernment concerns how the illumination is brought out of the realm of a revelation of sorts and into action in the world. It is intimately entwined with the first moment. If the illumination gets rightly attributed to the working of something beyond my own intelligence, a cosmic intelligence, then it would seem that it needs to stay there. What right do I have to try to make it apply to things of the earthly world? Such an attitude, however, makes an absolute separation between the earthly world and the spiritual worlds.

Letting discernment have its say, cosmic intelligence is allowed to play through the limitations of individual intelligence. But the two cannot be allowed to separate. Currently, for example, science allows them to separate. Thus, true moments of illumination achieved through deep meditative states brought about by concentrating for a long time on a problem lead to discoveries that are immediately put into practice. The illumination is never attributed to a spiritual world. Discernment is never even addressed. The primary questions are never asked: Where does this insight *originate?* What does it *want?*

A truly intelligent way to work with an illumination, a flash of insight, is to actively give it back to where it came from in the first place. Thank you for the insight. I return it to you, the true originator. Let it cook for a while. The mere fact that it entered my awareness has changed what I do. Am I saying it should not be applied? Not indiscriminately. On our own, any application, no matter the apparent humane values involved, will be indiscriminate. Here, at the level of our own resources, we can only speak of degrees of indiscrimination. This unfortunate range of choice is due to the fact that if illumination gets separated from intelligence, only half of the whole is being dealt with. The virtue of discernment requires working at each and every step with the whole.

Above, a central part of the process of discernment was described as acknowledging the source of our deepest insights and then returning them to this source rather than immediately seeking to apply them in our lives. This aspect of discernment needs clarification. This process is discernment's alchemical way. In alchemy, when a substance was heated in a hermetic vessel, the substance first transformed into a liquid, which then transformed into steam, rising in the vessel. The hermetic vessel, however, was shaped in such a manner that the distillate turned back on itself and was returned to the substance at the bottom of the vessel; it was heated again and recirculated over and over. One version of this vessel was called the "pelican" because it resembled the sacrificing, self-wounding pelican, arching its neck and piercing its own breast in order to feed its young with its own blood. The alchemical way of discernment follows this kind of process of drawing down an insight, returning it again to the spiritual realm, drawing it down again, returning it again, over and over. The circulation and recirculation of the insight in this manner constitutes a process of purification, a procedure absolutely crucial to discernment.

The recirculation process also extends the instant of discernment itself, which has been described above as the contradictory simultaneity of openness and containment. For a time, the two aspects, openness and containment, are to be somewhat separated, as in the hermetic vessel, just as in alchemy coagulation is separate from dissolution. So, with discernment, there is a momentary light of illumination/brilliance. An intelligence is operating. If we take it to be an illumination from above, it stays above. If we take it to be of our own doing, we do not have the kind of intelligence necessary to apply the insight in life or in the broader world without reducing the spiritual illumination into a self-centered, egotistical, personal notion.

A circulation is required between the two moments of insight, between the two levels at which it operates. What was one (illumination) becomes the two (illumination and intelligence), which becomes the three (illumination, intelligence, and intelligence returned to illumination), which becomes the four (discernment), to put the whole operation of discernment into the paradoxes of alchemy.

An interesting example of discernment gone indiscriminate can be found in the work of William Crookes (1832–1919). It is one of thousands that could be pointed to in the realm of science, but one that is equally illustrative of what happens in more personal ways every day in our own lives. William Crookes was the inventor of the cathode ray tube, which made possible everything we have today in the domain of television, computers, radar, and any electronic device dependent upon this technology of the vacuum, cathode ray tube. His research was also the starting point of the long train of inquiry that has now culminated in the release of atomic energy.

Little known is the fact that Crookes's scientific investigations were initiated by the loss of a much-beloved brother. At the sight of the dead body of his brother, Crookes came to the questions of whether spirit-life continues after death, how to find and make connection with such a realm, and how this life would manifest itself in the earthly world. He carried out a series of scientific experiments with Spiritualists, and in particular with one individual, Daniel Douglas Home. These experiments convinced Crookes that he had discovered a new form of energy, which he termed "psychic force." This force showed itself capable of movement in defiance of gravity, able to move objects, produce sound, and manifest light without any apparent source.

Crookes's scientific investigations of the phenomena of Spiritualism were soundly rejected by the scientists of the time. He dropped the direct investigations and continued with his researches into electricity. But in his subsequent scientific inquiries, he was always something of a Spiritualist. He indicated, for example, that he felt especially attracted by the strange effects arising when electricity passes through rarefied gases; that reminded him of certain luminous phenomena he had observed during his spiritistic investigations. These latter investigations led him to the discovery of the cathode ray tube. Crookes considered cathode rays to be of a double nature—they were both material and supermaterial at the same time. He termed these rays "Radiant Matter," or "The Fourth State of Matter." Of these rays, Crookes stated:

> We have seen that in some of its properties Radiant Matter is as material as this table, whilst in other properties it almost assumes the character of Radiant Energy. We have actually touched here the borderland where Matter and Force seem to merge into one another, the shadowy realm between Known and Unknown, which for me has always had peculiar temptations. . . . I venture to think that the greatest scientific problems of the future will find their solution in this Borderland, and even beyond; here, it seems to me, lie Ultimate Realities, subtle, far-reaching, wonderful.

This line of development can be seen as revealing an absence of discernment. The need for discernment began for Crookes at the bedside of his dead brother. There, a kind of illumination occurred: what happens after death? That was the question that came to Crookes with a great deal of force. He then became interested in Spiritualism, which at that time took the form of appearances of phantom beings in a fog at the séance table, tapping of tables, and the movement of objects in the room at the séance. The need for discernment became even greater: Is there a difference between true spiritual existence and materialistic manifestations of spiritual life? That was the question that needed to be held and meditated.

The illuminative moment, when Crookes had the insight that the dead may still be involved in matters of the Earth, turned into a brilliant idea with the exploration of cathode rays and the invention of the cathode ray tube. The whole matter of the relation of the living and the dead was degraded into a form of materialism. Had discernment operated, the initial insight that needed to be returned to the spiritual world in the form of meditation was the living question: What is the relation between the living and those who have died? This initial, illuminative question was instead taken by Crookes as the brilliant idea that light and electricity are somehow manifestations of the dead. This idea then got further application in the form of the cathode ray tube.

Thousands of people all over the world still think that spiritual energy is electrical in nature, or that it is manifested in material forms of one sort or another, from radio waves to the electrical activity of the body. Consider, for example, the research into Kirlian photography. The bulk of the research in this area takes the pictures of the light around the body made visible with Kirlian photography to be the aura, the spiritual light of the person. Actually, it is the electrical activity of the body that is being photographed.

Add to that the fact that, paradoxically, Crookes's investigations, which ultimately led to the project of the atomic bomb, have brought into the world not a way of relating with the dead but the most destructive death force imaginable. His spiritual investigations had the effect of bringing into the world great confusion concerning the nature of spiritual reality and an intensification of the forces of death.

We cannot look at this research one-sidedly without becoming equally caught in an absence of discernment. What about all of the positive developments resulting from Crookes's research? William Crookes can well be called the father of the Information Revolution. We would not have television, computer screens, radar, and many medical instruments without him. We would not have all the valuable benefits of atomic research.

The point of telling Crookes's story is not to say that what he did was wrong and should not have happened. It happened, and the tasks of discernment now take new forms. We now have to work at discerning true spirituality from simulated spirituality. We have to be perceptive enough to see, for example, that electronic technology is a kind of simulated spirituality, and that perhaps its tremendous attraction in our time is based in a deep spiritual longing. Through this technology we are able to be present to instantaneous thought, information, images; and it seems to offer the promise of relieving us from burdens, while giving pleasure and fulfillment. Perhaps we are called to extricate that longing from its misplacement so that it can be explored in terms equal to the realities prompting those longings.

Discernment is truly the virtue of our times, a primary interior quality asked of us all. What occurred for William Crookes is emblematic of what we each face now as an ongoing challenge—that of receiving spiritual insight, knowing that this illumination is not wholly of our own doing, but learning to be responsible for it and to take it into the world in a spiritual manner.

13 The Virtue of Love

Love is a vast topic and a vast experience, encompassing the whole of the aim and purpose of humanity. A consideration of love as a virtue takes one small, but as I hope to show, tremendously significant aspect of love and develops the practical means for concentrating that aspect and making it fully conscious. The virtue of love has nothing to do with being in love or falling in love, or wanting to love and be loved. It even goes beyond the ways in which we daily love someone. With the virtue we shift from the soul level of feeling to the level of spiritual action in the world in our relationships with others. How do you do love is the question posed to us when we encounter this virtue.

"Love" is one of those big words, in league with words like "soul" and "spirit," words that cannot be defined because they are symbols and as such embrace worlds of meaning. Unlike the words "*soul*" and "*spirit*," however, everyone wants, needs, longs for, and has some notion of what they think constitutes love. When I ask a group of people what constitutes soul or spirit, a good number do not know how to speak of such things. When I ask them what love is, they all have some notion. However, when I ask the group to define the virtue of love, few are able to speak with clarity.

Everyone knows that love is powerful, but we know very little about being conscious within the power of love. We still live as if love happens to us. A consideration of the virtue of love shows that while love does happen to us, we can come to attune to its presence in such a way that our relationships with others come to be ways of serving the soul of others and of the world and of deepening into the mysteries of our soul.

The experience we typically speak of as "loving someone" cannot be called the virtue of love; it remains too mixed with our own individual needs. Besides, this kind of love, strictly speaking, consists primarily of the emotional reaction to another person rather than the action of loving in an ongoing way that is for the sake of the other person. The virtue itself remains hidden and obscured unless deliberate work takes place to make it conscious. We have to do a good deal of inner work to come to the experience of love as the essential defining quality of what it is to be human. A human being is one who loves. Not only does love complete us in our humanity, it is the redeeming gift we are able to give to the world.

Love is always relationship. It is a relational phenomenon; it is not something that I have alone and then proffer to others. Nor it is something that others possess and can offer me as if it were a subtle commodity. The great task presented by this virtue is to develop the capacity to concentrate on, to learn to perceive, to live within the between space of the relation itself. Love never involves only a lover and a beloved. There is the third part of love, the relation itself that exists between the lover and the beloved. Becoming sensitive to this dimension, the charged field of the love, takes us into the virtue.

Relation does not exist in me alone, and it does not exist in the other alone. It is a soul space that exists between those in relationship and also encompasses their inner life. This soul space that exists between those in relationship also involves their mutual relation with the spiritual dimension of love. Love occurs between myself and another person or a task or a place or a creation such as a beautiful painting, a deeply moving book, or an inspired concert. This is the horizontal dimension of the love relationship. But love is also inherently spiritual. Through love we are always in connection with the divine worlds. The virtue involves the skill of being simultaneously present to both of these dimensions.

The "between" spoken of here defies all dualisms. The division between inner life and outer world dissolves in the midst of the phenomenon of the virtue of love; as well, the spiritual and the earthly come into living confluence. It is not possible, while experiencing the actual soul of relating, to know whether what we are experiencing is something inner, outer, or both. The virtue of love depends on our capacity to be able to live this soul space without becoming overwhelmed by feeling and shutting down our hearts. We often shut our hearts, either when the magnificence of love gets to be too much for us to hold, or when it seems that the force of love has been taken from us, though when this happens it is often because we have mishandled the mystery.

How many of us have experienced the actual relationship, something that goes beyond what I feel about another person and what another person feels about me? The relationship itself is a reality, able to be experienced in certain moments and certain situations. The virtue of love senses this interactive field and compels us to relate to others through the medium of this soul space. When this space is ignored we feel suffocated in our relating, or abused, or not cared for. At best, when this space is ignored we live in relationship as simply comfortable but without any sense of what we are doing together. It is the love itself that suffers when the medium of the soul space between people is disregarded.

How do we know when we are sensing the field of relationship? When we are with others in the ordinary circumstances of life, there is a felt separation between ourselves and others. They are "over there" and we are here, where our body is. What goes on between us is mainly functional or perhaps social, but the main interest is self-interest. The spiritual tone, the rhythm of the words each person speaks, the subtlety and nuance of the interaction goes unnoticed, or is noticed only at the edges. In this kind of interaction, there also exists a strong sense of the linear character of ordinary time. Our time together feels more like "doing time." What holds people together in this kind of situation are the mutual tasks, not the mutual love. A first signal of entering the field of love is the felt change of time.

When the connection with someone has more of a heart quality, then it is possible to sense the field. Time takes on a different quality. More duration is experienced, and sometimes it is almost as if we have entered a timeless realm with someone we love. In linear time, one event follows in sequence after the previous event. Things happen in a string, one after another. In the interactive field, time begins to feel more "friendly."

By this term I mean that there is a desire to linger with the other person. There is a deliciousness to being together, and if we have to leave and go our separate ways, it is as if a liquid exists between us that stretches and the field is carried with us wherever we go. The field is felt as a subtle change of consciousness and feeling. There is a break in our ordinary consciousness; a door opens and we begin to feel there is something between us. If you want to consciously cultivate the field of a relationship, you have to find this time quality by being attentive to the moment when there is a break in ordinary consciousness.

A break in ordinary consciousness is something different than a momentary pause, a blank spot, though if we are able to really notice those pauses and enter into the very space of the pause, that pause is the crack opening the door to friendly time. Ordinarily, in our connections with others, our consciousness is full of these breaks, which we take to be quite normal and natural, though if they are too long we begin to feel uncomfortable. We feel comfortable when our consciousness is experienced as seamless to us. Our attention may move from one thing to another, and we may lose consciousness of what we are doing from time to time, but on the whole there is not an experience of our breaking into a different realm.

This sense of our consciousness as continuous is an illusion. The illusion serves a purpose; it makes it seem as if consciousness serves our every need, whim, and purpose. When a break occurs, if we can really be present to it, we discover in a flash that consciousness is a gift that is being given to us. And there are many gifts; ordinary consciousness is just one of them. To receive the gift of a different mode of consciousness, there has to be a break.

Sometimes such a break gets extended in time and we find ourselves living in a kind of liminal state in which nothing makes sense. The extension of this break often means we are looking for what we left behind instead of what is trying to come in. If we follow the break in consciousness, instead of looking backward, we make connection with the interactive field where love does its work.

The interactive field is a fluid medium. It exists between whatever content goes on between myself and another individual, and when attended to, it amplifies and can be felt even more than the content of what we are doing with someone. When we feel this medium, we begin to know that it is the intervals that occur in our connections with others that are most important. The content of what we feel, think, speak, perceive, imagine is important, but primarily to us. We thus identify consciousness with a content, and even identify love as a kind of content—a content of certain kinds of feelings. The intervals are taken to be inconvenient interruptions. The intervals, though, are where love thrives.

An interval in consciousness is not the same as going unconscious. It is consciousness with a different timing. The work of consciously entering a field consists of becoming aware of the intervals and not just the content of what goes on between myself and another person. The virtue of love consists of working more and more into the intervals, to the point that whatever content occurs now emerges from the depths of the intervals.

The virtue concerns listening for the intervals when we are with someone, and gradually breaking through the tyranny of the content of what we may be talking about or doing. The content, of course, is still important, in itself, and also as the way to launch ourselves into the field. Staying in the field, and not immediately needing to refocus attention back on the content, is love in action, the virtue.

The play of content and interval, given equal significance, takes linear time sequence and bends it into an active spiral, a vortex. We may, for example, find that we begin to enjoy repetitions, things said one way and then another. We find joy in the rhythm of our interaction. We enjoy lingering in the moment. We hear more deeply and have intimations of the deepest soul-being of the person we are with. We experience a movement between us that has force; we are together in a force field.

This field can be felt in a very bodily way. It is as if there is a current of energy between us. It is not like electric energy. It is much more gentle, as if you could feel light's illumination as a force. It is more like an illumination than a electric current. Yet, this gentle force is strong and steady.

The practice of the virtue of love requires learning to give greater and greater intensity of attention to the intervals in our interactions with others. Doing so is an assault and an insult to our ordinary consciousness, which thrives on content, knowing, and efficiency of operation, even when we are being kind and feel treated with kindness. Perception of the soul space between myself and another individual requires not-knowing, but rather full presence. We know this field through the whole of our body, not with our mind. So, to the mind, what is happening is completely puzzling and even frightening. If fear begins to come, the thing to do is move consciousness from the head to the heart region of the body. Then the fear will stop and the subtle currents can be felt.

Stepping into the field is like stepping into another world. Perception alters. It is as if a soft mist enters the room where we are, diffusing the sharp edges between things ever so slightly. Accompanying the barely perceptible blurring of bodily boundaries is a sharpening of the individual interiority of each of the people so that they each become more centered in themselves while at the same time they are more open to the other person.

In the intervals in an encounter with another person through love, we find that our visual perception of the other person changes. The feeling aspect of perception, which usually lies in the background in our encounters, now comes to the foreground. The physiognomy of the individual becomes more apparent. It is as if we can see the soul of the other person shining in the countenance of the face. We intimately feel what is being expressed through the face and gestures of the other person.

We perceive physiognomy all the time, but unconsciously. Ordinarily, we focus on the body of a person as a content and are not aware of the light as it reflects the features of a person's face. Field perception consists of becoming sensitive to the interplay of the person's features with the light. It also concerns becoming sensitive to the light emanating from the person. In the light of love, people shine.

Perception in the interactive field of love takes on the character of wholeness, which entails the capacity to focus simultaneously on the content of what is going on between us and another and also on the perceptible soul life of the other person. Do not take this description as saying that everything becomes confused or indistinct. Much more precision of perceiving exists in the field of love than with our usual ways of perceiving. We usually see categories and not the essence of the person. We see, for example, our friend, our sweetheart, our wife or husband, but seldom see their essence shine because we do not concentrate on what goes on in the interactive space of love. We feel so separated and alone because we are relying on concepts rather than our heart, and the unique character of each person does not come through. It does come through in the field. Ordinarily, we look at others but we do not see them. To see and to be seen cannot be underestimated; when seeing and being seen take place, it is like a blessing; or we could say, it is a healing.

When we see the other person through the field of love, we see the other person in his or her potential. We perceive who that person can be; the virtue of love perceives the potentially present as actually present. This is a real perception and not just our hopes, wishes, or guesses concerning the future of the person. To be seen is to be seen in our potential, in our coming-to-be.

Enacting the virtue of love through perception of the field between myself and another person is not angelic perception. While the spirit of the other person becomes as if perceptibly present, it does so along with the pain, vulnerability, and woundedness each of us is. Without these tensions between seeing the spiritual perfection of the others along with their well-wrought pains of life experience, we are not in a field of force.

The virtue of love is the effort to be within the field and it is also the effort to retain the full presence of the soul-being of the other person as an afterimage when we are not with that person, or during those times when the interactive field is not strong. By the term "afterimage," I mean that the soul-being of the other person continues to have an effect on us when we are not with the person or when we return to the person and the field does not seem perceptible. This is the extended aspect of the virtue of love. The virtue, then, consists of shifting our attention to what goes on between myself and another person, and it also consists of allowing something of the soul life of the other person to live within me. I am speaking here of something more than a fond feeling or memory. The depth of soul of the other person continues to resonate within my soul.

The word "resonate" comes from the Latin verb "*resonare*," meaning to "return to sound." When we sound an object such as a bell, the bell continues to ring or resonate the original sound. There is another kind of resonance called sympathetic resonance. When a bell sounds and continues to resonate, another object with qualities of the same pitch as the bell will begin to vibrate with the bell. A type of sympathetic resonance characterizes the functioning of the soul space of the virtue of love.

Imagine walking along the ocean shore, holding hands with your lover. As you walk, the rhythm of your steps together begins to match the incoming and outgoing waves. As that happens you both feel intimately together with each other—and with the world. This is the resonance of the soul. And if we contemplate the phenomenon just a bit, we see that soul is not in me and in you separately. We are in soul and soul is in the world. When we are in soul, then we feel the innerness of our life, but also feel something of the mysterious qualities of the world. The interactive field of love brings in the world as our partner. We feel more connected with the beauty of the world and can sense it directly. We notice more, perceive more intently, feel the hallowing of the world.

A vital aspect of the virtue of love is to work to become sensitive to the ongoing reverberation that occurs when we have felt a field of love between ourselves and others.

To do so, it is necessary to understand that the soul is not something akin to a bell that picks up the similar vibrations from another soul. Thinking this way about the soul would be too materialistic. The description of the bell resonating is an analogy only. It helps attune us to the way soul functions. Except with soul we have a picture, not of something that resonates, but a pure resonating medium.

Think of soul this way—as pure resonance, not as something that resonates. Think of the action of love as intensifying or sometimes changing the pitch or the tone or the rhythm of the resonating medium. Think of the medium as the flow between all things, the great force of attraction. Soul, then, is not a subtle thing that resonates. Soul is resonance. We know we are in soul when there is the quality of resonance. Our perceptions, feelings, thoughts, sensations, reverberate because they are being carried on waves of love.

We come close here to developing the physics of love, but that is the only way to feel something of the force of the virtue of love. Love is a real force in the world, not just good feelings. It has the power to change the world. Shifting to the language of resonance and away from the language of sentimentality helps us sense the force of love. We often use the language of sympathetic resonance to describe soul phenomena without realizing we are doing so. We speak of "being in tune" with someone, or "being on the same wavelength." Something about a connection with another person feels just right. It clicks. Or there is the experience of dissonance. We look for experiences of resonance and flee from those of dissonance, though dissonance too belongs to the language of the virtue of love. The dissonances are necessary. They, in relation with resonance, give love its force.

When we experience the interactive field of active love, this experience continues on in resonance. But it is more than a matter of memory. Something more happens than having inner pictures and feelings. Engaging the virtue of love enacts a process of soul-making. Soul is not present without our interactions of love with others. These interactions can be small or large; I am talking about not only the love of our life, but rather the ongoing practice of the virtue of love even in everyday encounters. The love that exists between individuals continues as reverberation, and that is soul-making, not memory of something that happened. Living in this current contributes to each other's soul and to the soul of the world. It contributes not as a kind of addition to what is there, but as a creative reconfiguring. Our lives and the life of the world are transformed by love.

In the philosophy of Aristotle, a distinction is made between *potentia* and actuality. Things can exist in *potentia*—the word means "coming into being." The soul belongs to the realm of *potentia,* a domain of coming-into-being. Thus, soul is always connected with imagination, dream, creativity, possibility. The virtue of love activates these realms. *Potentia* is not on the way to becoming something real. It is of the soul's nature to be vibrating *potentia,* intermingling every moment with whatever is around, picking up the vibrations of the milieu. Soul lives in *sympathy, antipathy, empathy, telepathy,* and sometimes even in *apathy.* The key part of these words, the "pathy," refers to the soul's pathos, a word that means "to allow." Soul is the allowing of all sorts of resonances to flow through, chief of which is love.

Practice of the virtue of love begins with giving attention to the rhythmic elements of our interactions with others. Attend, for example, to the way you speak—the tones, the nuances, the rhythms, the space, the undertones and overtones—more even than to the content of what you say. Such attention changes the way we are with people from social nicety to acts of healing. *How* we are with others takes on equal importance with what we are doing in terms of content. The work of the virtue of love is to be present to these subtleties with utterly clear consciousness.

You will find that if you try to allow a more diffuse consciousness of the heart to exist alongside the content of what the interaction is about, there is a tendency to go toward a kind of hypnotic state or a light trance. We have to work to be aware when this is happening. The recovery from sliding into a light trance, however, does not consist of moving back into focused consciousness to the exclusion of resonance. Rather, when there is a feeling of slightly losing the content, then move consciousness, quite deliberately, to the region of the heart.

Living in the heart of love requires this kind of practice. Centering in the heart means that our interactions have a quality of reverence, and we can begin to attend to our speaking with someone as a listening rather than the kind of push-pull speaking that usually goes on between two people.

The virtue of love has nothing to do with sentimentality. Finding the way into the interactive field and living in soul resonance also mean that we are better able to hold experiences of dread, anxiety, anger, anguish, and confusion that happen between us and others. These emotions are usually considered a hindrance to a good relationship. When these qualities are excluded from our relating, or only come up when there are problems, then the virtue of love cannot operate with the vigor required. These forceful qualities give love its transformative and moral force. Without these qualities the interactive field disappears.

The virtue of love is not confined to our relationships with others. Try to imagine the interactive field as extending to occurrences other than our interpersonal connections. Maybe you hear a remarkable concert that continues to live within you and changes your life. Maybe you read a book that does something to you that goes far beyond the content. Maybe you undergo an experience in meditation. Maybe you study a virus in a laboratory and enter so deeply into what you are doing that you step into a field. These can all be experiences initiating the virtue of love. When such moments occur, and they occur far more often than we realize, it is of importance to recognize them as a strong impetus to change.

Love comes and invites us to change, to enter into our potential, to feel intensely the process of coming-to-be, even though we do not know where our unfolding will go. This same love invites the person or the event we are involved with to change too. The other person enters potential. And so does the world when approached in this manner. We simply have to suspend judgment concerning what is happening and allow the experience of this between realm to float vibratingly as if it were an undulating current in the center between ourselves and others.

I have drawn attention to the virtue of love as soul-making that transforms us. What is the direction of such transformation? The virtue transforms conflicting pairs of opposites that we feel in relation to another person. We may feel both love and hate for someone, despair and desire, daring and cowardice, anxiety and calmness. We begin to realize that the other person does not cause these conflicting feelings. Rather, the other person makes it possible that we discover these conflicting feelings within ourselves. The virtue does not take away such feelings, but something new comes into them. Let's look at an example.

Recall a time when someone you know, someone you love, said something to you, perhaps something complimentary, but when you heard the compliment you felt a conflict. Maybe the person said, "Oh, your friendship means so much, I have grown through my contact with you." But when the person said that, you felt a bodily tension and a desire to withdraw, as what the person was saying felt odd. You sensed that perhaps the person was using you for their growth. You felt both gratitude for the compliment and a desire to withdraw. A conflict of feeling.

If you are able to stay in the field and live in the resonance of the virtue of love, the conflict changes into a sensing of the dynamic flow between the opposites rather than remaining in conflict. The conflict indicates that there is engagement at the soul level. The tension, when felt with love, loosens into the flow of the field instead of the tension of polarities. This loosening is felt in the region of the heart and is not a cognitive knowing. The loosening can be felt in the body as the constriction of the tension eases. More is involved here than mere relaxation. The boundaries of the body expand and perception opens and the world appears more vivid and alive. The engagement with soul in this way opens to an engagement with the soul of the world.

The virtue of love does even more than transform conflicting feelings. The true aim of the virtue is to release the power of love into the world. Sensing the field and how it changes our experience of time and our perception of the world and how it transforms us is the preparation for its more mysterious work. We are invited to get close to the activity of love in the ways described, not only for what it brings to us, but so that we can be more consciously present to the force of love and release it into the world. This act of release can be an active, conscious practice. When we experience the field, we build it for a while, stay in it, let it amplify, and then consciously give it away to the world. Then the virtue is more complete.

14 **Working with the Virtues in Our Lives**

There are three ways we can engage the virtues in our life—an intellectual-spiritual way, a psychological way, and a spiritual-psychological way. The first way consists of knowing what the virtues are, studying each of them, discovering ways to meditate on them, and then beginning to observe how they function in life.

A second way does not begin by paying attention to anything like virtue at all. Here, the circumstances of our lives, from time to time, throw us into various kinds of confusion that can be times of being called to one virtue or another. If we learn to pay attention to these times of upset, through looking for the soul and spirit directions in them rather than fighting against what is happening or trying through all sorts of different means to restore life the way it used to be, then we can be taken into virtue in very specific ways. This more common way of encountering the entry into the virtues will be explored in the reflections in this chapter.

The third, spiritual-psychological, way begins with some knowledge and study of the virtues. Life taking its course will provide circumstances in which the possibility of the development of virtue will be presented to us. Here we can be much more conscious of the process we are engaged in. In contrast to the second way of proceeding, the strictly psychological way, with a spiritual-psychological approach we can recognize that opportunities for the development of specific virtues are presenting themselves when we find ourselves in confusion. Instead of letting the process take place randomly, reflection and meditation can be brought to bear so as to make the development of virtue a *conscious* process directly connected with life. The specific kind of meditation involved in this approach will be presented in what follows.

As a beginning point, the twelve virtues and some of their important characteristics have been summarized in table 1. We begin by placing the twelve virtues on the circle of the zodiac—column one, two, and three of the table. The correspondence of each virtue with a sign of the zodiac is something that is given from previous research—not mine but that of H. P. Blavatsky and Rudolf Steiner.

We begin to get a feeling for the virtue universe by relating one virtue to the virtue preceding and following it in the zodiac. Developing an inner feeling for the virtue, so that it is not just a word but begins to be an actual experience, requires meditating on the dynamic flow between the virtue before, the virtue in question, and the virtue after the virtue in question.

For example, we begin to get an inner feeling for the virtue of devotion by meditating on the flow of love to devotion to balance. These three words have to be pictured within, and then the flow from one to the other can be pictured in meditation. One way is to picture actual instances of being engaged in an action in life that expresses love; then one that expresses devotion; then one that expresses balance. An inner feeling of the virtue begins to develop. In the chart, this relation is given for each virtue under the heading "Before/After."

Under the heading "Opposite," the zodiac sign opposite in the zodiacal circle to the one in question is given, along with the virtue connected with that sign, and beneath that, the initial quality through which that opposite virtue typically manifests itself. A further sense of the virtue in question is given by meditating upon and feeling the line of tension between the virtue and its opposite.

For example, the virtue of equanimity is opposite the virtue of devotion. It is the tension between these two that leads to a feeling of devotion as having an ongoing steadiness. Opposites here do not mean contraries; rather, an opposite means that the virtue

Table 1: Working with the Virtues

Sign	Time	Virtue	Initial Quality	Before/After	Opposite	Image	Practice	Extremes
Aries	March 21–April 21	Devotion	unsettledness	love/balance	Libra (Equanimity) (indecision)	ability to love in a steady, ongoing, deep way	approach others and the world as sacred	malice, superficiality
Taurus	April 21–May 21	Balance	material comfort	devotion/faithfulness	Scorpio (Patience) (passion)	right relation between effort and grace	deepening into a sense of destiny	imposition, apathy
Gemini	May 21–June 21	Faithfulness	inattention	balance/selflessness	Sagittarius (Truth) (opinionated)	standing firm in soul and spirit	mindfulness in image and reverence	dogmatic, psychopathic
Cancer	June 21–July 21	Selflessness	self-protection	faithfulness/compassion	Capricorn (Courage) (stubborn)	adhering to inner soul and spirit while serving	vulnerability	self-abandon, egotism
Leo	July 21–Aug. 21	Compassion	power	selflessness/courtesy	Aquarius (Discernment) (confusion)	feeling suffering of other while allowing it to be	discern difference between one's suffering and the other's	contempt, numbness

Sign	Time	Virtue	Initial Quality	Before/After	Opposite	Image	Practice	Extremes
Virgo	Aug. 21–Sept. 21	Courtesy	control	compassion/equanimity	Pisces (Love) (sentimental)	holding back emotion to give soul life of others a place	practice soul and spirit perception	smothering, carelessness
Libra	Sept. 21–Oct. 21	Equanimity	indecision	courtesy/patience	Aries (Devotion) (unsettled)	evenness of emotion; honoring all emotion	befriend our vices	crudeness, aesthete
Scorpio	Oct. 21–Nov. 21	Patience	passion	equanimity/truth	Taurus (Balance) (comfort)	soul/spirit time/fecund void	waiting with open expectation	rigidity, impatience
Sagittarius	Nov. 21–Dec. 21	Truth	opinionated	patience/courage	Gemini (Faithfulness) (inattention)	feeling-toward; soul-touch; subtle; nuance	attention; focus; concentrate	judging and opinionated, gossiping and slanderous
Capricorn	Dec. 21–Jan. 21	Courage	stubborn	truth/discernment	Cancer (Selflessness) (self-protection)	engaged perception; persistence	facing abyss and continuing	ambition, timidity
Aquarius	Jan. 21–Feb. 21	Discernment	confusion	courage/love	Leo (Compassion) (power)	presence to desires; freedom	creative thinking	self-indulgence, self-denial
Pisces	Feb. 21–March 21	Love	sentimental	discernment/devotion	Virgo (Courtesy) (control)	doing love	universal friendliness	emotionality, hard-hearted

opposite the one being considered is a help in entering the virtue being considered. We need equanimity to practice devotion, and vice versa. In meditation, it is possible to feel the precise relation and difference between devotion and equanimity. The former carries strong feelings of the heart and a strong sense of having to be intensely present to the moment. Equanimity does not center so strongly in the region of the heart; it concerns more the whole of the emotional realm.

Under the heading "Image" is a short description of the essence of the virtue. These images come from meditating on each virtue and then through this meditation coming to see the particular essence of each virtue such that it can be stated in a few words.

Under the heading "Practice" is a short description of the kind of practice that can develop the consciousness of the virtue in question. The particular practice also comes from the phenomenological work of carefully describing each of the virtues. When the virtue itself is allowed to speak, to unveil itself, rather than us imposing some meaning on the virtues, the practice associated with the development of the virtue spontaneously follows.

Under the heading "Extremes" are the emotional extremes that typically come about when the "Initial Quality" of the virtue comes to us through some life circumstance. The particular extremes mentioned are also derived from meditating on each of the virtues and writing phenomenological descriptions of them. These extremes are immensely important. Each virtue must be understood as the full continuum from one extreme to the other. For example, the virtue of devotion is rightly understood and felt as an emotional quality only when imaged as the continuum malice to devotion to superficiality. When these three qualities are meditated upon, the full depth, force, and breadth of the quality of devotion can be felt in a way that is otherwise missed if you try to imagine devotion alone.

Perhaps the most interesting feature of the chart is under the heading "Initial Quality." I came to these qualities through realizing that the virtues associated with each of the signs of the zodiac, given through the spiritual research of Blavatsky and Steiner, are decidedly different than the qualities typically associated with each of the zodiac signs in astrology as commonly practiced. The major qualities under the heading "Initial Quality" describe the essence of the primary qualities given in astrology for each sign of the zodiac. These qualities are the undeveloped aspects of the virtues. That is, the typical characteristics listed in standard astrology for each of the signs of the zodiac can be considered to be the *initial* gifts we are given that prompt us toward the development of virtue in life. At certain times in life, it seems that one or more of these qualities are strongly stimulated, and at such times there is the possibility of consciously developing the quality into a living sense of the virtue.

It is the "Initial Quality" that makes possible the inner soul and spirit perception of virtue in the first place. We have to have the "organ," so to speak, for feeling the particularity of each virtue. We have twelve such organs, our participation in the twelve signs of the zodiac, given as soul and spirit equipment. It is through the qualities of these twelve signs that we can feel the stirrings of virtue. Otherwise, virtue would be no more than an intellectual schema.

In our lives there are particular emotional occurrences that signal the possibility of developing particular virtues. These occurrences are our typical *entry points* into the circle of virtues. In the chart, these entry points are under the heading "Initial Quality" in column four. Consider, for example, a time when you felt extremely unsettled in your life. I do not mean a momentary upset, but a time of prolonged life disorientation of an emotional nature.

For example, in a recent workshop I asked this question to a group. One woman told the story of her husband going off on a camping trip several years earlier. He did not say where he was going; he did not return home several days later, when he was due. After several more days, the police got involved, but they could do nothing because this woman could not tell them where they might look for her husband. She described how her life was completely thrown into turmoil. After a couple of weeks, she returned to work, still not having heard anything about her husband. She felt somewhat comforted by the stability of working day to day, but there was no doubt that this was a tremendously emotional upset. Had he abandoned her? Did some terrible thing happen to him, an accident, or perhaps he was murdered?

These kinds of thoughts and the feelings accompanying them sometimes shifted into moments of feeling that surely everything was fine and that he would return. She described how deeply she was moved by the support of all of her extended family, how a certain quality of calmness came about due to the prayers and the support of these people, as well as her friends, and the people she worked with. Then, after another few weeks, she was told the search parties found her husband at his campsite. He had died in his sleep of a heart attack.

As I listened closely to this woman's story, it was clear that, in the midst of all that was happening during that time, she was coming into the virtue of devotion. Through the support of those around her, the virtue opposite devotion on the zodiac, equanimity, was also working strongly. (In the table, the opposite virtue is listed under the heading "Opposite." Under this heading the zodiac sign of the opposite virtue is listed, and under this is listed the "Initial Quality" of that opposite virtue.)

She certainly went through emotional extremes: for example, having extreme malice toward some assailant when she imagined her husband had been attacked. (The extremes of each virtue are listed under the last column.) At other times, she felt everything was fine, which was a kind of superficial reaction. Surprisingly, after she learned of the death of her husband, she experienced a kind of inner balance.

Not everyone going through what this woman went through would respond in this manner. At the time this happened, the woman did not consciously think of virtue or of being virtuous. Nonetheless, among the significant soul qualities that were developed through this experience, a sense of devotion, of deepening in the capacity to love in a steady, ongoing, deep way, was primary. Years later, she radiates this quality, and we would have to say that she embodies this virtue.

Another individual in that same workshop described his situation of feeling tremendously emotionally unsettled. This individual, a young man, barely twenty, had gone to his parents several years before to ask them for advice and help in a matter that was troubling him deeply. Instead of helping him, they threw him out of the house. After wandering for several days, he got on a bus, deciding to move to a small town in California. He was determined that he would exist on his own, without the help of his parents. While on the long bus ride out West, he suddenly felt a strong inner sense of confidence and calmness, and knew he would be fine. These qualities of confidence and calmness do not have to do with the virtue of devotion, but are qualities more characteristic of equanimity.

I do not think that this person entered into the qualities of the virtue of devotion. Instead, he passed over into the opposite virtue, equanimity. In the table you will see that the virtues preceding and following the virtue of equanimity are courtesy and patience (listed under the column headed "Before/After"). It is likely that this young man was stronger in these qualities than in the virtues preceding and following the virtue of devotion—love and balance. Why his soul experienced equanimity rather than the "Initial Quality" of the virtue of equanimity, which would have been a strong emotion of indecision, tends to indicate that love and balance must have been fairly well developed in this individual.

For some people, undergoing the kind of experiences described in relation to these two people would not result in a movement toward a particular virtue at all. Instead, the individual would either stay in the Initial Quality or would pass into the Initial Quality of the virtue opposite to the Initial Quality encountered. The person could go into the extremes of the virtue he was coming into connection with. In the instance of approaching the virtue of devotion, typically when our life becomes completely unsettled, we undergo the extreme emotions of malice and superficiality. For a period of time, we may feel hostile toward others or approach others in extremely superficial ways. Unless we become aware of this behavior, through the suffering it brings or through the reactions it brings about in others, the possibility exists of remaining in these extremes of emotional life. These extremes of emotions are a necessary learning through which we gradually become able to find a mean between the extremes, which is the virtue.

Another possibility is that a person can be psychically pulled into the opposite Initial Quality, and instead of moving into the virtue associated with this quality, be pulled into the extremes of that virtue. For example, in the instance of confronting an Initial Quality of unsettledness in life, one may be pulled into the opposite qualities of indecision and go through the emotional extremes of crudeness, and alternately, a kind of aesthetic relation to others and the world, which is a kind of superficial indulgence in sensual pleasures. Notice the similarity between the extremes related to the Initial Quality of the virtue of devotion—malice and superficiality—and the emotional extremes related to the Initial Quality of the virtue opposite devotion, namely crudeness and aesthetic behavior. This similarity in qualities shows clearly that when we are being introduced to the development of one virtue, at the same time we have to contend with the pull of the opposite virtue and its extremes, or vices, if you will.

The precise ways in which these various relationships to the virtue of devotion may come about, and how the events of life may pull one toward the development of a particular virtue, and how that pull may be thwarted, are certainly more than likely to be more complex than presented here. Nonetheless, there is a psychic lawfulness to the development of the virtues, which occurs in the manner suggested.

Let us stay with the virtue of devotion and give some indications how development of this virtue can come about. If we have a good sense of love, that would constitute a first condition for the development of the virtue of devotion. On the other hand, if one is more developed in the virtue of equanimity, then the likely response will be equanimity. If this response occurs, does it mean that the opportunity to develop devotion will be bypassed? Perhaps. But there will be other possibilities for its development in the future.

In a situation of extreme emotional turbulence, once we have gone through experiences of emotional hostility toward others, or alternately, finding our emotional life to lie wholly on the surface, it is likely that we find life to be not working so well. At this point, a kind of inner wakening can occur. We can begin to consciously try to treat ourselves and others differently, with a deeper sense of honor and respect. This is the beginning of the development of the virtue of devotion. As this behavior deepens, it becomes a habit to approach oneself, others, and the world as sacred. We find that a new ability emerges, the ability to love deeply and steadily, and that this ability resolves the feeling of emotional turbulence.

A psychological approach to the virtues, one that approaches them from the viewpoint of the psyche, of what occurs in soul life, is important because such an approach describes how the circumstances of life bring us to the possibility of spiritual development. If a strictly spiritual approach is taken toward the virtues, certain inevitable difficulties develop. By "strictly spiritual," I mean an approach that describes the characteristics of each virtue and then relies upon the individual to develop the discipline to put each virtue into practice.

A difficulty with such an approach is that, in our time, very few people would take up the discipline and practices needed. An additional difficulty follows; without a sense of the psyche, of the soul, the virtues would be taken literalistically, that is, without any sense of how one particular virtue rather than another applies to the particular circumstances of one's life at a given time. Further, the ways a virtue may be lived by one person are unique and different than the manner the same virtue would be lived by another person. A strictly spiritual approach tends to convey a notion that a virtue has a single form.

At the same time, a psychological approach to the virtues also carries its own difficulties. The circumstances of life bring the possibility for the development of virtue, but one can be stuck for years without realizing that the turbulence of life may be an invitation to enter into a particular virtue process. In fact, in our time, such turbulence is typically met by standard psychotherapy and counseling, but these have little or no sense of the virtues.

A spiritual-psychological approach to the virtues consists of the following: Study is an important part of this approach; that is the only way we can be introduced into the variety of virtues and reintroduce a lost mode of soul work into cultural life. Study is also a grounding for the meditative work needed to see the particularity of each virtue in relation to one's own life and circumstances.

This needed aspect of study differs from academic study and is more in the realm of the proper and healthy preparation for spiritual work. In all spiritual schools of the past, prior to any initiatory experience, years of study preceded actual practices. Understanding this form of spiritual work from within such a tradition indicates that it would be decidedly unhealthy to provide practices oriented toward the virtues that would bypass the important preparation of study. On the other hand, it is equally important to indicate that such study, even if it takes a long while, is but a preparation of the spiritual work to be taken up.

After sufficient study of the virtues has taken place, when the circumstances of life then throw us into situations that are the invitation to take up the inner development of a virtue, practices can be entered into consciously. We take soul and spiritual development into our own hands. While study is the first phase of this development, the second phase consists of gradually developing the capacities of inner observation to the point that many of the qualities listed in the table can be experienced and identified. Some particular meditation practices can then take place.

While I am speaking as if a linear process characterizes this movement from one form of working with the virtues to another, this progression is due to the limits of language, where one thing has to be described before another. In life, there is no such progression, though an important differentiation of levels of awareness does exist. It is these different sectors of awareness that are at the heart of what I am describing and not the sequence in which they occur. Once we are attuned to the importance of the virtues, life circumstances sometimes lead the way, while at other times it may be study and other times deliberate meditative practice.

Spiritual awareness of the virtues consists of understanding virtue in its general significance for human beings and the particular nature and quality of each of the virtues. It also consists of seeing a direction for the development of each virtue in one's life. Psychological awareness of the virtues consists in recognizing that the turbulence in life is the invitation to develop virtue. This awareness consists of attending to the emotional range of responses brought about by particular upsets in life and seeing that this range of responses, while often extreme, is not abnormal.

Psychological awareness also consists of the intimations that our soul life—experiences of those things that grab us and hold us, that seem beyond our control, that continue to live on within us even when the outer prompting circumstances have passed—not only concerns what has already happened to us, but orients us to what is coming to meet us. The mode in which soul prepares to meet whatever comes is through virtue.

Spiritual-psychological awareness of the virtues consists of what occurs when the spiritual and the psychological dimensions surrounding virtue are brought into conscious conjunction. It is more than a combination of the two. A new freedom develops in which we consciously and receptively greet the upsets of life and work with them in light of virtue, in order to develop virtue, which is precisely the manner in which soul life comes into harmony with the life of spirit. In this mode of working with the virtues, we go through what life brings but do not get bogged down by it. Rather, we seek to lift these life difficulties up in an act of offering to the spirit, and then to wait receptively for a response. Let us look into how this way of working can be carried out.

While teaching workshops on the virtues with my partner, Cheryl Sanders, I began to realize that in addition to discussing the virtues, hearing stories of how they unfold in the lives of individuals, and developing an understanding of each of the matters listed in the previous table, it is also possible to develop a mode of image-based meditative practice that develops a spiritual-psychological experience of the virtues. The procedure is simple, but first it is necessary to clearly show how this meditative procedure differs from other forms of meditative work and other forms of image work, such as active imagination.

To develop an example of the form of image-based meditation on the virtues, let us continue to consider the virtue of devotion, recognizing that this procedure can be applied to each of the virtues. Indeed, this form of meditation, which I will call "imaginal meditation" to distinguish it from other forms of spiritual mediation and other forms of image work, has a wide range of application beyond work with the virtues.

The procedure of imaginal meditation, applied to the virtue of devotion, begins by making an inner image of doing an act of devotion in relation to another person. (Imaginal meditation with any of the other virtues would follow this same basic pattern.) This instruction needs to be clarified. There is the deliberate use of the word "making." Making an image is something different than remembering, letting an image come, or having an image. The word implies a specific act of will. This act of will differentiates imaginal meditation from other forms of inner image work such as visualization, or guided image work, or from procedures that begin with relaxation and then encourage and allow images of any sort to come forward.

While it is true that the material with which one might make an image of doing an act of devotion might originate, say, from a memory of an act one did, the procedure is not simply one of remembering. If, for example, one uses the material of memory, such material in this form of meditation is considered to be like the materials of an artist. In order to make an image, a painter needs the materials of paints, a knowledge of color, light, composition, a certain training, a brush and canvas. Our memories can be considered analogously as the materials we use to make an image.

For example, when someone is asked to make an inner image of doing an act of devotion in relation to another person, it often happens that a number of memory images form the initial response. Then, when one particular incident is selected, another series of images flows by related to that one incident. From this wealth of material the person engaged in imaginal meditation then makes *a single image*. This single image, we could say, is analogous to a painting, though now it is an inner painting. This inner image is not the same as a painting because in the case of making an inner image, the image consists of the act of making the image and the concomitant act of receiving the image, and it is also the canvas on which the image is made.

This particular procedure, imaginal meditation, begins with a conscious act of making an image. For example, a person might make the following inner image of doing an act of devotion in relation to another person: "In the image I am making my faithful weekly call to my son and I feel an inner awareness of wanting to encourage him to talk and tell me what is going on in his life. I am on the phone, listening intently, responding with intensity, as if I were with him."

An act of will is required to make this image. This inner image is then stabilized so that no other images enter, just as in any act of meditation it is necessary to focus and concentrate on one single thing to the exclusion of all else. When the image is stabilized, it is then held for five minutes as the focus of concentration. It is further helpful to move this image from being centered in the head to being centered in the region of the heart. It may take some time and practice to be able to do this readily and without effort.

Before describing the next phase of this process, I would like to indicate the reasons for developing this form of image-meditation work up to this point. When we engage in work with images, it is essential to know what imaginal world we are working with. When we image something, this is an act that not only takes place within us; it is also an act that takes us into something, takes us somewhere. This somewhere can be considered to be an imaginal world. However, there are many different imaginal worlds. For our purposes, let us here consider only three such worlds.

First, there is the imaginal world of waking, perceptual consciousness. Everything we perceive, we perceive by way of image, or else there would be no form, no pattern, and no meaning in our perception. This imaginal world combines strongly with sensation, so that the imaginal aspect of our perception is usually not recognized. When the soul is engaged with the ordinary world of waking life, it is filled with whatever surrounds us, and thus there is no particular awareness of soul in itself. Soul becomes completely filled with whatever we happen to be attending to—perception of something of the outer world, or with our thoughts, or with our feelings. All of our experiences occur through the soul, but there is not an awareness of soul itself.

The second imaginal world is best exemplified as the route traveled by the shaman. The shaman, through specific procedures such as chanting, drumming, or perhaps the use of certain drugs, finds the way into a different imaginal world. This world consists wholly of image; here, image is reality. This imaginal world is an already and completely formed world.

For example, this world can be mapped, and over the ages, the shamans of a given region developed a set of cultural symbols that provided guidelines for anyone entering into the already formed imaginal world. There are beings and powers there, the same beings and powers that operate invisibly within the realms of all natural phenomena such as the formation of the clouds and rain, the forces within mountains or deserts or rivers, the elemental forces within plants, animals, and the human body. This imaginal world is rightly called the world of elemental imagination. A shaman, engaging in imagination, knows exactly where he or she is going and how to successfully navigate the intricacies of these worlds.

Outside this specialized tradition in which a great deal is known about the elemental imaginal worlds—the powers there, and what can be done there, such as working with elemental beings to bring about healing of the physical body—these worlds are often touched into without knowing where one is or what is involved. We touch into this world of elemental imagination with all procedures that rely upon "having an image," or "waiting for an image to come," or procedures such as visualization or guided meditation.

These worlds are also touched upon in-depth psychological approaches to dreams, and techniques such as active imagination and various kinds of dream work. However, these worlds of elemental imagination are typically mixed, so to speak, with other imaginal worlds, without our recognizing that this is the case. Typically, the result of working with most modern techniques of imagination is that one does not know what worlds one is working with.

The third imaginal world is the soul's receptivity to the spiritual worlds. The spiritual imaginal worlds are not at all the same as the elemental imaginal worlds. The spiritual worlds are those traditionally encountered through the development of specific spiritual disciplines. Perhaps the most basic of these disciplines is prayer, which, viewed strictly as an imaginal technology, is concerned with turning attention directly toward the soul in its receptivity to the spiritual realms. A more developed technique is that of mysticism and its practices, which consist of deliberately turning away from the world and toward the soul and finding there a spark, an inner fire of the divine, and learning to concentrate in a devoted way on the presence of the divine. An even more developed technique consists of attending to spiritual presences and learning how to fan the inner flame, so to speak. By this I mean the development of specific meditative techniques through which one begins to be able to perceive the spiritual realms.

The imaginal worlds entered into by the deliberate development of spiritual capacities is a different world than the worlds of elemental imagination. The spiritual worlds, rather than being already formed imaginal worlds, are the worlds of the creating-beings who are engaged in the acts of creating imaginal worlds rather than existing as already formed worlds. In the spiritual worlds, everything is not already set; here, spiritual realities are all process, all action, all movement in the process. These worlds are far from chaotic, but the forms are forms in the making rather than forms already completed. It is these worlds that are touched into with the fullness of the virtues. Recall the meaning of the word virtue: "the powers or operations of divine beings."

The "imaginal technology" for making connection with the spiritual worlds is different from technologies of working with imagination in relation to our everyday waking world, and different also from the technologies of working with the realms of elemental imagination. Certainly, these realms are not clearly separated, but different procedures are required for clear work in relation to each realm.

An additional factor to consider concerns being clear about the stance one takes in relation to imaginal worlds. The stance of this work with the virtues is that of spiritual psychology. Here, the two terms, "spirit" and "psyche" (or "soul") are carefully chosen and put together in a way that indicates a particular stance. Spiritual psychology concerns developing the receptive capacities of the soul in such a manner as to be open to the spiritual worlds.

Spiritual psychology, as defined here, is different than many other spiritual disciplines. For example, the spiritual disciplines developed by masters such as Blavatsky and Steiner develop the capacities of the individual spirit in such a manner that it is possible to develop clairvoyant faculties of the spirit and thus explore the complex realms of the spiritual worlds. Spiritual psychology does not follow this line of development; it stands in and for the realm of the soul and develops soul capacities to be receptive to spiritual currents, but is clear about the difference and relation between soul and spirit.

Spiritual psychology, while differentiated from other spiritual practices, is at the same time differentiated from other kinds of soul practice. For example, the depth psychology of Jung is not clear concerning the relation between soul and spirit. The two realms are mixed together in depth psychology. Thus, taking up practices such as active imagination, or Jungian dream work, or following the path of individuation, while of great value, does not allow one to know what worlds one is working with because the elemental worlds are mixed together with the spiritual worlds.

This confusion occurs because in the practices of depth psychology, one always begins with and works with images that come or images that are given to one, thus implicating the worlds of elemental imagination as a primary focus. In depth psychology, the realm of elemental imagination is called the collective unconscious; this collective unconscious is also the realm of the archetypes. In Jung's understanding, the archetypes are already formed, completed, and essentially unchanging. Thus, this psychology speaks of archetypes such as the Old Wise Man, Trickster, anima, animus. This way of approaching the worlds of imagination parallels shamanic approaches to the worlds of elemental imagination and treats spiritual worlds as if they were the same in form, structure, and function as the worlds of elemental imagination.

Spiritual psychology does not mix together the realms of soul and spirit, but works to develop the capacities of soul to be open and receptive to spiritual realms. Through the practices of spiritual psychology, one does not develop the capacities to "leave the body" and cross into the spiritual realms. On the other hand, soul is not simply opened up to the inpouring of contents from the elemental realms.

The imaginal technology developed in our School of Spiritual Psychology since 1990 involves the clear and conscious making of inner images related to what one is researching. For example, in the example being employed here—working with the virtue of devotion—we begin the imaginal practice by making a conscious, inner image of doing an act of devotion in relation to another person. This act is a conscious act of the soul, if one makes an inner image and does not just think about doing such an act, or does not remember such an act, or does not wait for an image to appear. Making such an image, stabilizing it, and concentrating the image constitutes the soul aspect of the practice.

In such a practice, if the image does not remain stable but begins to change or move or take on any qualities that were not present in the act of making the image, then these changes indicate that the elemental imaginal world has entered into the work. For example, if one begins by making an inner image of something as simple as a rock that one has just held in hand and observed, and the inner image of the rock suddenly sprouts wings and begins to fly, or it begins to talk, or it simply disappears altogether, then the elemental imaginal world has been touched.

If such a mixing in of the influences of the elemental imaginal world occurs, it is an indication that a basic strengthening of the conscious soul life is needed. This strengthening can be developed by taking an everyday object such as a stone, pencil, or paper clip and each day spending five minutes making an inner image of that object and holding the inner image steady. When the capacity to make and hold an image steady is developed, the next phase of the process can proceed.

Suppose, then, one has come to the point of being able to make an inner image of doing an act of devotion in relation to another person. Out of an array of initial images, which may be memory images, or fantasy images, or images tinged with ideas, one comes to the point of making a single image. This single image is not static, as it is a dynamic condensation and creative expression of the array of images leading up to this moment of more intense concentration.

We have gone from following soul processes to an act that is a conscious soul process. This inner image, the image of doing an act of devotion in relation to another person, however, has not at this point yet found its relation to the spiritual worlds. The value of this part of the process is that it validates the particular and completely individual expression of a virtue.

In working with people on the virtue of devotion, I begin with a phenomenological description of devotion, trying to open up the actual experience of such an act. Then we do this first part of the image work. Here, the way devotion is experienced by one individual is different than that imaged by another. In fact, in many instances, the inner image of an act of devotion might not look like an act of devotion at all. If this part of the practice of working with virtues is bypassed, we have only generalized descriptions of virtues and not how they operate in individual instances. This part of imaginal-meditative work constitutes the soul aspect.

A second phase of the imaginal-meditative work concerns the specific practice needed to open the soul in receptivity to the spiritual worlds in relation to the specific theme that has been given image-form through the inner act of making an image.

To make an inner image and at the same time be able to be present to the image one is in the act of making, two delicately coordinated processes must occur simultaneously. There is the act of making the image, which is experienced as an act of the will. This act of the will has to be in exact balance with the act of receiving the image, the act of allowing the presence of the image for it to be there. If either of these acts is out of balance with the other one, the image will change from the image made.

If the act of will making the image does not have enough strength, the image will take on other characteristics on its own, an indication that the forces of the elemental imaginal worlds are acting on and within the image. If the act of will making the image is too strong, there will not be an inner appearance of the image because receptivity has been overwhelmed.

Similar changes can occur in relation to the act of receptivity, which is an active rather than passive act. If there is not full receptivity, there will not be an image; if receptivity is too open and not selective in relation to the image made, the image will take on other characteristics. In practice, one can tell whether changes taking place in the made image are due to will or receptivity by paying attention to the inner sense of tension exerted in making the image. If the image changes and one feels a strong inner tension or a weak inner tension in the act of making, then the difficulties lie on the side of the will, which can be corrected with practice. If the image changes and one feels something is blocking receptivity or one feels too open, then the difficulty lies on the side of receptivity.

After an inner image is made and held steady for a few minutes, the next part of the process consists of completely erasing the inner image upon which one has been focusing all one's powers of attention. Then one "listens" to the void. The void does not remain empty. If one gives attention to the subtle qualities of that inner void, something will take place: an image appears, or an insight, or a strong feeling tone. This "return" is the spiritual correspondence to the conscious soul image characterizing doing a particular virtue.

I want to clarify what occurs when an image that has been meditated on is then erased. Doing this act of erasing an image takes as much will activity as did making the image in the first place. The released image is given over to the spiritual worlds in a form that is understandable by the spiritual worlds, that is, in the form of an image. The image, insight, thought, or feeling that returns is not some sort of message from the spiritual worlds. The image that comes into the void can be best understood as the spiritual correspondence to the conscious soul activity of making an inner image, concentrating on it, and then releasing it.

Why do I not say that the inner image of the act of devotion is already spiritual? Why do we have to go through a particular additional procedure in order to become aware of the spiritual aspect of the image?

An inner image is something that belongs not to the natural world, but to the soul world. The procedure is necessary to consciously open the soul to be receptive to the spiritual realms, and it is also necessary to experience moments in which the spiritual and the soul realms coincide.

The procedure of imaginal meditation on the virtues has been worked with in numerous groups in workshops offered by our School of Spiritual Psychology. Some three hundred people have done this kind of meditation work. What actually occurs in terms of the images made and the kinds of experiences returned in the void are not spectacular in their content. Most often, what occurs during the time of concentration within the empty void after the image has been released are images that the individuals know in an inner way correspond with the image of the act of devotion made. When these images are reported, they usually do not form any kind of rational connection with the inner image that had been made.

However, a strong feeling response typically accompanies the image, thought, or insight, a feeling that can be best described as awe or reverence, or that of a feeling-recognition of the holiness of the act of virtue that had not been realized with the making of the inner image alone. This feeling response seems to be what is important, rather than the content of the image or thought or insight that comes. It is, in fact, better not to make too much of the content of what returns, because concentrating on the content can readily be turned into an act of interpretation, which does not seem to be particularly helpful.

To provide a flavor for what happens, let me present some instances:

A. Inner image of doing an act of devotion: "I am making my weekly faithful call to my son and I feel an inner awareness of wanting to encourage him to talk and tell me what is going on in his life. I am on the phone, listening intently, responding with intensity, as if I were with him."

Image received after erasing the meditated image: "A huge radiating presence in the sky, like an eye, though rays of light come from it; the rays of light shine on a field, and in the field there is a large ring of sunflowers, and the radiating light shines on these flowers which are intensely yellow."

B. Inner image of doing an act of devotion: "I am holding my sick grandbaby in my arms. She is crying, and I sit with her and sway back and forth, back and forth."

Image received after erasing the meditated image: "I did not get an image. I felt in my body the pain in my arms that I felt when I held my granddaughter, though it was more intense, and although it was in my arms the pain was not exactly physical and I had the inner feeling that this pain that was in my arms was the pain my granddaughter was in and it was leaving her and going into me."

C. Inner image of doing an act of devotion: "I am holding down a child, physically restraining her as she is in rage."

Image received after erasing the meditated image: "I felt an overwhelming sense of love flooding in that was so strong I did not think I could contain it."

Many more instances could be given. In every case several important features occur. The virtue of devotion takes as many forms as there are individuals. It is impossible to say in an abstract way what constitutes an act of devotion except in very general terms. Often, in fact, an act of devotion might be looked upon by others as anything but that. The third example above illustrates an instance that hardly anyone would say is an act of devotion. We can assume that this same variability, this individuality of the manner in which a virtue is lived, would be characteristic of all the virtues. In our groups this has proved to be the case.

Another characteristic concerns what returns in the void after the image has been erased. In all instances, the content of what returns—image, thought, insight, feeling—does not have a direct, logical connection with the virtue of devotion. At the same time, in all instances, when this procedure was carried out, the individuals understood the virtue of devotion in a deep way. This same recognition holds for all of the virtues.

A further characteristic is more difficult to describe, but is perhaps the most important result of this procedure. When this technique of imaginal meditation was carried out in groups, a new field was created in the room that was not present before we did these meditations together. This subtle field was felt when people reported the images, thoughts, insights, and feelings that came

225

when the inner created image was erased, and it was a field felt by everyone. There is nothing mystical about this. It seems to involve the quality of the imaginal spiritual worlds coming into conjunction with the imaginal conscious soul life. The presence of such a field is transformative and moves a group from talking about virtue into the dynamic field of virtue.

Epilogue

Everyone now agrees that the world changed on September 11, 2001. While for most people the tragedy means that we are now living in danger every moment, from the perspective of spiritual psychology, there is another side. The tragic events of terrorism in New York City, Washington, D.C., and the skies over Pennsylvania were an initiation moment. We entered the age of virtue.

Each of the virtues described in this book was enacted that day for the whole world to see. We saw a great power and desire for doing the good burst forth in the actions of all who responded to the terror. We saw the possible founding of a new culture of care. When tested, the love we have for our fellow human beings lights up, and the world is healed from our sleepy indifference, our unconscious paranoia, and our ingrained competitiveness. Such is the power of virtue.

While we continue at the surface level to get things back to normal, we now carry the potential of learning to live the virtues in daily life, consciously. An opening now stands waiting for us to enact the highest potential for love, courage, patience, selflessness, compassion, and courtesy.

The most significant act we can do for the healing of the world is to hold an afterimage of the terror in New York City, Washington, and Pennsylvania. The tragic events resonate in our hearts, and our hearts are linked with each other, and not just on a horizontal plane. The souls of the departed, wrenched suddenly from life in such a shocking manner, and those who have departed by all other causes since this moment in time also resonate not just with the repercussions of this horrific event, but with the magnitude of the possibility of such actions and worse in the future.

In addition to thoughts and actions of retaliation and protection, we would do well to enter into a new shaping of our lives, a shaping formed by the action of the virtues. We are now conscious of courage, devotion, and compassion in entirely new ways. This book has come from seeing these virtues come forth on that fateful day.

The time has come to acknowledge the power of the soul that acts in virtue. Education, business, politics, and economy can now move from competition-driven modes of operation to conducting daily affairs as if every other person truly mattered. Children can now be instilled with delight in life, not just the conquest of winning. Business can now grow a conscience, and politics can reawaken to its mission of service. Not much will change the hard edge of the social imperative to acquire, conquer, and prevail over others, however, unless the virtues hold our new attention.

Since September 11, 2001, we are able to find words to express feelings that were once thought to be too private for public expression. If these feelings are not educated into the life of virtue, they will quickly become platitudes. It is the work of those who live more on the edges of culture to see the possibilities that emerge from dire events and try to shape a new imagination that can restore the imaginative possibilities of the soul.

Many people do want to be responsible and are willing to forge a new relationship to the world and to other people. Our hearts were broken and shaken out of complacency. Our hearts were put on alert that we are all responsible for the future. We were thrust into seeing answers concerning how we will now live into the future. Developing the virtues within our everyday life, and pursuing the imminently practical work of inner transformation, affect every moment, every encounter, and every impact we have in the world.

Love is a new prospect since this day. Patience, compassion, and equanimity come to harbor our grief. Faithfulness and balance are now acceptable. Courage, devotion, and selflessness are gaining in popularity. Courtesy became surprisingly evident in the aftermath of September 11. Truth is harder to find in the collective world, but individuals are now asking if they are being truthful to their lives and what they are doing. Perhaps the most challenging virtue in this time is discernment, and it may be the one most needed. We have to discern the difference, for example, between revenge and protection. And we have to discern the difference between a lust for war that will spread a contagion for destruction and standing firm in the conviction that freedom must be preserved.

We have awakened from complacency and the illusion of having complete control over our destiny. Thrown into shock, grief, anger, and revenge, and humbled by the enormity of destruction, we cried, we rallied, and we set about the work of trying to make sure nothing of this sort ever happens again—to anyone. We began a war on terrorism. That needs to be balanced with a love of virtue. These twelve virtues are now given to each individual to develop as new capacities, as new ways of relating to others. We can emulate the example of hundreds of police, firefighters, citizens, and a courageous mayor whose sacrifice teaches us the way of virtue. Or we can fall into hatred. This is a decisive time. Virtue is no longer a passive, quiet simplicity of being that can be shrugged off as being only for the pious. We have seen proof that virtue is the only effective weapon against destructiveness. May this book be a force of love in the world.

Index

For information concerning the School of Spiritual Psychology, please contact

The School of Spiritual Psychology
P.O. Box 5099
Greensboro, N.C. 27435

Programs in spiritual development, sacred service, elder wisdom, correspondence courses, publications.
Web site: www.spiritualschool.org

Hampton Roads Publishing Company

. . . for the evolving human spirit

Hampton Roads Publishing Company
publishes books on a variety of subjects,
including metaphysics, health, visionary fiction,
and other related topics.

For a copy of our latest catalog, call toll-free
800-766-8009, or send your name and address to:

Hampton Roads Publishing Company, Inc.
1125 Stoney Ridge Road
Charlottesville, VA 22902

e-mail: hrpc@hrpub.com
www.hrpub.com